SCIENTOLOGY

THEOLOGY
&
PRACTICE
OF A
CONTEMPORARY
RELIGION

SCIENTOLOGY

A Reference Work
Presented by
The Church of Scientology
International

BRIDGE PUBLICATIONS, INC.
Los Angeles

Published by
Bridge Publications, Inc.
4751 Fountain Avenue
Los Angeles, California 90029

ISBN: 1-57318-145-5

This publication was made possible through the support of the U.S. IAS Members' Trust. Through its own activities and that of its members, the IAS embodies the concept of an international religious community. The IAS has undertaken special projects to further religious freedom and to ensure that Scientologists everywhere can carry forth and achieve their mission of spiritual salvation.

The Church of Scientology was established in 1954. Today its more than 3,000 churches, missions, related organizations, groups and activities span the globe and minister the religion to more than 8 million people in 100 countries in over 30 languages.

The rapid emergence of the Scientology religion within the world's changing spiritual community has led many to ask what kind of religion it is, how it compares with other faiths and in what ways it is different. What is its understanding of a Supreme Being and the spiritual aspects of life which transcend the temporal world? What social and community work do Scientologists do and how do these activities relate to its greater religious purpose?

This volume provides answers to these and other such questions about the religion and its members. In it, leading scholars provide diverse and insightful perspectives into Scientology, resulting in a unique and comprehensive overview of the religion.

The goal of the Scientology religion is to achieve complete certainty of one's spiritual existence, one's relationship to the Supreme Being and his role in eternity. In this regard, countless authorities have affirmed that Scientology sits squarely within the tradition of the world's major religions.

Church of Scientology International

The Creed of the Church of Scientology

The Creed of the Church of Scientology was written by L. Ron Hubbard shortly after the Church was formed in Los Angeles on February 18, 1954. After he issued this creed from his office in Phoenix, Arizona, the Church of Scientology adopted it as official because it succinctly states what Scientologists believe.

We of the Church believe:

That all men of whatever race, color or creed were created with equal rights;

That all men have inalienable rights to their own religious practices and their performance;

That all men have inalienable rights to their own lives;

That all men have inalienable rights to their sanity;

That all men have inalienable rights to their own defense;

That all men have inalienable rights to conceive, choose, assist or support their own organizations, churches and governments;

That all men have inalienable rights to think freely, to talk freely, to write freely their own opinions and to counter or utter or write upon the opinions of others;

That all men have inalienable rights to the creation of their own kind;

That the souls of men have the rights of men;

That the study of the mind and the healing of mentally caused ills

should not be alienated from religion
or condoned in nonreligious fields;

And that no agency less than God has
the power to suspend or set aside these
rights, overtly or covertly.

And we of the Church believe:

That man is basically good;

That he is seeking to survive;

That his survival depends upon himself
and upon his fellows and his
attainment of brotherhood with the
universe.

And we of the Church believe that the
laws of God forbid man:

To destroy his own kind;

To destroy the sanity of another;

To destroy or enslave another's soul;

To destroy or reduce the survival of
one's companions or one's group.

And we of the Church believe that the
spirit can be saved and that the spirit
alone may save or heal the body.

Table of Contents

Introduction

From a Western perspective, the 20th century has seen many changes in the role of religion. The rapid advance of technology has unquestionably played an important part. None of the world's great faiths — Christian and non-Christian — have escaped question. The Turin Shroud has faced radio carbon dating and the electron-scanning microscope, while biologists claim they can now create life. To those who have sought to question the fundamental tenets of religion itself, the glittering success of science has been a persuasive ally.

Yet, in all truth, the conflict between science and religion has spurious foundations. As Albert Einstein himself noted, "Science without religion is lame. Religion without science is blind."

While the religion of Scientology was born in the century of science's greatest ascendancy and has not been unaffected by this conflict, it believes (along with those such as Einstein) that these con-cocted issues arise from misunderstandings of the roles religion and science must play in these times of great change, and, indeed, misunderstanding of the very nature of religion itself.

Although the first Church of Scientology was established only in 1954, it has obviously met a religious need. Today, more than 3,000 churches, missions and related organizations, groups and activities span the globe, ministering to some 8 million people in more than 100 countries in over 30 languages.

Naturally, Scientology's rapid emergence within the world's changing religious community has led many to ask what kind of religion it is, how it "compares" with other faiths and in what ways it is different. What is its understanding of a Supreme Being and the spiritual aspects of life which transcend the temporal world, and what social and community work do Scientologists do?

To provide a definitive, objective view on these issues, the Church brought

together leading authorities on comparative religion, and other scholars, sociologists and experts to assemble and compose the text of the chapters which follow. Thus, what the Church now presents in this volume are the results of the most comprehensive study and analysis ever conducted of one of the world's most important religions.

Additionally, the authors of this book have also addressed the more basic question concerning religion itself: What is it? As one authority has noted, "If one investigates the texts of the fathers of the Christian Church and the texts of the great figures of theology in search of the original definition of religion, he will be disappointed." He added that until questioned from without, people consider their own religion self-evident and thus beyond need of definition.

Another recalled the Eastern view that all religions, despite diverse beliefs and practices, are merely different paths leading to the same ultimate reality. Citing an ancient Japanese poem, he noted that "there are many paths at the foot of the mountain, but the view of the moon is the same at the peak."

The subject matter of Scientology is wholly religious. Yet, to the degree that science and religion are concerned with truth, with knowledge and with what *is*, the Scientology religion has bridged the gap between the two. It addresses the most fundamental questions of life which no man can avoid, no matter how fascinated he may become with his presumed knowledge of the material world. The universe may have started with the astronomer's "big bang," but that hardly answers why. Nor does it tell us where the universe is proceeding, or if our lives fulfill some grander purpose.

Today, Scientology fulfills the goal of religion by addressing the spiritual nature of man and his role in eternity. Yet it approaches the traditional questions of religion from a standpoint of reason, an approach that science can hardly argue with.

The scope of Scientology is immense. The full body of knowledge that comprises the religious Scripture is contained in more than 40 million spoken and written words on the subject — all by L. Ron Hubbard, the source and founder of the Scientology religion. A lifetime of searching for truth and a deep examination of the wisdom to be found in both East and West led Mr. Hubbard to write, "And when we call Scientology a religion, we are calling it a religion out of a much deeper well than only the last two thousand years. It is a wisdom in the tradition of ten thousand years of search in Asia and in Western civilization."

Nevertheless, Scientology is a religion without dogma. There is nothing in Scientology that one is expected to take on faith or on the basis of arbitrary

Scientology fulfills the goal of religion by addressing the spiritual nature of man and his role in eternity.

authority. The goal of Scientology is to *know* — to achieve complete certainty of one's spiritual existence and one's relationship to the Supreme Being. While countless authorities have affirmed that Scientology sits squarely within the tradition of the world's major religions, one of the factors which clearly makes Scientology unique is the religious practice by which this spiritual certainty is attained.

The religious practices of Scientology include exact, precise methods by which a person achieves greater spiritual awareness. These practices are referred to collectively as the *technology* of the Scientology religion. "Technology" describes the *methods of application* of the principles of something, as opposed to mere knowledge of the subject itself.

Many of these methods have counterparts in other religions — such as the use of confessionals and other forms of spiritual counseling. However, the technology of Scientology was developed pragmatically, is based upon an understanding of the fundamental laws of life, and provides a predictable series of steps by which a person can progress to higher states of spiritual awareness.

Although certainly not unique in the field of religion, another aspect essential to an understanding of the Scientology religion is the extent to which Scientologists all over the world are found working with other religious and social groups in all manner of community programs — caring for the environment, helping those who have fallen into the trap of drugs, supporting human rights campaigns and many other such activities.

Again, these activities are not pursued on faith alone, or under an authoritative edict that one should "do good." It is simply that as he reaches higher levels of spiritual awareness, the Scientologist invariably begins to recognize that his responsibilities extend far beyond the sphere of his own life, or even that of his immediate family.

L. Ron Hubbard once wrote, "The first principle of my own philosophy is that wisdom is meant for anyone who wishes to reach for it. It is the servant of commoner and king alike and should never be regarded with awe."

In this spirit, the Church of Scientology has an open-door policy for anyone who seeks a better understanding of the religion — whether from a personal, a scholarly or an official perspective. It is our hope that this book will help with such understanding. For those desiring a more in-depth view, the Church has also produced *What Is Scientology?* — a truly encyclopedic volume which addresses, in detail, all aspects of Scientology, including answers to common questions. Copies of this book are available from any Church of Scientology and from many libraries.

Should any questions remain, we welcome your communication.

Church of Scientology
International

CHAPTER ONE

Defining Religion in a Pluralistic Society

Religious scholars faced with the question of how to define religious practice in today's changing and pluralistic society have examined the essential characteristics of all faiths and how these factors are manifested in the Scientology religion.

Many consider they already know the answer to the question, "What is a religion?"

The definitions employed from one person to the next almost always are defined by personal religious heritage and experience, yet history has demonstrated that this perspective is a perilous one. Such approaches have given us the Crusades, the Spanish Inquisition, hundreds of years of bloodshed in the Netherlands and elsewhere in Europe, and the troubles of Northern Ireland.

More commonly, restrictive approaches to defining religion lead to less violent but nonetheless equally destructive forms of discrimination and other violations of human rights — particularly against members of new or unfamiliar faiths.

For centuries Western thinkers approached the subject from the unique perspective of Judeo-Christian tradition. This approach revolved around two fundamental but related doctrinal concepts — a belief that there is a personal creator God separate and distinct from man, and that man's highest activity is the worship, supplication and veneration of this god. If a set of beliefs did not manifest these doctrines, it was not regarded as a religion.

This doctrinal approach also reflected the way Western scholars analyzed religious thought and practice from the very beginning of civilized society until only relatively recently. For hundreds of years the terms "religion" and "Christianity" were virtually synonymous. Henry Fielding's sarcasm in "By religion I mean Christianity, by Christianity I mean Protestantism, by Protestantism I mean the Church of England as established by law" aptly caught the prevailing belief of the times. In fact, England refused to treat Judaism as a proper religion for purposes of charity law until as late as 1837.

This deceptively simple standard by which religions were judged not only closed the doors to many religions but opened the doors to persecution — underscoring that "defining" religion is far more than an issue of academic concern. From it, uneven treatment, discrimination and even violence have flowed.

Fortunately, as contemporary society became more global and the variety of religious expression in the West blossomed, scholars and others began to

It is the Eastern view that all religions, despite diverse beliefs and practices, are merely different paths leading to the same ultimate reality. As an ancient Japanese poem states, "there are many paths at the foot of the mountain, but the view of the moon is the same at the peak."

discover that the doctrinal approach could not be applied easily to religions not grounded in the Judeo-Christian tradition — a discovery that eventually brought about an enlightened change in view. The inherent bias of the traditional approach to defining religion was

of Theravada Buddhism and Jainism, which have no Supreme Being, when both predate Christianity by five centuries? What of the many Hindu sects which, while recognizing numerous gods, clearly subordinate them to the ultimate goal — union of the "Self" with the "Absolute"? And what of Taoism, which cannot be defined but only "discerned," or Confucianism, where character is the goal and wisdom the path to attaining it?

Modern religious scholars now agree that the test for religion must be objective and cannot be based on concepts drawn from any one particular tradition. Use of a definition that is biased toward a particular religious tradition is certain to discriminate among religions, and has indeed resulted in varying levels of religious persecution. Rather, experts have broadened their view to achieve what Professor Bryan Wilson, Reader Emeritus in Sociology, Oxford University, calls "ethically neutral definitions" consisting of "elements [which] came to be recognized as constituting religion, regardless of the substance of the beliefs, the nature of the actual practices, or the formal status of the functionaries in their service." In this way a religion's beliefs and practices can be interpreted fairly and without bias.

There still are many different ways of defining religion. In more recent years the trend has been toward analysis through "comparative religion," which approaches the understanding of a religion through cross-cultural comparisons of its component parts. This approach and the context from which it developed are discussed below.

particularly obvious when indigenous or Eastern religions were at issue, since many of them either have no God or Supreme Being, let alone a personal creator God, or tend to view religion as an integral part of everyday life.

Indeed, in many indigenous religions there is little belief structure, and some Eastern religions such as Zen Buddhism and Hindu Bhakti view doctrine as ancillary and even a hindrance to spiritual advancement. Moreover, how could anyone deny the religiosity

APPROACHES TO DEFINING RELIGION BY WESTERN SCHOLARS

For hundreds of years religion had been defined on the basis of doctrine, and primarily on whether the doctrine in question exhibited the same characteristics as Christianity. The earliest attempts to go beyond the confines of the doctrinal test occurred in the early 1800s when scholars began considering intuitive and experiential factors in order to give more emphasis to man's inner religious feelings, which was fundamental to Asian religions but missing from the Western modes of analysis. This resulted in a more inward approach exemplified by the German theologian Friedrich Schleiermacher's definition of religion as a "feeling of absolute dependence" — as opposed to a feeling of "relative" dependence on something else, something divine.

For many years religions were interpreted by methods such as this which often were based more on speculation than actual knowledge of the true facts, particularly of Eastern religions. Eventually, in the 1860s the Oxford scholar Max Muller called for the creation of a "science of religion" that would interpret religion through an objective test based on actual facts and fair and accurate methods of comparison.

Anthropologists and sociologists in the 1900s argued that religious belief and practice could be understood only within the cultural context from which they grew. Led by sociologists Emile Durkheim and Max Weber, they posited that religion should be analyzed on the basis of its component societal factors, and they reduced religious belief to its social, economic, political, psychological and cultural components. But many of the approaches they advocated were subject to criticism on the ground that they did not address what many considered the essential element of religions: *transcendence*.

This concept of transcendence, which means "to go beyond," "to bridge" or "to cross over," is a fundamental characteristic of all religious belief systems and a central element in every modern approach to defining religion. Transcendence creates the connection between the natural world and the supernatural, allowing man to pass through the limitations of his biological or physical state to the place of the divine. This place may be physical, as a temple or a church, or conceptual, as an image or principle — or both.

The distinction between the divine or the supernatural and the physical world — between the "sacred" and the "profane" — is another fundamental characteristic of religious belief and an inherent concept in most definitions of religion. This separation is most obvious in religious rituals, customs and trappings that appear distinctly religious.

Soon other broader approaches to defining religion were developed that drew on the work of Schleiermacher but avoided the "reductive" method that focused so much on societal factors. Two of the most widely known exponents of this new approach, Rudolf Otto and Mircea Eliade, advocated defining religion in terms of how one experienced the sacred, an awareness of which they described as an intensely deep religious feeling. They focused more on the objects that individuals believed were sacred or endowed with supernatural power, whether an object, a person, an activity or a structure.

Another approach, advocated by the religious historian Joachim Wach, also analyzed religion in terms of objects and religious symbols. Wach expanded the ordinary notion of symbols to include people and activities, even institutions — thus, any activity, thing or person could serve as a bridge or connection between the sacred and the material world. He called these activating links "forms of religious expression" and grouped them into three main categories: (1) theoretical forms of religious expression — doctrines, beliefs, myths and sayings; (2) practical forms of religious expression — services, rites and practices; and (3) sociological forms of religious expression — organizations, relationships and authority.

While contemporary religious scholars certainly have not settled upon a universal definition of religion, it appears that a consensus believes these three categories of religious expression accurately reflect the essential common features of religions. Their basic approach looks for:

• A belief that deals with the supernatural, some "ultimate reality" that transcends the physical world. This ultimate reality may be a God, gods or Supreme Being, or it may simply be some supernatural principle such as a belief in the transmigration of one's spirit;

• Religious practices that enable man to contact, understand, attain a union or commune with this ultimate reality; and

• A community of believers who join together in pursuing this ultimate reality.

Thus most scholars of comparative religion now agree with this three-pronged

The concept of transcendence, which means "to go beyond" or "to cross over," is a fundamental characteristic of all religious belief systems. It allows man to pass through the limitations of his physical state to a place of the divine.

approach because it is free of religious bias, is not intrusive and avoids evaluation of religious belief or practice. It is, in the words of Dr. Wilson, a truly "ethically neutral" definition.

OVERRIDING INTERNATIONAL STANDARDS

While such a definition of religion may have been embraced by modern scholars as the correct approach to the subject, international human rights law mandates it as the only approach. And while international human rights instruments purposely do not define religion, they do establish core international standards requiring that governments not use discriminatory definitions or apply objective definitions in discriminatory ways.

Unfortunately, it is all too apparent that religious discrimination occurs, even in democratic societies. The internationally acclaimed 1997 study *Freedom of Religion and Belief: A World Report*, prepared by the University of Essex Human Rights Centre in conjunction with experts from 50 countries, has found that religious discrimination and repression is broadly occurring through the application of "narrow interpretations" of the concept of religion.

Some of the most important international standards to guard against this discrimination were developed by the

The United Nations' International Covenant on Civil and Political Rights, and other human rights treaties, protect and guarantee the wide variety of freedom of thought, conscience and religion which is found in the 137 countries around the world that have signed these covenants.

United Nations, which seeks as one of its primary aims to encourage "respect for human rights and for fundamental freedoms for all without distinction as to race, sex, language, or religion." (Art. 1(3) of the Charter). These principles of equality and non-discrimination are of such fundamental importance that they are regarded as *principles of customary international law,* binding on all civilized nations.

To further these principles, United Nations human rights treaties, resolutions and reports call upon all member states to use a definition of religion that is sufficiently objective and expansive to avoid discrimination among religions. For this reason, the United Nations has rejected tests derived from Judeo-Christian concepts as outdated and unduly restrictive and suggested instead an inclusive and "ethically neutral" approach like that followed by religious scholars.

This mandate for religious tolerance is clearly evident in authoritative guidelines the United Nations Human Rights Committee adopted regarding Article 18 of the International Covenant on Civil and Political Rights, which guarantees freedom of thought, conscience and religion in each of the 137 countries which signed and ratified it. The UN's Human Rights Committee, responsible for ensuring that the Covenant's signatories comply with its obligations, has expressly warned them not to discriminate against any religion. The Committee has directed the signatories to treat all religions equally, particularly those that are "newly established, or represent religious minorities that may be the subject of hostility by a predominant religious community," and

those that may have a "nontheistic" system of beliefs. (para. 2)

The UN's foremost authority on religious matters, the Special Rapporteur on Religious Intolerance, has underscored this mandate for a broad approach to defining religion, stating that a group which goes "beyond simple belief and appeals to a divinity, or at the very least, to the supernatural, the transcendent, the absolute, or the sacred, enters into the religious sphere." The UN Religious Rapporteur also has pointedly rejected standards used by some national governments for granting religious recognition that were based on the size of the group or the number of years it existed.

Other international authorities working in this area take this same approach. The European Court of Human Rights, for example, routinely issues decisions that recognize and protect the rights of minority religions. A related organization, the Human Rights Information Centre of the Directorate of Human Rights of the Council of Europe, has noted that the broad concept of religion under the European Convention on Human Rights is "not confined to widespread and globally recognized religions but also applies to rare and virtually unknown faiths" and that religion must "thus be understood in a broad sense." And in April 1997, a body of religious experts convened by the Organization for Security and Cooperation in Europe, a group of more than 50 countries, confirmed that the United Nations' broad standards should apply to any definition of religion in order to protect nontraditional and minority religions.

COMMON FUNCTIONS OF RELIGIONS

An understanding of the essential characteristics of religion is crucial to identifying religion but falls short of a full grasp of what religion means in modern society. In this regard, the learning of religious scholars and sociologists is again instructive. Beyond isolating the *sine qua non* qualities of religion, many also point to common functions present in modern religion.

Probably the most important function of every religion — in fact, their primary concern — is *salvation*. This is not limited to spiritual salvation which, in the Judeo-Christian tradition, focuses primarily on man's ultimate destiny. Rather, the true meaning of salvation is found in the origin of the word, from the Latin word "salutas," meaning "safety" or "wholeness." Thus, salvation actually has to do with making man "safe" or "whole" in his present life. Religions accomplish this by giving their followers the means to ward off difficulty or by showing what they must do or believe to have a meaningful existence, safe from the major vicissitudes of life.

Of course, the different paths to salvation vary greatly from religion to religion and range from placing one's faith in a "saving" god to sacrificing to various gods, worshiping ancestors, conforming to specific standards of conduct, practicing certain rituals, and meditation.

Another related and equally important function of every religion is to put forth *cosmology*. Every religion has its own distinctive view of the cosmos — the nature of the physical universe, including time and space, the world we live in, and man's place in it. This cosmology forms the philosophical underpinning on which that religion is based and, in effect, becomes its "religious philosophy". This religious philosophy, in turn, determines the religion's doctrine and belief systems, provides its uniqueness, and frequently is the single most feature that attracts new members. As India's noted Hindu scholar Sri Aurobindo stated, "A religion that is not the expression of philosophic truth degenerates into superstition and obscurantism."

Similarly, *preservation of orthodoxy* is a common feature of almost every religion, and a religion's measures to ensure the integrity of its beliefs, practices, traditions and scripture range from the very simple to the legally sophisticated. *Revelations 22:18* strongly admonishes against alteration or deletion of Christian religious text. In Catholicism, the entire Jesuit religious order is charged with seeing to the integrity of scripture. And the Christian Science Church, among many others, has employed legal devices such as copyright laws to ensure sacred works are not perverted or improperly used.

Establishment of ethical and moral codes and guidelines governing behavior and "right conduct" figure prominently in virtually all religions, and is expressed in such varied forms as the Ten Commandments in Judaism, and the Golden Rule in Christianity, the Noble Eightfold Path in Buddhism and the way of the dharma in Hinduism. The late religious scholar and author Mircea Eliade noted that while religion concerns the sacred, it also guides human conduct: "By imitating the divine behavior, man puts and keeps himself close to the gods — that is, in the real and the significant."

A *spiritual healing element* is one of the most ancient and fundamental religious functions, found in many of the ayurvedic practices of Hinduism, early Christianity, some schools of Buddhism, and in many modern religious denominations such as Christian Science and Pentecostal. "[A] religion that does not heal cannot long survive," says Professor David Chidester of the University of Capetown, South Africa, noting that it is only in the modern world that religion relinquished primary responsibility for healing the body and the mind.

Almost every religion also provides some way to help members *resolve personal problems.* In religions from the Judeo-Christian tradition, this often takes the form of pastoral counseling, particularly when the parishioner's problem has to do with marital difficulties, problems at work or at school, antisocial or self-destructive behavior such as drug or alcohol abuse, or simply the stress of day-to-day life. Increasingly, churches encourage members to resolve problems through methods such as reading books or listening to recorded lectures in the privacy of their homes. Other religions prescribe following special rituals as a way to resolve personal problems. Catholics often use the confessional for this purpose. Dr. Wilson has described this function as providing "proximate salvation from immediate suffering and travail."

Numerous other functions of religion could be noted here. But scholars and historians have stressed that the presence or absence of one or more of these or other functions should not be mistaken as a factor in "defining" religion. Rather, they furnish a deeper understanding of the greater meaning of religion in modern society, and what particular religions mean to their adherents.

Every religion has its own distinctive view of the cosmos — the nature of the physical universe, including time and space, the world we live in and man's place in it.

APPROACHES BY GOVERNMENT BODIES TO DEFINING RELIGION

There is another source of definitions of religion — governmental bodies. Government officials regularly must determine whether a particular group is religious and therefore qualifies for some privilege accorded only to religious organizations. This privilege may be a special zoning variance, exemption from taxes, the authorization to perform marriages, or in some localities just the simple right to provide spiritual healing to the ill or distressed. In some countries, particularly those dominated by a state religion, religious groups are required to register and be approved by the government before they may function or even hold religious services.

Despite the specific cultural differences among countries, contemporary court decisions are adopting expansive definitions of religion that appear to fit perfectly within the "ethically neutral" approach taken by scholars of comparative religion. In just the past several years the highest courts in Italy, the United States, Australia, New Zealand and India all have rejected an exclusively theistic definition of religion. The Italian Supreme Court specifically directed that courts look to the opinions of religious experts when determining whether a set of beliefs is religious.

In fact, the definition of religion adopted by the High Court of Australia in *Church of the New Faith v. Commissioner for Pay-Roll Tax* (1983) 154 CLR 120, could well have been written by a scholar of religion. In that opinion, the Court set forth a series of four indicia derived from an empirical analysis of accepted religions: (1) a belief in something supernatural, some reality beyond that which can be conceived by the senses; (2) that the belief in question relates to man's nature and place in the universe and his relationship to things supernatural; (3) as a result of this belief adherents are required or encouraged to observe particular codes of conduct or engage in particular practices that have supernatural significance; and (4) the adherents comprise one or more identifiable groups.

Yet many if not most governmental officials and judges who have to make these decisions are not always familiar with the nuances of the variety of religious thought. And in all likelihood, their views of religion have been framed by their own experience, by the concepts, practices and trappings of the religious world in which they were born and raised. Thus, it would not be unusual to have as many definitions of religion as there are decision makers. With this lack of objective uniformity, it also is easy to see how discrimination among religions can occur, unintentional or not.

BONA FIDES OF THE SCIENTOLOGY RELIGION — AN OVERVIEW

Even with the growing preponderance of an ethically neutral and informed approach to religiosity by academia and governments, the Church of Scientology sometimes is asked why it should be treated as a religion if all of its beliefs and practices do not fit within the Judeo-Christian tradition. As explained later in this book, although Scientologists believe in the existence of a Supreme Being, which is placed at the apex of Scientology's cosmology, Scientology religious practices do not include worship, supplication or veneration, which are primary religious practices of the Judeo-Christian tradition. Scientology religious practices "differ" from practices of the traditional Western religions in that they seek to better one's understanding of and relationship with the Supreme Being, as well as the entire cosmos, rather than simply reflecting worship and adoration. In this respect Scientology is more like many Eastern religions, which seek to better one's understanding of and relation to some other supernatural being, principle or power.

To assist others to understand how Scientology compares with other religions, the Church of Scientology asked a number of internationally recognized religious scholars and experts from diverse disciplines to examine Scientology beliefs, practices and organizations and give their opinion as to its religiosity. These experts, all of whom examined Scientology from an "ethically neutral" standpoint, agree that it is a religion.

The opinions of several of these experts are published as Appendices to this book. They are:

1. **Dr. Bryan Wilson**
Reader Emeritus in Sociology,
Oxford University
Professor Wilson is one of the most distinguished authorities on comparative religion in the world and has been studying Scientology for over 20 years, writing extensively about the religion. In applying the three-pronged approach, Dr. Wilson utilized a "probabilistic inventory" of 20 factors that he finds are characteristic of any religion in one combination or another.

Dr. Wilson wrote an extensive opinion, analyzing the major features of Scientology as well as the other important religions of the world. Finding that "Scientology is a genuine system of religious belief and practice which evokes from its votaries deep and earnest commitment," he ultimately concluded that "it is clear to me that Scientology is a bona fide religion and should be considered as such."

2. Dr. M. Darrol Bryant
*Professor of Religion
and Culture, Renison College,
University of Waterloo, Canada*

Since first becoming aware of Scientology in the mid-1970s, Dr. Bryant has conducted a lengthy review of the religion. His test for religiosity is an adaptation of the three-pronged approach, which he defines as "a community of men and women bound together by a complex of beliefs, practices, behaviours, and rituals that seek, through this Way, to relate human to sacred/divine life." Like Dr. Wilson, Dr. Bryant concluded that "Scientology is a religion. It has its own distinctive beliefs in and account of an unseen spiritual order, its own distinctive religious practice and ritual life, it has its own authoritative texts and community-building activity."

3. Dr. Régis Dericquebourg
*Professor of Sociology
of Religion at the University
of Lille III, France*

Dr. Dericquebourg's religiosity test is another modification of the three-pronged approach that looked for: (1) a cosmology in which the universe takes on meaning regarding one or more supernatural forces, (2) a moral that stems from this cosmology that supplies direction and guid-

ance, (3) tools or practices which put human beings in contact with the supernatural principle, and (4) a community of followers. After studying Scientology Scripture and practice and interviewing almost 300 French Scientologists, Dr. Dericquebourg easily concluded that Scientology is a bona fide religion: "Scientology has the characteristics of a religion. It has a theology, a set of exercises making it possible to reach the spiritual part in every human being, a 'very bureaucratized' church structure, and religious rites. . . . Scientologists extend the use of instruments of rationality in the service of a mystical path, a self-transformation and a transformation of the world. It is probably for this reason that it appears unique among religions."

4. Dr. Alejandro Frigerio
*Associate Professor of Sociology,
Catholic University of Argentina*

Dr. Frigerio took a more expansive approach to analyzing Scientology, utilizing five different methodologies used by social scientists: (1) a "substantive" approach, which examines a religion by the religious experiences of its practitioners, (2) a "comparative" approach, which distinguishes religion from other systems of meaning, (3) a "functional" approach, which examines religion in terms of the consequences it holds in other areas of life, (4) an "analytical" approach, which examines religion through the different ways that it expresses itself, and (5) what is called the "emic" approach, which focuses on aspects that culture acknowledges as religious. At the end of his exhaustive analysis, Dr. Frigerio concluded that "Scientology is a religion from all perspectives which exist in the current discussion of the definition of the term in the social sciences...."

5. Dr. Frank K. Flinn
Adjunct Professor in
Religious Studies,
Washington University,
Missouri

Dr. Flinn has been studying emerging religions since 1962. He took the classic three-pronged approach discussed above, concluding that Scientology unquestionably is a religion: "I can state without hesitation that the Church of Scientology constitutes a bona fide religion. It possesses all the essential marks of religions known around the world; (1) a well-defined belief system, (2) which issues into religious practices (positive and negative norms for behavior, religious rites and ceremonies, acts and observances), and (3) which sustain a body of believers in an identifiable religious community, distinguishable from other religious communities."

6. Mr. Fumio Sawada
Eighth Holder of the Secrets
of Yu-Itsu Shinto

Mr. Sawada is one of Japan's foremost authorities on religion and a former director of the Sophis University. Mr. Sawada, as an Asian scholar and a leader of the oldest religion in Japan, brought a unique perspective to the analysis of Scientology. He approached his task from the standpoint of the Japanese definition of religion, which is "to teach the origin, teach the source of the origin." In addition to satisfying this test, to be recognized as a religion in Japan the religious organization must also "disseminate the teachings, perform religious ceremonies, and train parishioners." Mr. Sawada unequivocally concluded that "Scientology does all these things." As he went on to note, "Japan is a country where religions place an accent on the raising of one's spiritual ability. From a Japanese point of view, Scientology is indeed a similar religion to others already here. ... It has more similarities to Japanese religions than Western religions, and for this reason it may be misunderstood in the West for not being similar to other mainstream religions."

7. Prof. Urbano Alonso Galan
Theologian and Philosopher,
Madrid

Prof. Alonso also utilized an adaptation of the three-pronged approach, focusing on doctrine, ritual, organization and spiritual objective. He found that Scientology comprises a "community of persons united with a complex body of beliefs, in its search for the infinite, the sacred, searching to place man into his proper relationship with the divine," and concluded that "Scientology fulfills completely the requirements that can be asked of any religion."

These well-grounded, thorough and balanced expert opinions are supported by dozens of others. Together they illustrate the wide variety of approaches to the analysis of religious thought and practice utilizing "ethically neutral" standards. And they are unequivocal in their findings that Scientology is a bona fide religion in every respect.

Each of these expert opinions gives a fascinating depiction of the essential characteristics of any religion and how these characteristics are manifested in Scientology. While much can be gained by reading them, a further dimension can be gained by what follows: a description of the Scientology religion that plainly shows the transcendent dimension of its beliefs, practices and organization. In reading these chapters you will easily see how Scientology shares fundamental characteristics with other religions and serves the common functions described above. You also will see something even more important — how Scientology is dedicated to offering man a practical and attainable path to spiritual salvation.

Doctrine of the Scientology Religion

■

While Scientology owes a spiritual debt to the Eastern faiths,
it was born in the West and its beliefs are expressed
in the technological language of the mid-Twentieth Century.
Scientology adds to these spiritual concepts, a precise and workable technology
for applying those concepts to life.

Scientology religious doctrine includes certain fundamental truths. Prime among them are that man is a spiritual being whose existence spans more than one life and who is endowed with abilities well beyond those which he normally considers he possesses. He is not only able to solve his own problems, accomplish his goals and gain lasting happiness, but also to achieve new states of spiritual awareness he may never have dreamed possible.

Scientology holds that man is basically good, and that his spiritual salvation depends upon himself, his relationships with his fellows and his attainment of brotherhood with the universe. In that regard, Scientology is a religious philosophy in the most profound sense of the word, for it is concerned with no less than the full rehabilitation of man's innate spiritual self — his capabilities, his awareness, and his certainty of his own immortality.

And, in the wider arena, through the spiritual salvation of the individual, Scientology seeks the ultimate transformation — "a civilization without insanity, without criminals and without war, where the able can prosper and honest beings can have rights, and where man is free to rise to greater heights."

In one form or another, all great religions have held the hope of spiritual freedom — a condition free of material limitations and suffering. Scientology offers a very practical approach to attaining this spiritual aim. Of this, L. Ron Hubbard wrote: "For countless ages a goal of religion has been the salvage of the human spirit. Man has tried by many practices to find the pathway to salvation. He has held the imperishable hope that someday in some way he would be free." Mr. Hubbard continued, "And here, after these ages of grief and suffering, through terrible wars and catastrophe, the hope still lives — and with that hope, accomplishment."

Thus, while the hope for such freedom is ancient, what Scientology is doing to bring about that freedom is new. And the technologies with which it can bring about a new state of being in man are likewise new. An understanding of these beliefs will illustrate how Scientology fits within the religious and spiritual traditions of the world.

DIANETICS

L. Ron Hubbard's path to the founding of the Scientology religion began with certain discoveries he made in his research into the nature of man. He announced his findings in 1948 as "Dianetics," a word which means "through the soul" or what the spirit is doing to the body.

With Dianetics, Mr. Hubbard discovered a previously unknown and harmful part of the mind which contains recordings of past experiences of loss, pain and unconsciousness in the form of mental image pictures. These incidents of spiritual trauma are recorded along with all other experiences of one's life in sequential order on what Scientologists call the *time track*. The painful incidents recorded on this time track exist below a person's level of awareness and collectively accumulate to make up what is called the *reactive mind*, the source of all travail, unwanted fears, emotions, pains, and psychosomatic illnesses — as distinct from the *analytical mind*, that portion of the mind which thinks, observes data, remembers it and resolves problems.

Dianetics provided a method to address the reactive mind by uncovering this previously unknown spiritual trauma and erasing its harmful effects on an individual. When this occurs, one has achieved a new state of spiritual awareness called *Clear*. One's basic and fundamental spirituality, personality, his artistry, personal force and individual character, his inherent goodness and decency, are all restored.

While the Clear is analogous to the state of awareness in Buddhism called the Bodhi, or enlightened one, the Clear is a permanent level of spiritual awareness never attainable prior to Dianetics and Scientology.

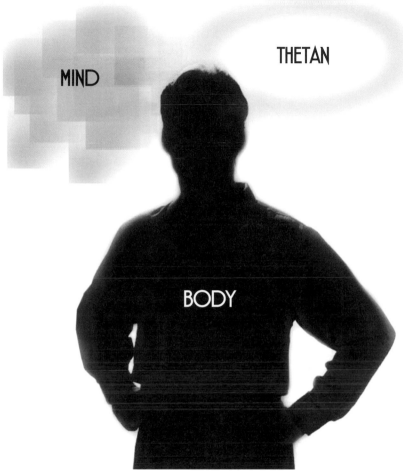

MIND

THETAN

BODY

A man is composed of three parts:
A body, a mind and the individual himself — the spiritual being or thetan.

THE THETAN

For all that Dianetics resolved, the actual nature of the spiritual being was still unknown, even though it was apparent from the beginning that this was a question which would one day need resolution. The breakthrough from Dianetics to Scientology came in the autumn of 1951, after Mr. Hubbard observed many people practicing Dianetics and found a commonality of experience and phenomena which were of a profoundly spiritual nature — contact with past-life experiences. After carefully reviewing all relevant research

data, Mr. Hubbard isolated the answer: Man had been misled by the idea that he *had* a soul. In fact, man *is* a spiritual being, who has a mind and a body. The spirit is the source of all that is good, decent and creative in the world: it is the individual being himself. With this discovery, Mr. Hubbard founded the religion of Scientology, for he had moved firmly into the field traditionally belonging to religion — the realm of the human spirit.

Awareness of the human spirit has existed as a universal ingredient of almost every religion in every culture. However, each defined the spiritual essence of man differ-

In the Scientology view, as expressed in the Axioms and the Factors,
if there was a "spark" that brought a first primeval brew of chemicals to life, that spark was not the
MEST energy of electricity, mindlessly contributing some "lucky" voltage, but the volitional,
spiritual element of theta taking an elemental step in the creation and conquest of MEST.

ently. Terms such as "spirit" and "soul" were encumbered by centuries of various meanings. A new word was needed. Mr. Hubbard adopted the Greek letter theta (θ), which he had assigned in 1950 to represent the transcendent "life force." By adding an "n," the word "thetan" thus described the individual unit of "life force" — the spiritual being — which is the person.

THETA AND MEST

In more general terms, the term *theta* describes the life force which animates all living things. This life force is separate from, but acts upon, the physical universe, which consists of matter, energy, space and time (called "MEST" in Scientology). Scientology is built on a series of fundamental truths called the Axioms, which define *theta* and MEST and describe how the two interrelate to form life as we know it. The Axioms comprise the fundamental elements of the beliefs of the Scientology religion. (See Appendix 1.)

First published in 1954, the Axioms of Scientology present this doctrinal foundation with a definition of theta as a "life static" which has no mass, no wavelength, no location in space or in time. It has the ability to influence and change its environment and achieve total knowingness.

CREATION

Scientology holds that it is the action of this non-material life static, playing upon the kinetic of the physical universe, which results in the manifestation of life. All living organisms are composed of matter and energy existing in space and time, animated by theta.

To a Scientologist, life is thus neither accidental nor purposeless, and the answers to questions of creation and evolution are found in Scientology. Materialists have sought to explain life as a spontaneous accident and evolution as a haphazard process of "natural selection." But these theories never ruled out that additional factors may be merely using such processes as evolution.

Most of the world's religions express some view of the creation of the world. Some religious traditions, such as Hindu and Buddhist, see the universe as essentially eternal, without beginning or end in the stream of time as we perceive it. The first books of the Bible contain an account of the creation of the universe which some Christian faiths hold to be allegorical and some hold to be an expression of literal fact. Other religious traditions have other views, but each attempts to explain this ultimate question of where we came from and how it occurred. In Scientology, this view flows from the theory of theta creating MEST; in fact, it could be said that the creation of the universe is an inseparable part of that theory. The origins of theta and the creation of the physical universe set forth in Scientology are described in *The Factors*, written by Mr. Hubbard in 1953. (See Appendix 1.)

In the Scientology view, as expressed in the Axioms and the Factors, if there was a "spark" that brought a first primeval brew of chemicals to life, that spark was not the MEST energy of electricity, mindlessly contributing some "lucky" voltage, but the volitional, spiritual element of theta taking an elemental step in the creation and conquest of MEST.

Just as the combination of theta and MEST produces life, their separation is synonymous with death of the organism. The human body, like all life forms, follows a cycle of birth, growth and survival, and ultimately death. The thetan, however — the individualized "unit" of life energy which is the person — is not of the universe of matter, energy, space and time and thus does not cease to exist when the body dies. It is immortal.

As Mr. Hubbard observed, "A Scientologist, before he has gone very far, begins to realize the nature of the universe. He realizes this didn't all just occur spontaneously one fine day out of some scientific formula, and he realizes there must have been an Author to all of these things. And he also realizes, oddly enough, in his own participation."

SPIRITUAL ENTRAPMENT BY MEST

The creation and animation of life forms is part of the process by which theta accomplishes its goal in the physical universe, which is the conquest of MEST — expressed in some religions as a conflict between order and chaos. This goal is made necessary by the fact that the physical universe — MEST — tends to encumber the thetan and cause it to act contrary to its true spiritual nature.

Although Scientologists hold that the immortal thetan is intrinsically good,

Scientology posits that he has lost his spiritual identity and operates at a small fraction of his natural ability. It is this loss of spiritual identity that causes man to be unhappy or to act irrationally and with evil intent, even though he is inherently good and highly ethical.

This "fall from perfection" is not due to Satan's intervention or man's natural evil impulses, as Judeo-Christian-Muslim religious theology maintains. Rather, Scientology postulates that it is caused by the thetan's own experiences, whether in current or prior lives. As these experiences accumulate over time, they cause the thetan to become enmeshed with the material universe.

It is through Scientology's central religious practices, as described in Chapter 3, that the thetan is able to extricate himself from this entrapment. This is analogous to the concept of salvation found in other religions.

SALVATION

Scientology's path to spiritual salvation differs from that taken by religions of the Judeo-Christian tradition. In part, this is due to Mr. Hubbard's discovery of the thetan's immortality and its separateness from the mind and the body. This fact aligns Scientology much more to Eastern traditions of religious thought in many ways, including their concepts of salvation.

Jews and Christians believe the soul lives only once, and Christians believe that upon death the soul is resurrected as a spiritual body in heaven or hell.

Like the Buddhist, the Hindu, and even some early Christians, Scientologists believe that the thetan assumes many bodies through its repeated contacts with the physical universe.

Scientologists also believe that the thetan, and therefore man, is basically good. In contrast, Jews and Christians follow the Old Testament teaching that man has two intrinsic impulses — one good and the other evil — that are constantly competing, just as the perceived cosmic struggle between God and Satan.

According to this Judeo-Christian framework, man's plight is to overcome his evil side. Jewish theology states he can do this by observing the finely crafted rules of the Torah. Christian theology teaches he must, at minimum, accept Christ's resurrection as a matter of faith. In either case, the promise of salvation is not realized until death.

Salvation in the Scientology religion is much different and much more immediate. In the tradition of certain Eastern religions, Scientology teaches that salvation is attained through increasing one's spiritual awareness. The complete salvation of the thetan, called "Total Freedom" in Scientology, is attainable through the practice of Scientology religious services.

As one's spiritual awareness grows through practicing Scientology, so does his ability to determine his own answers and solutions about life, the spirit and eternity, and to know them with absolute certainty. Ultimately, the individual is aware of himself as a spirit, independent of the flesh, and that he will survive with memory and identity intact.

Second Dynamic

First Dynamic

THE EIGHT DYNAMICS

One fundamental and unifying factor that runs throughout Scientology's view of the universe is that the primary goal of all life forms —including the thetan — is towards infinite *survival*. The urge is so powerful and so universal that it is known as the "dynamic principle of existence." This dynamic principle of existence is itself divided into eight distinct parts, called the "eight dynamics," each representing one aspect of the survival dynamic. Viewed as concentric circles expanding outward from a common center, the eight dynamics represent an increasing awareness of and participation in all of life's elements. These dynamics represent Scientology's view of the cosmos.

The first dynamic is SELF. This is the urge toward existence and survival as an individual, to be an individual, and to attain the highest level of survival for the longest possible time for self. Here we have individuality expressed fully.

The second dynamic is FAMILY. This is the urge toward existence and survival through sex and the rearing of children.

Third Dynamic

Fourth Dynamic

It stands for creativity, for making things for the future, and it includes the family unit.

The third dynamic is GROUPS. This is the urge toward existence and survival through a group of individuals, with the group tending to take on a life and existence of its own. A group can be a club, friends, a community, a company, a social lodge, a state, a nation, or even a race.

The fourth dynamic is SPECIES. This is the urge toward existence and survival through all mankind and as all mankind.

The fifth dynamic is LIFE FORMS. This is the urge toward existence and survival as life forms and with the help of life forms such as all animals, birds, insects, fish and vegetation, or anything motivated by life. It is, in short, the effort to survive for any and every form of life. It is the interest in life as such.

The sixth dynamic is PHYSICAL UNIVERSE. This is the urge toward existence and survival of the physical universe, by the physical universe itself and with the help of the physical universe and each one of its component parts — matter, energy, space and time.

Fifth Dynamic

Sixth Dynamic

The seventh dynamic is SPIRITS. This is the urge toward existence and survival as spiritual beings or the urge for life itself to survive. Anything spiritual, with or without identity, would come under the heading of the seventh dynamic. The seventh dynamic is the life source, or theta. This is separate from the physical universe and is the source of life itself. Thus, there is an effort for the survival of theta as theta.

The eighth dynamic is the urge toward existence and survival as INFINITY. The eighth dynamic also is commonly called God, the Supreme Being or Creator, but it is correctly defined as Infinity. It actually embraces the "All-ness" of All.

Mr. Hubbard wrote about the interrelationship of the sixth, seventh and eighth dynamics:

"The theta universe is a postulated reality for which there exists much evidence. If one were going to draw a diagram of this, it would be a triangle with the Supreme Being at one corner, the MEST universe at another and the theta universe at the third. Too much evidence is forthcoming in research to

Seventh Dynamic

Eighth Dynamic

permit us to overlook this reality. Indeed, the assumption of this reality is solving some of the major problems of the humanities...."

Because the fundamentals upon which Scientology rests embrace all aspects of life, certain key principles which permeate the religion can also be broadly employed to better any aspect of life. Moreover, the principles greatly clarify what is so often confusing and bewildering. And, through Scientology, a person realizes that his life and influence extend far beyond himself. He becomes aware also of the necessity to participate in a much broader spectrum. By understanding each of these dynamics and their relationship, one to the other, he is able to do so, and thus increase survival on and participation in all these dynamics.

Thus, as a Scientologist expands his awareness, participation and responsibility outward along the dynamics, he will ultimately arrive at the eighth dynamic, survival through Infinity, or the Supreme Being. That is why, according to Mr. Hubbard, "When the seventh dynamic is reached in its entirety, one will only then discover the true eighth dynamic."

SUPREME
BEING

There are probably at least as many concepts of the Supreme Being or ultimate reality as there are religions. Christianity is monotheistic. Hinduism is a polytheistic faith. Branches of Buddhism do not believe in a Supreme Being in any form whatsoever. As many religious scholars note, Scientology in this respect is more like Western religions and shares their view that places the Supreme Being at the pinnacle of the cosmos.

According to Mr. Hubbard, a man who does not share a belief in a Supreme Being is not really a man. Mr. Hubbard wrote:

"No culture in the history of the world, save the thoroughly depraved and expiring ones, has failed to affirm the existence of a Supreme Being. It is an empirical observation that men without a strong and lasting faith in a Supreme Being are less capable, less ethical and less valuable to themselves and society. ... A man without an abiding faith is, by observation alone, more a thing than a man."

Many religions characterize the Supreme Being (whether called Yahweh, God, Allah, or something else) in such terms as omnipotent, omniscient, beneficent, judgmental, demanding, or attribute to the Supreme Being other generally anthropomorphic qualities.

Scientology differs from these other religions in that it makes no effort to describe the exact nature or character of God. In Scientology, each individual is expected to reach his own personal conclusions regarding all eight dynamics, including God, through the practice of the religion. Thus, an individual's understanding as to his relationship with the Supreme Being is developed over time as he comes to understand and participate more fully in each of the preceding seven dynamics.

This is a necessary approach, for in Scientology no one is asked to accept anything on faith. Instead, everyone is expected to test beliefs for themselves, on a purely personal level. A belief — or knowledge — will be true for someone only when that person actually observes it and determines that it is true according to his own observation. Thus, by following the Scientology religious path, one comes to a relationship with the Supreme Being that is truly personal and individual. In this regard, Scientology is in some respects similar to those religions such as Unitarianism and other faiths which are wary of providing dogmatic definitions or descriptions of God.

SCIENTOLOGY
ETHICS

Scientology shares the view of many religions that no person can be spiritually free — or even successful in everyday life — if he is only interested in himself, his first dynamic. From a Scientology perspective, such a person would be considered to have lost his native spiritual awareness of and responsibility for the other seven dynamics.

As a person becomes more spiritually aware through Scientology, he inevitably experiences a reawakening of his own interests and responsibilities in these other areas of life. Thus, as one progresses in Scientology, one normally develops a stronger sense of the importance of the family, and the need to contribute to one's community and take part in activities that assist mankind as a whole. Rather than accepting such duties as a burden, the Scientologist sees responsibility on the eight dynamics as a natural and necessary progression of his own spiritual growth.

Scientology teaches that one must always take these dynamics into account in deciding any course of action, even in seemingly mundane, day-to-day matters. Indeed, one of the cardinal pillars of Scientology thought and the standard by which it encourages individuals to guide their conduct is that the "optimum solution" for any problem is the one that does the "greatest good for the greatest number of dynamics."

It is this interrelationship of the eight dynamics which provides the foundation of Scientology's system of ethics. Indeed, in Scientology, ethical conduct is defined as conduct which maximizes one's growth and participation along each of the dynamics, the most ethical action being that action which enhances the survival and growth of all dynamics, and the least ethical action being that which causes the most destruction along the dynamics, with infinite gradations in between. Good and evil are thus defined, and from them a system of right conduct which enables an individual to maximize the survival of himself, his family, community and society as a whole.

Ethics plays a large role in the life of a Scientologist, as these beliefs govern conduct. Having embraced a yardstick by which to gauge their conduct, Scientologists strive to live honest, ethical lives, to better conditions not only as far as their own lives are concerned, but for their family, community, nation, and all of society. A Scientologist is not following his religion if he is seeking only his own spiritual enhancement. Thus, Scientology doctrine repeatedly emphasizes the need for individuals to apply its religious wisdom to better the conditions of their family, neighbors, their friends and society at large.

Scientology encourages its members to take the principles they have learned through the practice of the religion and apply them to help others to have a better life. Moreover, according to Scientology doctrine, the individual bears a responsibility for bettering the community as surely as he is responsible for taking care of himself, for the Scientologist knows his spiritual salvation depends on it. Some of the many ways in which individual Scientologists work to better their communities are described in Chapter 4.

Communication

Affinity

Reality

In Scientology the components of understanding
— an important part of spiritual well-being — are viewed
as a triangle consisting of Affinity, Reality and Communication,
known as the ARC Triangle.

UNDERSTANDING LIFE

Because the ultimate goal of an immortal spiritual being — infinite survival — can be attained only by maximizing one's participation along all eight dynamics, the question arises as to how, then, an individual accomplishes this.

Scientology teaches that by increasing understanding along all eight dynamics, the thetan can increase his participation and survival potential. Scientology defines understanding as being composed of three elements: affinity, reality and communication. These three interdependent factors may be expressed as a triangle and are examined at great length in Scientology Scripture. Each element occupies a corner of the triangle, known as the *ARC triangle*.

The first element is affinity, which is the degree of liking or affection. It is the emotional state of the individual, the feeling of love or liking for something or someone. The second element is called reality, which could be defined as "that which appears to be." At bottom, reality is actually a form of agreement. What we agree to be real is real. The third element is communication, the interchange of ideas. These three concepts — affinity, reality and communication — are the component parts of understanding. They are interdependent one upon the other, and when one drops, the other two drop; when one rises, the other two also rise.

Of the three elements, communication is by far the most important, and a substantial portion of the Scientology Scriptures are devoted to the understanding and application of communication.

An individual's communication level is a primary index of his spiritual state. To the degree that a person is withdrawn, introverted or uncommunicative he may have many problems in life. Experience shows that many of these problems can be alleviated simply by knowing the various components of communication, thus raising one's ability to communicate.

In Scientology, as a person's spiritual awareness increases, his level of affinity, reality and communication — and thus his understanding — expands. Indeed, Scientology teaches that when a thetan has total affinity, reality and communication across all eight dynamics, complete understanding of the entirety of life and full spiritual awareness follow.

Thus it can be seen that the doctrines of Scientology address ultimate concerns — the relationship of man as a spiritual being to all aspects of life and the universe, and finally his salvation through a route to higher states of spiritual existence. To fully appreciate the depth and scope of the religion, it is necessary to gain some understanding of the most important and unique aspect of Scientology: its practices which are the subject of the next chapter.

CHAPTER THREE

The Religious Practices of Scientology

While the goal of salvation — expressed in Scientology as
Total Freedom — is common to all religions, Scientology offers mankind a precise
and practical route to attaining it through personal revelation.
This route, called Scientology's "Bridge to Total Freedom," follows
a specific sequence of levels of spiritual awareness attained as the Scientologist
participates in the two central practices of the religion
— auditing and training.

The Scientology religion embodies a rich tradition of ceremonies, rites and services. Yet the religious practices of auditing and training are by far the most significant. They are the *sine qua non* of Scientology, for they light the path to higher states of spiritual awareness and ability and, eventually, to spiritual salvation.

While Churches of Scientology hold congregational services to celebrate religious holidays, perform rites of passage and acknowledge other significant dates and events, the essence of Scientology lies in the distinctive methods by which its principles can be applied to the betterment of individual lives.

In auditing, the Scientology minister or auditor (on the left) applies the basic truths of the Scientology religion to the parishioner (on the right) toward the rehabilitation of the human spirit. This is accomplished by helping the individual examine his own existence and improve his ability to face what he is and where he is. The terms auditing and auditor come from the Latin audire, "to listen."

AUDITING

The central religious practice of Scientology is *auditing* (from Latin *audire*, "to listen"), which is a precise form of spiritual counseling between a Scientology minister and a parishioner.

It is readily apparent that, in many respects, man's efforts fall short of the ideal of infinite spiritual survival. He has lost sight of the Supreme Being, lost awareness of his own spiritual nature and, in most cases, forgotten that life requires successful participation in all eight dynamics. Rather than playing his part in the conquest of the physical universe, he suffers failures, to a greater or lesser degree, resulting in pain, unconsciousness and unwillingness to face the challenge of existence.

In the course of an average life as man, the thetan is certain to encounter many experiences that can reduce his level of spiritual awareness. Over the course of many lifetimes, he may entirely lose sight of his true nature, and with that fall from spirituality, the level and quality of his participation in all eight dynamics is diminished.

Auditing reverses this decline. It enables the being to cast off the spiritual chains that grow heavier from lifetime to lifetime — the accumulation of his pains and misfortunes, confusions and his own moral transgressions.

Just as these experiences bring about his fall from spiritual awareness, trapping and enmeshing him in the material universe, auditing provides the route to spiritual salvation by restoring the thetan's full awareness of his essential identity and abilities.

The *practice* of auditing was developed from the understanding of the fundamental laws of life contained in the Scientology Axioms. It is based on the principle that only the truth can set one free, and it enables the person to come to terms with the truth of his own existence — past, present and future. Through auditing, the person regains an understanding of and responsibility for his relationship to all of life and the Supreme Being. With full spiritual awareness and responsibility restored comes complete spiritual freedom — Scientology's spiritual salvation.

During auditing, a person can have many realizations about life. By honestly looking at the factors which have inhibited his spiritual growth, he is able to overcome them and experience a true spiritual resurgence. When auditing is understood as a spiritual practice that incorporates the theta-MEST theory and the concept of the eight dynamics, it is apparent that increased spiritual awareness brings about greater responsibility and participation as regards one's family, one's group and all the other dynamics, including the Supreme Being.

HOW AN AUDITING SESSION IS CONDUCTED

In auditing, the minister, or *auditor* ("one who listens") asks the parishioner a series of specific questions in the area of spiritual travail being addressed in that particular session. Once the auditor locates the area of spiritual trauma, he will ask further specific questions or give directions needed to help the parishioner address and come to grips with that incident, experience or area of life.

The minister does not offer any "advice" to the parishioner. One of the essential principles of Scientology is that an individual can advance spiritually only if he is allowed to find his own answers to life's problems. This is accomplished by helping one to examine his own existence and improve his ability to face what he is and where he is — peeling away the layers of experience that have weighed so heavily upon him.

THE ROLE OF COMMUNICATION IN AUDITING

The brilliance preceding great discoveries is often the insight which posed the right question — perhaps one so "obvious" it never occurred to anyone to ask. Newton may have "discovered" gravity only because he was the first to question why all bodies fall to the Earth.

In a similar way, but in the spiritual realm, auditing leads to personal revela-

tion by posing *precise* questions based on the Scientology cosmology. In seeking for his answer, the parishioner discovers intrinsic truths about life and the underlying factors of existence which transcend the physical universe.

Yet there is another factor in auditing which is even more important: the role of communication itself.

Communication is indeed necessary to all aspects of life; but the understanding of communication in Scientology goes far beyond any ordinary concept of the commonplace exchange of ideas in social intercourse.

One of the Axioms of Scientology, Axiom 28, presents the fundamental principle of communication, and a substantial portion of Scientology Scripture is devoted to its application in auditing. In fact, auditing and spiritual salvation through Scientology practices *only* become possible through the proper application of communication as defined in Axiom 28.

Through communication, the auditor directs the parishioner's attention to confront aspects of his existence to find the answers to auditing questions, erase the harmful mental and spiritual energy in which the thetan is enmeshed, and thus experience relief from spiritual travail.

This precise process of communication, as practiced in auditing, is essential for one to come to a complete understanding of life. As discussed in Chapter 2, understanding exists to the degree that one can have affinity for something, can perceive or experience its reality, and can communicate with it or about it. The precision of communication in auditing therefore plays a direct role in raising a person's understanding and spiritual state.

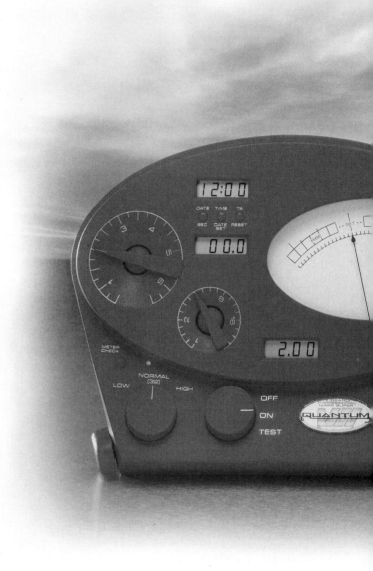

THE ELECTROPSYCHOMETER — AN AID TO AUDITING

Most auditors use a special electropsychometer — called an "E-meter" — to assist them in helping parishioners address experiences which lie at the root of spiritual travail. (Electro-psych-ometer, from *electrometer*: a calibrated device used for measuring extremely low voltages, and

In auditing, the E-meter, or electropsychometer, is used to measure the mental state or change of state of a person, helping the auditor and parishioner locate and handle areas of spiritual distress existing below the individual's current awareness.

HIGHER STATES OF EXISTENCE

Auditing ranges from very simple and basic to more searching and intensive religious experiences as one participates in further and higher level services. Auditing enables an individual to achieve the spiritual state of Clear. In this state the individual is no longer trapped by the prior traumas recorded on his time track and is capable of living a rational, more spiritual existence.

Beyond Clear, one attains higher states of awareness called Operating Thetan. In this spiritual state it is possible for the thetan to possess complete spiritual ability, freedom, independence and serenity, to be freed from the endless cycle of birth and death, and to have full awareness and ability independent of the body.

The Advanced Levels of auditing employ a special auditing procedure which the individual conducts alone; the person acts as his own auditor, alternately posing precise questions and then seeking their answers.

These levels deal with the highest truths of existence. The ability to conduct "solo" auditing presupposes a thorough and intimate knowledge of all fundamental Axioms and principles of Scientology. The Advanced Levels therefore appear at the very top of the Bridge to Total Freedom and are open to those who have completed the lower training and auditing levels necessary for full understanding of these advanced procedures. These individuals are not only spiritually prepared but are required to meet high ethical standards.

psyche: the human soul, spirit or mind.)

This religious instrument is vital because the mental image pictures that harbor these experiences also hold very minute amounts of electrical energy that can be detected with the E-meter. As this charge varies or dissipates, the auditor knows the parishioner has successfully addressed — and resolved — the source of that aspect of his spiritual entrapment. Thus, while the E-meter by itself does nothing, it is an invaluable guide for the auditor.

SCIENTOLOGY RELIGIOUS TRAINING

As described above, the Bridge to Total Freedom is a spiritual path consisting of the two complementary religious practices of auditing and training. Participation in both is essential for the attainment of a complete understanding of all life — all eight dynamics.

While auditing enables the individual to inspect and overcome spiritual encumbrances and rise through a series of ascending levels of spiritual awareness, *training* consists of the intensive study of the tenets of the religion.

Study of the Axioms and fundamental truths contained in Scientology Scripture leads to a complete understanding of man's spiritual nature — the relationship between thetan, mind and body; the relationship between theta and MEST; and the precise means by which a thetan becomes entrapped in the physical universe.

There is no part of life that Scientology training fails to address — from the seemingly mundane to the highest truths of existence. Studying these truths invariably answers many questions the individual has had about himself, his fellows, and the universe in which he finds himself. Training is thus a path of personal revelation and an indispensable part of an individual's personal progress up the Bridge.

An important practice of the Scientology religion is the study of the works of L. Ron Hubbard, which constitute the Scripture of the religion. Studying these truths invariably answers many questions the individual has had about himself and his fellows and the universe in which he finds himself.

But training is also the route by which Scientology ministers acquire the knowledge and skill to conduct auditing. The Scripture studied in training is organized into courses that align with the specific levels of spiritual awareness through which auditing progresses. As the minister completes each level in training, he acquires the knowledge and exact skills required to conduct auditing up to that level.

And as Scientologists become more spiritually aware, they translate this awareness into direct action to help others. Training enables the Scientologist to do that in the most valuable way possible — auditing others to help them achieve their own total spiritual freedom.

Training materials contain all of Mr. Hubbard's books and other written materials, tape-recorded lectures and technical training films that are necessary to impart a complete understanding of Scientology theory and technique.

Mr. Hubbard stressed that the disciplines of Scientology are just as important as its Scripture, and thus training places great emphasis on mastery of the skills of auditing.

HOW SCIENTOLOGY TRAINING IS CONDUCTED

Scientology training allows each individual to progress at his own rate. Each course is organized around a *checksheet* — a list laying out the books and scriptures to be studied, the practical exercises to be completed, and the sequence in which these steps are to be done.

Scientology ministers perform many of the same ceremonies and services as ministers, priests and rabbis of other faiths. Scientology wedding ceremonies, similar in form to those in other religions, draw upon Scientology scriptural concepts which bring heightened spiritual significance to the union.

There are no teachers in a Scientology course room. Instead, students make their own progress through their checksheets, assisted by a Course Supervisor. The Supervisor does not

SCIENTOLOGY CHURCH CEREMONIES

Scientology ministers perform many of the same types of ceremonies and services that ministers, rabbis and priests of other religions perform. Each Sunday, the Church's Chaplain, or another minister, conducts a service for members of the Church, which is open to nonmembers as well. At this service, the minister speaks about a topic related to an important Scientology principle or practice and discusses how it can be applied in daily life. A typical Scientology sermon may address the simple fact that a person is a spiritual being, certain of the Axioms of Scientology, or perhaps the Creed of the Church.

Scientology holds that man determines his own spiritual future through his actions towards others as well as his observance of the rules of conduct as expressed in the Creed of the Church. Consequently, the Sunday sermon often encourages conduct constructive on all dynamics. This message is presented within the framework of Scientology Scripture, and its relevance to everyday life is explained. Thus, the sermon may also be comforting and spiritually uplifting for non-Scientologists, who are always welcome to attend.

On Fridays, church services are held to celebrate and acknowledge those who have completed a church service in the preceding week.

In addition, Scientology congregations celebrate weddings and naming ceremonies for the newborn (similar to christenings in the Christian church) with their own formal ceremonies and mark the passing of their fellows with funeral rites. These services draw on Scientology's rich scriptural material to convey the relevance of these significant occasions from the special perspective of the beliefs of those involved in the ceremony.

lecture, or give his own rendition of Scripture. However unintentional, such interpretations would inevitably include alterations from the original. Instead, the Supervisor assists the student to apply the study principles developed by L. Ron Hubbard, so that he overcomes any misunderstanding and grasps the meaning directly from the Scripture.

The Chaplain often conducts these ceremonies, although any ordained Scientology minister is empowered to officiate. These services, which address the spirit in accordance with the religion's teachings, impart a special quality to these occasions.

NAMING CEREMONY

Although the Scientology naming ceremony for newborn children is comparable to a christening, it expresses the Scientology belief that the baby is a spiritual being who has lived before and will live again. The minister introduces the child to his parents and godparents, tells the child the name he has been given, and welcomes him to the congregation.

Parents and godparents are reminded that their responsibilities include:

That he/she [the child]
be given every chance to understand
the rules by which we
play this game called Life, and further
that we all here present
arrange within his scope
the guidance and the knowledge
that we along our path
already trod, have gained.
Yet always remember this:
Young [child's] life is HIS
and, in the final account
it is for him to make the choice
what path he choose;
what game he play.

Scientology pervades all planes of existence. It encourages and provides a route to achieve increased spiritual awareness and abilities, knowledge of the Supreme Being and the ultimate attainment of total spiritual freedom.

WEDDINGS

There are several different Scientology wedding ceremonies offering varying degrees of formality. Generally, services are familiar in form and appearance: a minister officiates, describes the responsibilities of the union being created, and invites bride and groom to publicly confirm their love for each other and to promise enduring honor and faithfulness. Traditional wedding dress is usual, and bride and groom normally exchange rings.

However, Scientology wedding ceremonies also draw upon scriptural concepts to add spiritual significance. For example, in one traditional ceremony the minister reminds all present of the concept of the ARC triangle. The minister then invites bride and groom to imagine an ARC triangle contained within the circle of the wedding rings they are about to exchange. He then observes, "I should like to see you make a pact between you that you will never close your eyes in sleep on a broken triangle. Heal any breach with the reality of your love through communication."

FUNERAL SERVICE

Similarly, the Scientology funeral service clearly recognizes that the deceased has, as a spiritual being, moved on to assume a new life. The service exhorts those in attendance to remember this fact, and to wish the departed well in his new life.

This sentiment is clear in the following extract:

> Our loss is gain
> In wisdom and in skill
> To future dates and other smiles
> And so we send into the
> Chain of all enduring time
> Our heritage
> Our hope
> Our friend.
> Goodbye, [deceased].
> Your people thank you for
>   having lived.
> Earth is better for your having lived.
> Men, women and children
>   are alive today
> Because you lived.
> We thank you for coming to us.
> We do not contest your right
>   to go away.
> Your debts are paid.
> This chapter of thy life is shut.
> Go now, dear [deceased] and live
>   once more
> In happier time and place.

CHAPLAIN SERVICES

Scientology ministers have always acted to ease suffering and provide succor and guidance to those in need or in distress, whether a member of their congregation or simply someone in the community who may require their help. In fact Scientology ministers traditionally have seen their mission as easing temporal suffering, helping where help is required and restoring dignity to men and women at pivotal points in their lives.

Ministerial services are important for any religion, but for individual Scientologists they take on special significance: It is by helping others that ministers help accomplish the Scientology goal of making this world a better place for everyone.

For example, if a couple are experiencing marital discord and find that it is affecting their progress in auditing and training, they can turn to the Chaplain to help them work through their difficulties. Chaplains are trained in ministering Scientology marriage counseling, an exact technology for alleviating marital problems that addresses the root of all such difficulties: transgressions against the couple's previously agreed moral code which now inhibits their communication. Or the Chaplain may help the young student suffering through his studies. Chaplains may also help the ill or injured, or a teen who cannot get along with his parents, identify, address and resolve the source of his problems.

Possessing the knowledge of Scientology Scripture, the Chaplain is well-equipped to counsel anyone through the trials and tribulations of modern life.

SCOPE OF PRACTICES

Scientology pervades all planes of existence. It encourages, and provides a route to achieve, improved family life and relationships, good health and prosperity, and primarily, increased spiritual awareness and abilities, knowledge of the Supreme Being and the ultimate attainment of spiritual freedom.

From the ultimate questions of existence to the day-to-day problems of real people, Scientology brings answers. It encompasses all life because it defines, clarifies and ultimately resolves what life is.

CHAPTER FOUR

Scripture and Symbols of the Scientology Religion

The Scripture of the Scientology religion consists of the writings and recorded spoken words of L. Ron Hubbard on the subjects of Dianetics and Scientology. This Scripture includes more than half a million written pages, over 3,000 tape-recorded lectures and some 100 films.

This Scripture is the sole source of all doctrine regarding the religion of Scientology and it is an inherent principle of the religion that only by exactly following the path it outlines can mankind achieve spiritual salvation. This concept of orthodoxy in religious practice is fundamental to Scientology. Thus, any attempt to alter or misrepresent the Scripture is regarded as a most severe breach of ecclesiastical ethics.

To ensure the purity and orthodoxy of the Scripture, the copyrights on all of its published works, which are owned exclusively by the Church for the benefit of the religion, have been registered in all relevant countries. These registrations ensure that the Scripture cannot be altered, perverted or taken out of context for improper or harmful ends.

AN OVERVIEW OF THE SCRIPTURE

It is only possible for the thetan to extricate himself from the shackles of the material universe because the fundamental laws which govern the relationship between theta and MEST have been isolated. These laws, discovered by Mr. Hubbard and fully articulated in his writings and lectures, form a crucial part of the Scripture and are used in auditing to enable an individual to discover the truth about his own spiritual nature and his relationship to the physical universe. It is this understanding of truth which ultimately brings freedom.

Information about some of the most important materials which comprise the Scripture follows.

BOOKS

One or more sacred texts are commonly identified with world religions. While other religions have a strong emphasis on belief or faith, the articles of which are usually contained in one or a small number of books, the Scientology religion's emphasis on precise application of doctrine both in services and in life gives rise to a comparatively expansive series of books and other publicly available texts.

Mr. Hubbard's numerous books on different aspects of Scientology and his

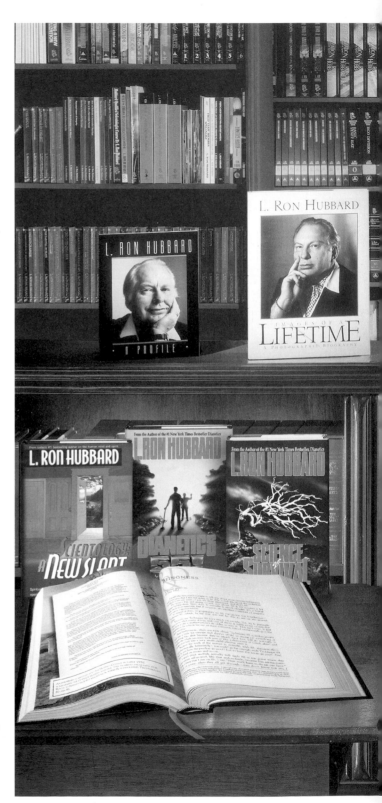

The religious works by L. Ron Hubbard comprise the Scripture of the Scientology religion, and thus the foundation upon which the Church is built. They include lectures, written words and films in 30 languages totaling 35 million words.

researches into the human spirit serve as texts for auditors and for Scientologists generally. These include:

• *Scientology, the Fundamentals of Thought* introduces many of the basic principles of the Scientology religion. It describes the nature of the thetan and the fundamental laws of theta from which stem many of the basic tenets of Scientology, including the dynamics, the fundamentals of affinity, reality and communication, and the three parts of man — thetan, mind and body.

These basic principles delineate how life works, and why, and provide an individual with a greater understanding of his real identity as a spiritual being.

• *Scientology 8-80* is a work concerned with the discovery and increase of the energy of the thetan. A thetan uses energy in the effort to bring order out of the chaos of the MEST universe, as detailed at page 108. When a spiritual being misuses his energy, he can become trapped by his own transgressions and thus become the effect of the material universe. The "8-8" stands for "infinity-infinity" upright, the "0" represents theta, the static.

• *Scientology 8-8008* first set forth The Factors, which comprise a vision of the beginning of life, the creation of the universe and the role of man in it. This text represents a study in how to free the human spirit from the debilitating effects

These basic principles delineate how life works and why and provide an individual with a greater understanding of his real identity as a spiritual being.

of matter, energy, space and time, and a full description of the theta-MEST theory, a core Scientology doctrine. Through the procedures described in this book, one fully awakens the near-ultimate capabilities of the spirit.

• *The Creation of Human Ability* sets out important Scientology religious codes as well as the transcripts of a number of sermons given by L. Ron Hubbard which trace the roots of Scientology through the earliest recorded formulations of Eastern wisdom in the Veda, through the Tao, Buddhism, the Judeo-Christian tradition and culminating in the works of Western seekers of truth.

This book also contains some of the fundamental auditing procedures which are used in the ministration of Scientology and which comprise the Scientology route to spiritual freedom.

• *Scientology, a New Slant on Life*, consists of a series of essays which provide both a discussion on the profound principles and concepts on which Scientology is based and practical techniques which can be used to improve life.

It provides answers to questions with which philosophers and religious men have struggled for centuries, including how to change destructive behavior patterns, the relationship of knowledge and sanity, rules for happy living, the exact anatomy of failure, how to live with children so they grow up intelligent and happy, and a description of what constitutes true greatness.

Mr. Hubbard's books on Dianetics also form part of the Scripture. Probably the most widely known work in the Scientology Scripture is *Dianetics: the Modern Science of Mental Health*, first published in 1950. Although this book predates the full knowledge of the spirit that made the religious nature of Scientology fully evident, it catalogues an important part of Mr. Hubbard's search for the truth of man's spirituality and is still the bedrock which contains many of the fundamental principles which underlie Dianetics and Scientology. Scientologists refer to *Dianetics* as "Book One" and annually celebrate its publication date, May 9, throughout the world.

• *Science of Survival* introduces the concept of how life suffers encumbrances when interacting with the physical universe. This subsequently evolved further into understanding the thetan as something apart from the material universe. The more the life force believes itself to be the effect of the physical universe and hopelessly controlled by it, the more heavily the impediments of the reactive mind weigh on him and affect his level of ARC.

This text contains a complete description of the emotional tone scale, which measures impact of the physical universe upon the thetan by providing a measurement of the level of ARC present in any individual. The survival potential of the life force can be measured by its position on the emotional tone scale and can be increased by moving the thetan up to higher levels of ARC, thus restoring its position of control over the physical universe.

• *Advanced Procedure and Axioms* tenders axioms which give a structure to man's knowledge of his spiritual self and the relationship of the spirit with the physical universe. These axioms contain the fundamental principles which govern the mind and life and describe how the power of a thetan's thoughts and decisions shape existence.

This text outlines counseling methods which return to the individual his own power of self-determinism. With these techniques, the emphasis shifts from addressing the encumbrances of the spirit to include direct communication with the thetan to raise his own awareness and ability.

• *Dianetics '55!* examines at length the importance of communication to the freeing of the human spirit and is the definitive Scripture regarding communication. The text describes universal laws which govern communication and discusses the practical and procedural uses of these laws in auditing at every level of the Bridge.

It further explores the capabilities of the thetan and defines the components of freedom and entrapment. The final chapter is devoted to exteriorization, that state of the spirit existing outside of the body, separate and apart from the material universe.

TECHNICAL AND ADMINISTRATIVE VOLUMES

As he made new discoveries and advances, Mr. Hubbard would release issues of varying length on different aspects of religious practice. The purpose of these was to keep Scientologists apprised of breakthroughs and ensure that auditors could make use of the latest information and counseling techniques as soon as they became known. Ecclesiastical policy concerning the management of church organizations was similarly issued. These are compiled into reference volumes and also into special course materials for the training of auditors and church staff members, and all are publicly available.

There are many other books and pamphlets by Mr. Hubbard which are similarly central to the religion. All are publicly available through any church or mission of Scientology. Many are also available in public libraries and bookstores. (For a full list of these works, see page 243.)

RECORDED LECTURES

Mr. Hubbard's discovery of the true nature of Man as an immortal spiritual being of near infinite capacity, senior to the mechanics of the material universe, opened new and unexpected horizons. During the more than half-century in which he conducted his researches into the human spirit, Mr. Hubbard delivered some 3,000 lectures to Scientologists and to the general public in many different parts of the world. The largest portion of the Scripture is contained in these lectures.

The largest single group of Mr. Hubbard's lectures are the *Saint Hill Special Briefing Course Lectures*, which he delivered from 1961 to 1966 to Scientologists gathered from around the world at Saint Hill, England. These 447 lectures comprise the most comprehensive series ever delivered on the philosophy and practice of Dianetics and Scientology.

During this period, Mr. Hubbard also began to codify the most advanced levels of Scientology. These researches culminated in mapping out the exact and certain route one takes to reach the states of Clear and Operating Thetan and in defining the exact path which is today followed by any Scientologist seeking to attain true spiritual freedom.

Another important series of lectures is *The Philadelphia Doctorate Course*. These provide the most comprehensive statement of the spirit in relation to the physical universe, and what the spirit is capable of achieving. These lectures explore and answer fundamentals about existence, including the true nature of reality, the anatomy of universes and their construction, maintenance and destruction.

By applying the spiritual truths contained in these lectures, an individual can undo the agreements which trap him in MEST and thus step outside of the physical universe and begin to operate fully as a spirit, independent of the traps of materiality.

The traps of the MEST universe are also the subject of a series of recorded lectures known as *Exteriorization and the Phenomena of Space*, which describe how a thetan, under the constant bombardment of the physical universe, becomes unable to emanate energy and so collapses in on himself like a dark star. Thus he becomes the effect of the material universe. These lectures demonstrate how to reverse this process and restore a thetan's ability to emanate and to create space.

The Phoenix Lectures mapped out the religious and philosophical roots of the Scientology religion, going back to the ancient Vedic Hymns. Mr. Hubbard also showed how Scientology effectively combined the methodology as well as the "impatience and urgency" of Western technology with the wisdom of the East.

In these lectures, Mr. Hubbard explored four basic attitudes toward existence or reality and described the methods used by a thetan to create any desired reality through the creation of self-evident considerations which form the very fabric of existence.

There are many, many other public lectures available at churches of Scientology.

FILMS

Mr. Hubbard also wrote a number of film scripts to teach Scientology ministers various auditing techniques. He wrote other film scripts depicting social and personal problems and how Scientology principles can be applied to resolve them. The films are intended for Scientology parishioners and for others interested in learning about the religion. More than 30 of the films written by Mr. Hubbard have been produced and made available to Scientologists. Several that

In order to disseminate the Scientology Scripture as broadly as possible, the Church has established two publishing companies, a film studio and a tape production facility.

impart basic principles of the religion and introduce people to the subject of Scientology are offered for viewing to the general public.

DISSEMINATION AND PRESERVATION OF THE SCRIPTURE

To disseminate the Scientology Scripture as broadly as possible, the Church has established two publishing companies, a film studio and a tape production facility. Other Church personnel involved in making Scientology Scripture available include those who compile existing Scriptural material into special-purpose publications, and translators who currently make the Scripture available in more than 30 languages.

The Church is also involved in extensive activities to preserve the Scripture for eternity. The Church's preservation program has developed and utilized special archival quality paper for books, and is also recording the texts onto stainless steel plates. The recorded lectures are being put onto special long-lasting compact disks as well as a back-up set of specially designed long-playing records. They are also being transcribed and preserved on the same archival paper as the written materials. Combined with advanced storage techniques the Church has developed, these actions will ensure that the Scripture is preserved for many millennia.

SYMBOLS OF THE RELIGION

Through its preservation and dissemination of the Scripture, the Church ensures the widespread practice of the Scientology religion in the exact manner described by Mr. Hubbard. To represent the quest for the spiritual freedom of mankind as well as the orthodox practice of the religion, churches of Scientology use a number of symbols which represent different aspects and concepts of the Scientology religion.

To represent the quest for spiritual freedom and the orthodox practice of the religion, Churches of Scientology use symbols which represent various aspects of the religion. The Scientology cross symbolizes the eight dynamics and the triumph of the spirit. The ARC triangle represents the relationship between Affinity, Reality and Communication. In the "S" and double triangle, the "S" stands for Scientology; the top triangle is the KRC triangle, Knowledge-Responsibility-Control; and the bottom triangle is the ARC triangle. The Dianetics symbol is a triangle divided into four segments which represent growth and life on the first four dynamics. The OT symbol represents the state of Operating Thetan, a being able to operate free of the encumbrances of the physical universe.

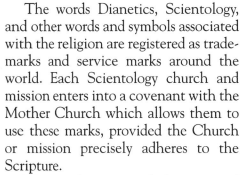

The words Dianetics, Scientology, and other words and symbols associated with the religion are registered as trademarks and service marks around the world. Each Scientology church and mission enters into a covenant with the Mother Church which allows them to use these marks, provided the Church or mission precisely adheres to the Scripture.

Thus, when a symbol associated with the Scientology religion is displayed in connection with the ministry of religious services, those participating in the services are assured that they are being ministered in exact accordance with the Scientology Scripture. In this way they can know with certainty that they are on the true path to spiritual freedom.

SCIENTOLOGY CROSS

The cross, a symbol which predates Christianity by thousands of years, and versions of which have been used by such diverse ancient peoples as the Phoenicians, Hindus, Navajos and Aztecs, has a special design and significance in the Scientology religion.

The Scientology religion divides the life force of the thetan into eight subdivisions called dynamics. Thus, in addition to the four arms of the cross, the

Scientology cross also has four rays which emanate diagonally from the center. Together, the arms and rays symbolize the eight dynamics.

The most basic religious significance of the Scientology cross is that of the spirit and the difficulties of its progression through the material universe. The horizontal bar represents the material universe, and the vertical bar represents the spirit. Thus, the spirit is seen to be rising triumphantly, ultimately transcending the turmoil of the physical universe to achieve salvation.

The cross has other messages as well. The four arms point to the four main points of the compass and thus symbolize the idea that spiritual development extends in all directions and encompasses all of life. Both the horizontal and vertical arms end in the standard heraldic symbols for leaves and flowers, known as the "Cross Fleury" or "Flowery Cross." This symbolizes the full flowering of the individual.

THE ARC TRIANGLE

ARC is one of the central concepts of the religious thought of Scientology. Thus, Scientologists realize that as part of their path to spiritual salvation they must work to continually improve their ARC for all areas of life.

The horizontal bar of the Scientology Cross represents the material universe and the vertical bar represents the spirit. The cross is symbolic of the difficulties of the spirit in its progression through the physical universe, to eventually transcend the turmoil of the material world and achieve salvation.

ARC is represented as a triangle with each of its three components, affinity, reality and communication, as one of the points. Thus, this symbol is often used to show understanding and positive emotion.

SCIENTOLOGY SYMBOL

The Scientology symbol consists of the S for Scientology and two triangles.

The lower of the triangles is the ARC triangle, described above. The top triangle is called the KRC triangle. The K stands for knowledge, the R for responsibility and C for control. As with ARC, these three elements interact; increasing one's sense of responsibility for something will lead to one's ability to increase his knowledge and will then result in an increased ability to control. In that manner, by raising each point of the KRC triangle, the individual is able to be in control of his or her life in all of its aspects.

Thus, the Scientology symbol shows that through participation in the Scientology religion, one can continually raise his ARC or understanding for life and also his sense of responsibility, his knowledge of and ability to control his life. Thus, through Scientology he is on an ascending path that will ultimately result in spiritual freedom and salvation.

DIANETICS SYMBOL

The earliest symbol in the history of Scientology is the Dianetics symbol. The symbol is a triangle divided into four segments, representing one of each of the first four dynamics (self, family, groups, species). The triangle is the shape of the Greek letter delta. Each of the segments is green, symbolizing growth. The space between the segments is yellow, symbolizing life.

OPERATING THETAN (OT) SYMBOL

The state of Operating Thetan — a being able to operate free of the encumbrances of the material universe — is a central part of the ultimate salvation sought in the Scientology religion. This state is represented by a symbol consisting of the letters OT with the T inside the O and each of the points of the T ending at the O's circumference.

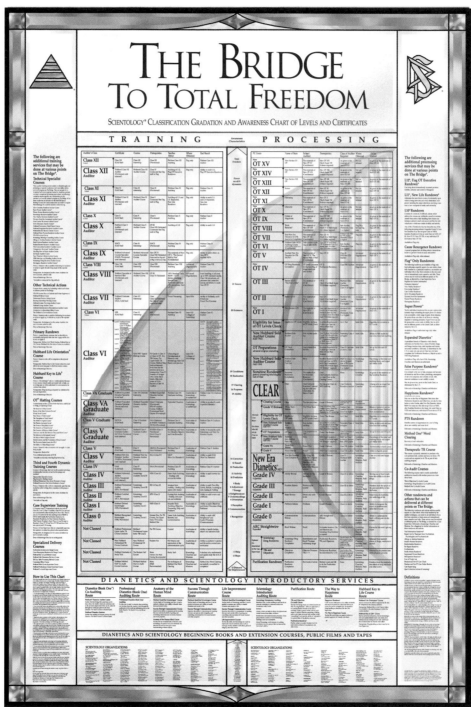

The Bridge to Total Freedom: The Classification and Gradation Chart shows the gradient path an individual takes to reach higher states of awareness, achieved through the two central practices of the Scientology religion. The left side lays out the training route to spiritual freedom, which is attained through study of Scientology Scripture. The right side lays out the auditing route, which is achieved with the help of a minister of Scientology.

THE BRIDGE

That man can improve himself and attain higher states of spirituality, ethics and reason both individually and as a civilization is a basic belief of every Scientologist and part of the underlying foundation of Dianetics and Scientology.

The metaphor which Scientologists use to describe their spiritual progress is that of a Bridge, taking one across the chasm of entrapment in the physical universe to higher states of existence — from unknowingness to revelation. This exact, gradient path to salvation is depicted graphically and is even more frequently used as a descriptive term.

The Scripture of the religion, when followed exactly, offers a route of continually increasing awareness. Thus, while each of the symbols described above represents some aspect of the Scripture, it is the symbol of the Bridge which represents the path that they offer to a better world.

Organizations of the Scientology Religion

The Church of Scientology is formed into an ecclesiastical structure which unifies and aligns a multitude of diverse religious activities including not only auditing and training, but proselytization, ecclesiastical management, relay of communication, production of dissemination materials and many other functions. Thus the Scientology religious community is united both by common beliefs and practices and an organizational form uniquely suited to its religious mission.

Scientologists come together in a worldwide hierarchical religious community. The structure of this community is an important, functional part of the Scientology religion. Because Scientology Scripture requires that its religious practices be ministered in an orthodox manner, the hierarchical structure helps ensure that individual churches receive the support and guidance needed to do this. All Scientologists are thus assured of an orthodox religious observance in every church around the world.

This ecclesiastical structure also helps unify and align a multitude of diverse activities in addition to the core religious services of auditing and training — such as proselytization, ecclesiastical management, relay of communication, production of dissemination materials, and many other functions.

Thus, the Scientology religious community is united not only by shared beliefs and practices, but also by an organizational form uniquely suited to forwarding its religious mission.

This structure also helps bring parishioners together in other ways, such as annual celebrations of Scientology holidays, including the founder's birthday and a day set aside to acknowledge the works of ministers. Tens of thousands attend such occasions, which are hosted by churches at all levels of the hierarchy.

THE SCIENTOLOGY ECCLESIASTICAL HIERARCHY

The ecclesiastical hierarchy of Scientology is made up of hundreds of churches and missions (the smallest churches of the religion), which minister Scientology religious services to their parishioners. There are also churches across the world that provide ecclesiastical management and support services to other churches. Individual churches are housed in their own distinct non-profit corporations or associations, which provide a legal framework from which to conduct their day-to-day affairs in relation to the secular society.

The Church of Scientology International is the Mother Church of the Scientology religion. As such, it is the most senior ecclesiastical management body for the religion throughout the world.

Church of Scientology International's primary function is to coordinate the activities of the churches, missions and field ministers which form the hierarchy, and to ensure they are working in harmony toward Scientology's ultimate goal of creating a better civilization.

The Mother Church furthers this religious purpose by guiding, supporting and coordinating activities throughout the hierarchy on matters concerning the ministry of religious services, training of clergy and other staff, dissemination and ecclesiastical administration as well as social betterment activities.

Church of Scientology International also sees to the publication and distribution of Scientology Scripture throughout the world through two publishing houses, one located in the United States and the other in Denmark, and one internal division, Golden Era Productions, which produces religious films, videotapes, audio tapes and laser discs at its own film studio.

The churches that provide religious services to parishioners are arranged in a hierarchy that reflects the gradient nature of the religion's spiritual levels. As discussed below, Scientology religious services are ministered by independent field ministers and churches of all sizes.

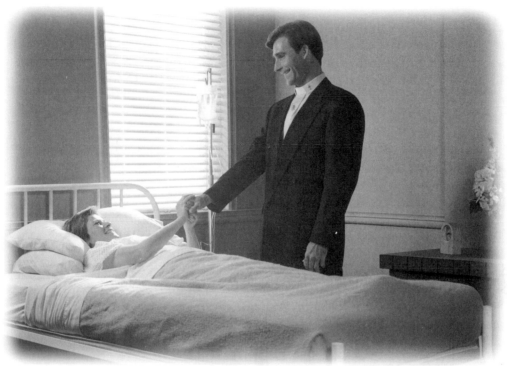

The Church's Volunteer Ministers, using Scientology technology, lend assistance to those in need to improve their lives and have provided tens of thousands of hours of assistance for those less fortunate.

FIELD MINISTERS

At the first level of the Scientology ecclesiastical hierarchy are the individual ministers of Scientology who do not serve on the staff of a church or mission. These field ministers provide introductory religious services to their families, friends and members of their communities. They minister auditing and provide their parishioners marriage counseling, help in overcoming drug problems, assist in dealing with basic distress of life, and are involved in the many other aspects one traditionally associates with a community ministry.

Field auditors sometimes join together to form Auditors Associations or Dianetics Counseling Groups, thereby expanding their activities to include organized lectures, seminars and other means of proselytization.

MISSIONS

Scientology missions reach out into their communities to bring new people into contact with Scientology and encourage their spiritual advancement through the higher levels of the religion. Missions minister basic Scientology religious services including the lower levels of auditing and introductory training.

Missions often are established in parts of the world which are new to Scientology, where they engage in missionary and dissemination activities on a broad scale. Scientology missions can be found in nations from Russia to India, Canada to Chile and from Ghana to Malaysia.

Church of Scientology of Tokyo.

Church of Scientology of Milan.

The Founding Church of Scientology in Washington, D.C., offers a spiritual center for business and government leaders in the nation's capital.

CLASS V CHURCHES

Class V churches minister beginning and intermediate religious services and have the authority to train and ordain ministers. These churches are so named because the highest level of training they provide is designated "Class V" within the progression of Scientology religious services. Class V churches generally are much larger than field groups and missions, and therefore act as the hub for their community of Scientologists. They are a place where Scientologists from all walks of life can gather to share common experiences. Scientologists attend their churches to participate in auditing and training as well as Sunday services, weddings, funerals and naming services, regular Friday evening gatherings and the celebration of Scientology holidays. Some of these churches, called Celebrity Centres, have congregations composed primarily of artists, professionals or community leaders, although, like all other Class V churches, their doors are open to anyone.

Scientology churches are sustained through the contributions of their parishioners. They are supported by the donations their parishioners make in order to participate in specific religious services. These donations are used exclusively to advance the religious, charitable and other public benefit activities that churches of Scientology carry out.

Located in the heart of Hollywood, the Church of Scientology Celebrity Centre International is an oasis for artists seeking spiritual freedom through application of the technologies of Dianetics and Scientology.

SAINT HILL AND ADVANCED ORGANIZATIONS

The original Saint Hill Church is located in East Grinstead, Sussex, England, where Mr. Hubbard resided from 1959 to 1966. Here, he made some of his most significant discoveries on the nature of the mind and spirit and regularly released these in daily lectures attended by advanced students of Scientology who had come from around the globe to study under him. Today this body of scripture, known as the Saint Hill Special Briefing Course, is the most extensive auditor training course in Scientology and comprises nearly 450 recorded lectures as well as other written materials.

There are now Saint Hill Churches in Copenhagen, Los Angeles and Sydney. The next level above Class V churches, in addition to ministering the advanced training services of the Saint Hill Special Briefing Course, these Churches also minister some of the most advanced levels of auditing.

Scientology Advanced Organizations minister very advanced levels of auditing and training, including the first levels of Operating Thetan. Advanced Organizations are located in Los Angeles, East Grinstead, Copenhagen and Sydney.

Saint Hill churches and Advanced Organizations generally minister to Scientologists from the missions and Class V churches in their respective continental areas, although Scientologists may choose to attend any one they wish.

Church of Scientology Advanced Organizations and Saint Hills provide services to parishioners around the world. Pictured counter clockwise from the top are the Advanced Organization/Saint Hill in East Grinstead, England; the Advanced Organization of Los Angeles, California; the American Saint Hill Organization of Los Angeles; and the Advanced Organization/Saint Hill Europe in Copenhagen, Denmark.

The Flag Service Organization in Clearwater, Florida, occupies more than 30 buildings. The Fort Harrison (above) is a religious retreat for parishioners who come from around the world. Here, parishioners participate in advanced auditing levels, some of which are available only at this Church of Scientology.

CHURCH OF SCIENTOLOGY FLAG SERVICE ORGANIZATION

At the next higher level of the Scientology religious hierarchy is Church of Scientology Flag Service Organization, located in Clearwater, Florida, the largest single Church of Scientology in the world.

The "Flag" in this church's name originates from its beginnings in 1967 aboard the *Apollo*, which served as the flagship of a small fleet of ships used in the 1960s and 1970s as religious retreats and training vessels. The name was maintained as tradition when this church moved ashore.

This church ministers the highest levels of auditor training, and Class V churches and missions regularly send their staff there for this special training. The Church of Scientology Flag Service Organization also ministers auditing services, including very advanced OT levels.

Known as the "mecca" of Scientology, this church is the spiritual headquarters for Scientologists from all over the world who travel there to participate in religious services in its unique environment. It has approximately 800 staff, many of whom are fluent in several languages to make it possible to minister to its international congregation.

The highest levels of Scientology auditing are made available to parishioners aboard the 440-foot Motor Vessel Freewinds, *home of the Church of Scientology Flag Ship Service Organization.*

CHURCH OF SCIENTOLOGY FLAG SHIP SERVICE ORGANIZATION

At the next level of the hierarchy is Church of Scientology Flag Ship Service Organization, which ministers the highest level of Scientology auditing as well as special Scientology religious courses not available elsewhere. This church is also unique in that it conducts its services aboard the Motor Vessel *Freewinds*, a 440-foot ship based in the Caribbean. The *Freewinds* serves as the ideal religious retreat where parishioners may devote their full attention to spiritual advancement in a complete Scientology environment.

STAFF OF SCIENTOLOGY ORGANIZATIONS

Local churches and missions of Scientology are administered by Scientologists who have dedicated themselves to full-time service to their religion. Staff duties vary considerably, although all positions directly or indirectly support the ministry of Scientology religious services to parishioners. Some staff are responsible for maintenance, others for dissemination. Some serve executive functions. Others directly offer the services of Scientology: the course supervisors who minister Dianetics and Scientology training and the auditors

The most dedicated staff within the Church are members of the Sea Organization, so named because its original members lived and worked aboard a small fleet of ships. The Sea Organization Coat of Arms symbolizes the dedication of that religious order to the aims of Scientology. The motto "Revenimus," meaning "We come back," underscores the eternal commitment of the individual Sea Org member to the Scientology religion.

who provide religious counseling. These staff obviously are important to the ministry of the religion, but they could not perform their responsibilities without the support of all the other staff of the church. Clearly, all staff of a Scientology church are dedicated individuals who hold their positions with a view toward serving their fellow man.

THE SEA ORGANIZATION

The most dedicated staff within the Church are members of the Sea Organization (or "Sea Org"), a fraternal religious order numbering more than 5,000 internationally. The Sea Org, an unincorporated association with no formal or informal ecclesiastical or secular structure, is a religious fellowship with a unique tradition. It began in 1967 when, after having resigned from all corporate and management positions, L. Ron Hubbard set to sea with a handful of experienced Scientologists to continue his research on advanced levels of auditing. Sea Org members originally lived and worked aboard a small fleet of ships, headed by its flagship, the *Apollo*.

As the Sea Org grew, it expanded to land bases such as the Advanced Organizations in Los Angeles and Denmark. Today, Sea Org members continue to care for the upper levels of Scientology, and so all church organizations above the level of Class V are staffed by Sea Organization members.

The main quality setting Sea Org members apart from other Scientology staff is their eternal commitment to the religion. Sea Org members sign a billion-year covenant, a pledge which has an intensely personal and deeply religious significance to a Scientologist. Sea Org members also share a unique tradition and lifestyle. They live communally in church-provided housing and eat in common dining halls. They receive only modest compensation for their work. But material remuneration is of little importance to members of the Sea Org. They view the privilege of serving their religion at the highest and most dedicated levels as the greatest reward they can ever receive.

Sea Org members are held in high esteem by all Scientologists who recognize the important role they play in the religion.

CONCLUSION

Scientology churches and their related organizations operate exclusively to accomplish the purposes and aims of the religion. They are staffed by committed individuals who apply Scientology Scripture both in administrative activities and in the ministry of religious services. These churches are always open to all and are there to help. They form the focus of religious life for the communities of Scientologists they serve, providing for the salvation of the individual and the means to achieve Scientology's broader goals in society.

RELIGIOUS TECHNOLOGY CENTER

While Church of Scientology International and the churches, missions and field auditor groups which comprise the hierarchy of the religion carry out the traditional function of churches — the ministry of religious services and ecclesiastical management — there is another Church of Scientology that has a unique role in maintaining the very foundation of the religion. That church is Religious Technology Center, which performs the essential function of preserving, maintaining and protecting the orthodoxy of the Scientology religion for eternity.

Monitoring and enforcing the purity of the Scripture is no small task. Historically, almost every religion has experienced periods of growth that have been accompanied by alterations of religious doctrine and practice, sometimes even outright departure from its initial mission.

Initially, Mr. Hubbard personally oversaw the orthodox practice of Scientology. As an integral part of that endeavor, he also registered as trademarks many of the religion's identifying words and symbols, including the word Scientology. These registered marks provided a legal mechanism for ensuring that the Scientology religious technologies could be ministered in exact accordance with the Scripture and not altered by misappropriation or improper use.

In 1982, Mr. Hubbard donated these religious marks to the newly formed Religious Technology Center and entrusted it with the responsibility of protecting the religion of Scientology by enforcing the pure and ethical use and orthodox practice of his religious technologies. Religious Technology Center thus maintains the purity of the Scientology technology and guards against any misuse or misrepresentation by legally registering, and where necessary enforcing, certain Scientology words and symbols as religious trademarks and service marks in countries around the world.

Religious Technology Center is not involved in the day-to-day affairs of churches. Its sole concern is protecting the technology of Scientology so it can always be properly ministered.

THE SCIENTOLOGY MEMBERSHIP ASSOCIATION

The International Association of Scientologists ("IAS") is the international membership organization for Scientologists. It is composed of individuals, churches of Scientology and national associations of Scientology. The IAS, through its own activities and that of its members, embodies the concept of an international religious community.

The purpose of the IAS is to unite, advance, support and protect the Scientology religion in all parts of the world so the Aims of Scientology can be achieved. It also supports churches of Scientology and individual Scientologists who have undertaken special projects to improve their communities or the world in general, particularly projects that further religious freedom. The IAS ensures that the religion is adequately defended and protected so that Scientologists everywhere can carry forth and achieve their mission of spiritual salvation. The IAS unites Scientologists around the world in activities that promote Scientology's aims, bringing freedom and hope to the peoples of earth.

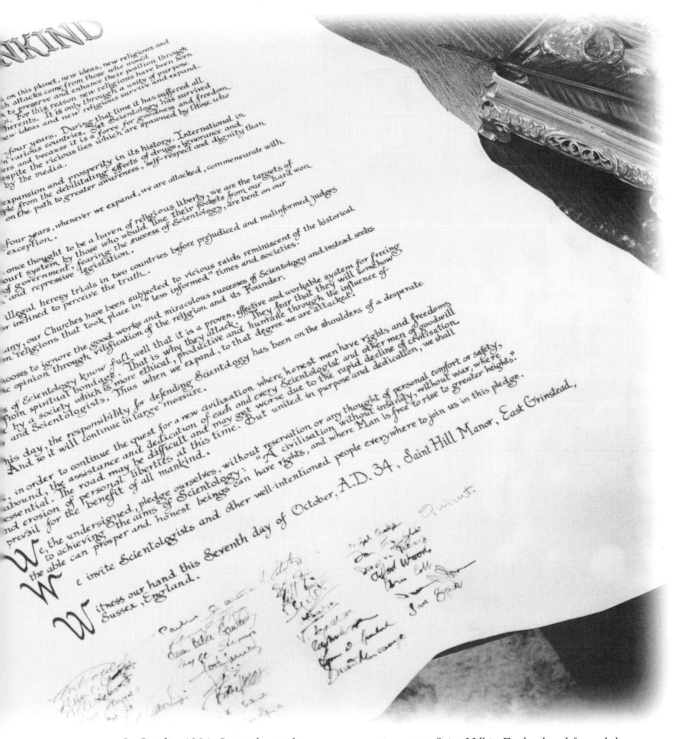

In October 1984, Scientologists from many countries met at Saint Hill in England and formed the
International Association of Scientologists. They signed the Pledge to Mankind, dedicating
themselves to achieving the Aims of Scientology — "A civilization without insanity, without
criminals and without war, where the able can prosper and honest beings can have rights, and
where man is free to rise to greater heights, are the aims of Scientology."

CHAPTER SIX

Scientologists' Community Activities

*As Scientologists continue to improve themselves spiritually,
they assume more and more responsibility for both themselves and their fellow man.
Thus the Church and its members have initiated a number of social benefit
programs to accomplish Scientology's mission to better society.*

The Scientology religion has a strong ethical and moral component that offers very workable guidelines for improving one's own life as well as the lives of others. This reflects the very essence of Scientology teaching: to go out and improve conditions to make this world a better place for all.

Scientology Scripture repeatedly emphasizes the need for individuals to apply its wisdom to better the conditions of their family, neighbors, their friends and society at large.

Thus, Scientologists are not following the scriptural mandate of their religion to the extent they seek only the spiritual enhancement of themselves. As Scientologists continue their spiritual ascent up the Bridge, they assume more and more responsibility for both themselves and their fellow man.

Volunteer Ministers are involved in a
variety of community assistance
programs such as working with the
Red Cross to provide food and clothing
to those in need. Volunteer Ministers
teach study skills to teachers and pupils
(center and bottom right). Using
techniques known as "assists," a
Volunteer Minister can bring spiritual
and physical relief to a person suffering
trauma (bottom left). Others help the
elderly with entertainment, visits and
good cheer.

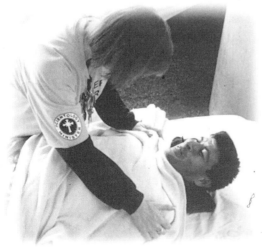

As the *Scientology Handbook* explains:

If no dynamic other than the first existed, you would have no responsibility other than to help yourself. But there are seven more dynamics and, as you have read, if you reduce them to nothing, sooner or later the first dynamic reduces to nothing. Therefore, one cannot sit back and watch his family, his work environment, his community, even his society or culture go downhill. The most wrong thing one can do is to do nothing. (*Scientology Handbook*, 1994, page 764)

Scientologists translate this teaching into direct action by working with other individuals and organizations in broad-based public benefit programs as well as through their own volunteer community activities.

Churches of Scientology are naturally a focal point for their members' volunteer actions, and provide encouragement and guidance to these efforts. Churches also sponsor their own public benefit activities for members' involvement, from drug education and crime prevention campaigns to community improvement projects and charity drives.

VOLUNTEER MINISTERIAL PROGRAM

One way Scientologists help their communities is through the Scientology Volunteer Ministers Program, which is sponsored by every local Church of Scientology.

Volunteer Scientology ministers offer care and aid to neighbors, friends and fellow employees, even strangers.

Volunteer ministers may work on their own or together with other volunteer ministers, attending to those in need at hospitals and retirement homes, providing succor and entertainment. They have aided residents in places as diverse as Japan, Germany, France, United States, Italy and the Olympic Village in Atlanta, Georgia, and victims of every possible tragedy, whether natural or man-made.

In their ministries, volunteer ministers use the fundamental Scientology principles and techniques found in *The Scientology Handbook*. One very important technique every volunteer minister uses is the Scientology "assist," a procedure L. Ron Hubbard developed to alleviate the spiritual component of physical pain, shock and emotional trauma. Assists work on the principle that one tends to withdraw spiritually from an injured area of the body. By restoring communication with this area, one can bring the spiritual element into healing, thereby greatly speeding the healing process.

Volunteer ministers also gather to help improve their communities through special projects such as cleaning up parks, revitalizing neighborhoods and erasing graffiti from public buildings. They may scour parks and beaches for used syringes as they do in Spain and Italy, to help alleviate the threat of AIDS infection to people at play. Or they may distribute food and clothing to the poor, as they do in France, Germany and all over Europe.

Volunteer ministers often join with their churches to support other established community benefit programs such as the Red Cross, Cystic Fibrosis Foundation, the Salvation Army and local community groups by participating in drug-free blood drives, collecting holiday toys for needy children, and donating food and clothing for underprivileged families.

SCIENTOLOGY SOCIAL BENEFIT PROGRAMS

Scientologists and others soon found that the principles and techniques discovered by Mr. Hubbard that form the foundation of Scientology Scripture and practice also could be adapted for use in two broad-based areas of significant social concern — drug rehabilitation and education. Over the years, the various activities Scientologists have conducted in these two areas have become the cardinal points of extensive social benefit programs churches of Scientology and individual Scientologists have undertaken to accomplish Scientology's mission to better society.

Another social benefit program that has popular support among Scientologists centers on a non-sectarian moral code that Mr. Hubbard wrote called *The Way to Happiness*. Scientologists use the code in social benefit programs that have helped raise moral standards throughout all levels of society.

DRUG REHABILITATION AND EDUCATION

One of the most widely known of these social benefit programs is the residential drug rehabilitation and public education program conducted under the name "Narconon" (meaning "non-narcosis" or "no drugs"). The Narconon drug rehabilitation program uses a detoxification procedure that Mr. Hubbard originally developed for use in churches of Scientology as a means of overcoming chemical deposits in the body — often the result of prior drug use — that serve as a barrier to spiritual development.

Other Scientology techniques and principles used in the program address the causes and effects of drug addiction and help participants become contributing members of society. These program components include helping participants learn how to communicate, cope with the pressures of life, and regain higher standards of self-esteem and honesty.

This program has been proven to be highly successful. Independent studies have shown that as many as 76 percent of Narconon participants were still drug-free four years later. Penal program administrators have found that *not one* of their inmates who graduate from a Narconon program returns to a life of crime.

It therefore is not surprising that Narconon programs have received the imprimatur of many governmental bodies. Narconon programs in Switzerland, Denmark, Sweden, Italy and the Netherlands receive public funding. And judges and governmental agencies in countries such as Denmark, Germany, Italy, the Netherlands, Spain, Sweden and the United States are now referring drug addicts to Narconon for rehabilitation, rather than to jail or prison.

It is not unusual for a highly successful Narconon program to be started by the efforts of just one individual. For example, one Scientologist decided to do something about the conditions in a Mexican jail where almost every inmate was a heroin user. When he began discussing the possibility of starting a Narconon program with the prison's officials, he was warned not only that it would be difficult, but that his life could be in danger. Nevertheless,

Scientologists around the world are involved in many different anti-drug efforts. Children in Spain receive special recognitions from a mayor for their anti-drug activities (top left). In Germany, Denmark, Canada and in many other countries Scientologists hold special events to promote the benefits of drug-free living and invite those in their communities to sign the "Say No to Drugs" pledge.

he went ahead. Today, illegal drug use in the prison has virtually stopped and the inmates are learning valuable life skills to prepare for their re-entry to society.

Stories like this have happened around the world. At present, there are 32 residential Narconon programs in 15 countries, including the United States, Canada, Australia, the Netherlands, Spain, Italy, Switzerland, France, Germany, Sweden and Denmark. In all, more than 30,000 former drug addicts have graduated from the Narconon program since its inception.

Scientologists, working in conjunction with Narconon, conduct a wide variety of public drug-education programs. One of these, "The Truth About Drugs," has been presented at schools, corporations, correctional institutions and rehabilitation centers in 11 countries, including Sweden, Brazil, Russia, Holland and Mexico. Started in 1979, this program has reached more than 1 million individuals, primarily children.

Churches of Scientology throughout the world also conduct their own drug-education program separate from those conducted by Narconon. In 1993, the Church of Scientology International launched an educational project called the Drug-Free Marshals Campaign to encourage young people to take responsibility for creating their own drug-free generation. Today the program is one of the most successful campaigns of its kind — more than 20,000 school children and adults have signed pledges to remain drug-free. International in scope, it goes by a variety of different names in many countries. "Ambassadors for a World Without Drugs" in France, "Drug-Free Kids" in Germany, "Guardians for a Life Without Drugs" in Switzerland, "Drug-Free Sheriffs" in Belgium and "Drug-Free Youth" in Denmark.

Churches of Scientology also sponsor an international anti-drug program that

Students in schools throughout Europe, the United Kingdom and around the world use the educational breakthroughs developed by L. Ron Hubbard and sponsored by Applied Scholastics — a separate and autonomous charitable program independent of the Church of Scientology but supported by the Church and its members.

enlists celebrities to give concerts with anti-drug themes, as well as high-profile conferences of community leaders involved in anti-drug activities.

EDUCATION

In the early 1960s, Mr. Hubbard conducted extensive research in the field of learning in order to develop better ways to instruct Scientologists in the tenets of the Scientology religion. Through this research, he discovered a number of basic yet powerful and widely applicable principles that he developed into a technology of study.

Scientologists have utilized these techniques in grassroots educational programs in various areas of education. These include teacher training, schools, community education programs, English as a second language programs and tutorials.

These programs can consist of an entire school of professional educators or just one or two concerned individuals. For example, one British Scientologist took it upon herself to do something about the plight of young children in Zimbabwe after she learned of the severe inadequacy of the educational facilities and resources there. Over a three-year period she made it her personal mission to bring to as many children as possible the rudiments of education and the encouragement to continue. By 1997, after constant travel between her home and Zimbabwe, she had trained more than 1,000 teachers. Local officials estimate that through her efforts alone more than 30,000 students have been reached with her program.

Today, more than 3 million people have participated in these educational programs. Mr. Hubbard's study technology is used by hundreds of organizations and schools in 30 countries on six continents, including China, Pakistan, Australia, South Africa, the United States and much of Europe. The study technology has recently been introduced in Russia and Uganda.

IMPROVING PUBLIC MORALITY

In 1981, Mr. Hubbard wrote a basic, common-sense moral code of fundamental principles and values for living an ethical and happy life that has been published as the book *The Way To Happiness*. This moral code consists of 21 precepts such as "take care of yourself," "be temperate," "love and help children," "set a good example," and "fulfill your obligations." Because the code is entirely non-religious in nature, Scientologists have been able to use it as the genesis of numerous nonsectarian community programs to combat moral decline.

Churches of Scientology and their members have received thousands of awards from local, state and national officials and community leaders in recognition of their valuable outreach contributions.

Through the efforts of thousands of Scientologists, more than 53 million copies of *The Way to Happiness* have been distributed throughout the world in 23 languages. In many countries, Scientology volunteers have formed The Way To Happiness organizations and groups to distribute the moral code locally. Often these groups work closely with other local charitable organizations, media and governmental bodies to maximize distribution to the public.

CRIMINAL REHABILITATION

Scientologists also have adopted principles from Mr. Hubbard's writings to help prison inmates and juvenile delinquents become productive members of society. This social benefit program called "Criminon" consists of a series of supervised and self-directed courses that help program participants develop communication skills, learn how to study, identify anti-social traits, and adopt higher standards of honesty and integrity. An integral part of the Criminon program is a correspondence course based on *The Way to Happiness*.

Since the Criminon program officially began in 1967, it has reached more than 10,000 prisoners and juvenile offenders in prison facilities in the United Kingdom, United States, Mexico, Argentina, Hungary, Poland, Sweden and Africa.

Feedback on the program's results has been overwhelmingly positive. Without exception, graduates of Criminon programs report a new feeling of self-respect, a new sense of meaning in life, and a

Churches of Scientology organize and coordinate public benefit activities as diverse as the needs of their communities and the talents and skills of the membership.

newly found commitment to do better in life. Prison officials and probation officers alike note a marked improvement in the behavior of the offenders in their charge as well as significant drops in recidivism.

COORDINATION AND GUIDANCE

In 1988, the Church formed a separate, non-profit charitable organization called Association for Better Living and Education ("ABLE") to provide overall guidance of the various social benefit programs churches of Scientology and individual Scientologists had been conducting over the years. This enabled the Church to concentrate its charitable and social benefit effort in a separate organization that could focus exclusively on accomplishing these goals. Since then, ABLE has continued to support and promote the public benefit programs with which the Church traditionally has been concerned and enabled them to expand greatly.

ABLE assists local social betterment programs through four social benefit organizations that are international in scope. These are Narconon International, which works in the field of drug abuse and education; Criminon International, which works in the field of criminal rehabilitation; Applied Scholastics International, which works in the field of education; and The Way To Happiness Foundation International, which seeks to raise society's moral standards.

Although the social betterment organizations are organized as separate, independent entities, they work closely with local churches by coordinating their activities wherever possible.

Churches of Scientology organize and coordinate a wide range of public benefit activities as diverse as the needs of their communities and the talents and skills of the membership. Among the common activities are community beautification projects to transform public eyesores into pleasing environments, fundraisers for police-sponsored youth programs, blood drives for the Red Cross, holiday toy and clothing drives, neighborhood anti-crime programs, entertainment for children's hospitals and elderly homes, and assistance to local government and civic community betterment campaigns.

CONCLUSION

Churches of Scientology and individual Scientologists work tirelessly to improve mankind's spiritual and moral well-being. Many work in the formal social betterment programs described above. But Scientology's greatest impact on society may well be at a much more personal level, through the one-on-one interaction that happens every time a Scientologist helps one other person in the community. It is these individual instances of seemingly small benefits that truly affect the spirits of others. Although unsung for the most part, they are certain never to be forgotten by the person helped.

Saint Hill Manor, in West Sussex, England. L. Ron Hubbard's home from 1959 through 1966. Saint Hill also served as the international training and administrative headquarters for the Church of Scientology.

CHAPTER SEVEN

L. Ron Hubbard

Founder
of
Scientology

■

As the founder of the Scientology religion and the sole author of its Scripture,
L. Ron Hubbard is respected by Scientologists
throughout the world, and he has no successor. He is remembered not as one
to be idolized or worshiped but as a man whose legacy is the religion
of Scientology which still lives on. Some understanding of his background serves
to illustrate how he came to discover the truths
of the Scientology religion.

EARLY YEARS

Son of United States naval commander Harry Ross and Ledora May Hubbard, L. Ron Hubbard was born March 13, 1911, in Tilden, Nebraska. Frequent travel was the rule rather than the exception for a military family, and shortly thereafter, the Hubbards settled in Helena, Montana. While there, Mr. Hubbard became friendly with the indigenous Blackfeet, and particularly a tribal medicine man, who was ultimately to honor the young Hubbard with the unique status of blood brother.

With his father's posting to the U.S. naval station on the island of Guam in

1927, L. Ron Hubbard began a period of travel that would consume the next several years. Included were extended voyages throughout the South Pacific and South China Sea and treks across China to its western hills.

He was later to write of his intense curiosity and this examination of Asian culture, that "my basic interest was the field of religion. Buddhism, Taoism were fascinating to me." As a circumstance of that interest, he was puzzled by the human suffering he found rife amongst those who claimed to practice these Eastern faiths. He soon concluded that his searches would need to go further, and deeper.

He returned to the United States and subsequently enrolled at George Washington University where he studied engineering. As a natural result of the interest that was kindled in Asia, he soon embarked on a search for what he then termed "the Life essence."

To that end, he enrolled in one of the nation's first nuclear physics classes where he examined the possibility that life might be explained in terms of small energy particles. "Is it possible," he asked, "that with this new branch of physics we might be able to locate the energy of life?" It opened a small crack in the door, but it was methodology such as this that led him to take a wholly scientific approach to inherently spiritual questions.

Following his stint at George Washington University, he embarked on international ethnological expeditions to the Caribbean and then to Puerto Rico.

Returning to the United States in 1933, Mr. Hubbard launched his literary career. His work spanned all genres, and between 1934 and 1950, he was to author more than 200 novels, stories and screenplays.

Mr. Hubbard's literary career was his means to continue his research into what he now spoke of in terms of the "common denominator of life." In the late 1930s, he conducted experiments concerning cellular memory retention and memory transmission to later generations, concluding that some unknown factor was capable of recording and transmitting the memory of a single event from one cellular generation to the next.

MILESTONES

In 1938, the first summary of these and other findings appeared in his unpublished manuscript, *Excalibur*. The work proposed that the dynamic thrust of all life is the urge to survive. The scope of *Excalibur* was immense and proposed not only the means of placing all life into a definitive framework of survival, but a method of resolving any problems related to existence. Mr. Hubbard chose not to publish it, however, as it did not also offer a workable therapy.

His research thus continued along two broad veins: to further confirm his theory on survival as life's single dynamic thrust, and to determine what inter-

As Mr. Hubbard's research continued, he encountered increasing evidence of man as a wholly spiritual entity and his findings suggested potential states of existence far beyond those previously envisaged — what followed was the foundation of all that is addressed by Scientology.

nal mechanism within the human mind tended to inhibit that thrust.

With the outbreak of the Second World War, Mr. Hubbard was commissioned a lieutenant (junior grade) in the United States Navy, and saw service in the Pacific and Atlantic. By early 1945, he was adjudged partially blind from injured optic nerves and lame from hip and back injuries, and admitted to Oak Knoll Naval Hospital in Oakland, California, for treatment.

While at Oak Knoll, Mr. Hubbard began his first concerted test of therapeutic techniques he had developed during the course of his research. His subjects were drawn from former prisoners of Japanese internment camps, and particularly those with an inexplicable inability to assimilate protein in spite of hormone treatments. Utilizing an early version of Dianetics, Mr. Hubbard proceeded to determine if there were not some sort of "mental block" inhibiting normal recovery. What he found was that thought did indeed regulate endocrinal function and not, as then commonly held, the reverse. Utilizing these same techniques, Mr. Hubbard was eventually able to restore his own health.

At war's end, Mr. Hubbard embarked upon an intensive testing program and continually refined Dianetics techniques. In essence, those techniques addressed what he defined as the sole source of all psychosomatic ills and mental aberration, or what he termed the reactive mind.

DIANETICS GOES PUBLIC

The first summary of Mr. Hubbard's findings was informally presented to friends and colleagues in a manuscript entitled *Dianetics: The Original Thesis.* Response was immediate and considerable, and eventually Mr. Hubbard was persuaded to write a full-length handbook, showing how Dianetics could be employed. This was published on May 9, 1950, under the title *Dianetics: The Modern Science of Mental Health.*

Dianetics was an overnight success and L. Ron Hubbard found himself the subject of immense public demand for personal instruction in Dianetics techniques. Soon, six Dianetics Research Foundations were formed throughout the United States.

Concurrent with his extensive instruction and lecturing, Mr. Hubbard continued his research, and by 1951 he authored his second book on Dianetics: *Science of Survival.* In this book he described in detail the precise nature of the relationship between the fundamental life force — the spirit — and the physical universe. *Science of Survival* also explained how this relationship can lead to unwanted encumbrances of the spirit as well as the means for overcoming these barriers to spiritual freedom.

THE SPIRITUAL ESSENCE OF MAN

As Mr. Hubbard's research continued, he encountered increasing evidence of man as a wholly spiritual entity with experiences extending well beyond the current lifetime. His research also suggested potential states of existence far beyond those previously envisaged.

What followed was the foundation of all that is addressed by Scientology — his definition of that seemingly immortal life-source he eventually termed the *thetan,* a potentially omnipotent and limitless being that was, in fact, the source of life.

Given the inherently religious nature of these discoveries, it was not surprising that those studying Scientology came to see themselves as members of a new religion. Consequently, in 1954, Scientologists established the first Church of Scientology in Los Angeles.

With the founding of Scientology, the impact of Mr. Hubbard's work increased internationally, as did his movements. By the mid-1950s, he was regularly traveling between lectures in Europe and instruction at the Founding Church of Washington, D. C. As Executive Director, he also saw to the worldwide administration of Scientology through these years, and drafted the organizational policies that still form the basis of Church administration.

In 1959, Mr. Hubbard moved to Saint Hill Manor in East Grinstead, Sussex, where he established his home and continued research, instruction and lectures into the spirit. Among the significant developments in the early 1960s were the inauguration of the Saint Hill Special Briefing Course lectures, the delineation of the Scientology Bridge to Total Freedom and the gradual increments of that Bridge to increasingly higher levels of spiritual gain.

To accommodate his research into Scientology's highest levels of spiritual attainment, Mr. Hubbard resigned as Executive Director of the worldwide network of Scientology churches, and moved to sea in 1967 to focus on his research in a distraction-free environment.

While on board the 3,200-ton *Apollo,* Mr. Hubbard streamlined the lower levels of Scientology and continued his research toward the attainment of higher spiritual

levels. He also began to search out solutions to society's more salient problems. In 1969, for example, he noted what recreational drug abuse spelled in terms of cultural and spiritual decline, and commenced work on what would ultimately become the Hubbard Drug Rehabilitation Program. Similarly, after noting the widespread illiteracy and societal waste which flowed from a failing educational system, he began developing methods of study for secular use. Mr. Hubbard's discoveries in these areas formed the genesis of many of the community betterment programs that have since become a worldwide Church effort.

Returning to the United States in 1975, Mr. Hubbard devoted his energies to the founding of the Church of Scientology's Flag Land Base in Clearwater, Florida. To fulfill a pressing need for instructional films on the disciplines of Scientology, he then moved to Southern California, where he wrote and produced numerous such films for the religion.

The 1980s culminated in Mr. Hubbard's completion of his research into man's ultimate spiritual potentials. After finalizing that research, and, in fact, all the Scientology Scripture he had spent most of his life developing, Mr. Hubbard departed this life on January 24, 1986.

"I like to help others, and count it as my greatest pleasure in life to see a person free himself of the shadows which darken his days." — L. Ron Hubbard

THE LEGACY

Today, the Scripture of Scientology comprises tens of millions of words in books and lectures by L. Ron Hubbard. In all, there are more than 120 million copies of L. Ron Hubbard books in circulation.

And Mr. Hubbard's legacy extends beyond Scientology *per se*. His educational discoveries have been used to help millions of children better read, write and comprehend. Hundreds of thousands of men and women have ended their substance abuse or prevented themselves from falling into the trap of abuse through his discoveries in drug rehabilitation. And literally more than 50 million have been reached through his non-religious moral code.

But for Mr. Hubbard, what was important was not acclaim or recognition, but that he achieved his intended aim of helping man "become a better being" by founding the religion of Scientology.

Appendices

The Theological Fundamentals of the Scientology Religion

The Aims of Scientology

By L. Ron Hubbard

A civilization without insanity, without criminals and without war, where the able can prosper and honest beings can have rights, and where man is free to rise to greater heights, are the aims of Scientology.

First announced to an enturbulated world in 1950, these aims are well within the grasp of our technology.

Nonpolitical in nature, Scientology welcomes any individual of any creed, race or nation.

We seek no revolution. We seek only evolution to higher states of being for the individual and for society.

We are achieving our aims.

After endless millennia of ignorance about himself, his mind and the universe, a breakthrough has been made for man.

Other efforts man has made have been surpassed.

The combined truths of fifty thousand years of thinking men, distilled and ampified by new discoveries about man, have made for this success.

We welcome you to Scientology. We only expect of you your help in achieving our aims and helping others. We expect you to be helped.

Scientology is the most vital movement on Earth today.

In a turbulent world, the job is not easy. But then, if it were, we wouldn't have to be doing it.

We respect man and believe he is worthy of help. We respect you and believe you, too, can help.

Scientology does not owe its help. We have done nothing to cause us to propitiate. Had we done so, we would not now be bright enough to do what we are doing.

Man suspects all offers of help. He has often been betrayed, his confidence shattered. Too frequently he has given his trust and been betrayed. We may err, for we build a world with broken straws. But we will never betray your faith in us so long as you are one of us.

The sun never sets on Scientology.

And may a new day dawn for you, for those you love and for man.

Our aims are simple, if great.

And we will succeed, and are succeeding at each new revolution of the Earth.

Your help is acceptable to us.

Our help is yours.

The Factors

*Summation
of the considerations and
examinations of the human
spirit and the material
universe completed between
A.D. 1923 and 1953.*

1 Before the beginning was a Cause and the entire purpose of the Cause was the creation of effect.

2 In the beginning and forever is the decision and the decision is TO BE.

3 The first action of beingness is to assume a viewpoint.

4 The second action of beingness is to extend from the viewpoint, points to view, which are dimension points.

5 Thus there is space created, for the definition of space is: viewpoint of dimension. And the purpose of a dimension point is space and a point of view.

6 The action of a dimension point is reaching and withdrawing.

7 And from the viewpoint to the dimension points there are connection and interchange. Thus new dimension points are made. Thus there is communication.

8 And thus there is light.

9 And thus there is energy.

10 And thus there is life.

11 But there are other viewpoints and these viewpoints outthrust points to view. And there comes about an interchange amongst viewpoints; but the interchange is never otherwise than in terms of exchanging dimension points.

12 The dimension point can be moved by the viewpoint, for the viewpoint, in addition to creative ability and consideration, possesses volition and potential independence of action; and the viewpoint, viewing dimension points, can change in relation to its own or other dimension points or viewpoints. Thus comes about all the fundamentals there are to motion.

13 The dimension points are each and every one, whether large or small, *solid*. And they are solid solely because the viewpoints say they are solid.

14 Many dimension points combine into larger gases, fluids or solids. Thus there is matter. But the most valued point is admiration, and admiration is so strong its absence alone permits persistence.

15 The dimension point can be different from other dimension points and thus can possess an individual quality. And many dimension points can possess a similar quality, and others can possess a similar quality unto themselves. Thus comes about the quality of classes of matter.

16 The viewpoint can combine dimension points into forms and the forms can be simple or complex and can be at different distances from the viewpoints and so there can be combinations of form. And the forms are capable of motion and the viewpoints are capable of motion and so there can be motion of forms.

17 And the opinion of the viewpoint regulates the consideration of the forms, their stillness or their motion, and

these considerations consist of assignment of beauty or ugliness to the forms and these considerations alone are art.

18 It is the opinions of the viewpoints that some of these forms should endure. Thus there is survival.

19 And the viewpoint can never perish; but the form can perish.

20 And the many viewpoints, interacting, become dependent upon one another's forms and do not choose to distinguish completely the ownership of dimension points and so comes about a dependency upon the dimension points and upon the other viewpoints.

21 From this comes a consistency of viewpoint of the interaction of dimension points and this, regulated, is TIME.

22 And there are universes.

23 The universes, then, are three in number: the universe created by one viewpoint, the universe created by every other viewpoint, the universe created by the mutual action of viewpoints which is agreed to be upheld—the physical universe.

24 And the viewpoints are never seen. And the viewpoints consider more and more that the dimension points are valuable. And the viewpoints try to become the anchor points and forget that they can create more points and space and forms. Thus comes about scarcity. And the dimension points can perish and so the viewpoints assume that they, too, can perish.

25 Thus comes about death.

26 The manifestations of pleasure and pain, of thought, emotion and effort, of thinking, of sensation, of affinity, reality, communication, of behavior and

being are thus derived and the riddles of our universe are apparently contained and answered herein.

27 There *is* beingness, but man believes there is only becomingness.

28 The resolution of any problem posed hereby is the establishment of viewpoints and dimension points, the betterment of condition and concourse amongst dimension points, and, thereby, viewpoints, and the remedy of abundance or scarcity in all things, pleasant or ugly, by the rehabilitation of the ability of the viewpoint to assume points of view and create and uncreate, neglect, start, change and stop dimension points of any kind at the determinism of the viewpoint. Certainty in all three universes must be regained, for certainty, not data, is knowledge.

29 In the opinion of the viewpoint, any beingness, any thing, is better than no thing, any effect is better than no effect, any universe better than no universe, any particle better than no particle, but the particle of admiration is best of all.

30 And above these things there might be speculation only. And below these things there is the playing of the game. But these things which are written here man can experience and know. And some may care to teach these things and some may care to use them to assist those in distress and some may desire to employ them to make individuals and organizations more able and so give to Earth a culture of which we can be proud.

*Humbly tendered as a gift
to man by L. Ron Hubbard,
23 April 1953*

The Scientology Axioms

Written by Mr. Hubbard in 1954, the Scientology Axioms are a condensation of all earlier Axioms and Logics. These Axioms are truths which are proven by all of life and which represent the most succinct distillation of wisdom regarding the nature of the human spirit.

Axiom 1 Life is basically a static.

DEFINITION: *a life static has no mass, no motion, no wavelength, no location in space or in time. It has the ability to postulate and to perceive.*

Axiom 2 The static is capable of considerations, postulates and opinions.

Axiom 3 Space, energy, objects, form and time are the result of considerations made and/or agreed upon by the static and are perceived solely because the static considers that it can perceive them.

Axiom 4 Space is a viewpoint of dimension.

Axiom 5 Energy consists of postulated particles in space.

Axiom 6 Objects consist of grouped particles.

Axiom 7 Time is basically a postulate that space and particles will persist.

Axiom 8 The apparency of time is the change of position of particles in space.

Axiom 9 Change is the primary manifestation of time.

Axiom 10 The highest purpose in the universe is the creation of an effect.

Axiom 11 The considerations resulting in conditions of existence are fourfold:

a. AS-ISNESS *is the condition of immediate creation without persistence, and is the condition of existence which exists at the moment of creation and the moment of destruction, and is different from other considerations in that it does not contain survival.*

b. ALTER-ISNESS *is the consideration which introduces change, and therefore time and persistence, into an AS-ISNESS to obtain persistency.*

c. ISNESS *is an apparency of existence brought about by the continuous alteration of an AS-ISNESS. This is called, when agreed upon, reality.*

d. NOT-ISNESS *is the effort to handle ISNESS by reducing its condition through the use of force. It is an apparency and cannot entirely vanquish an ISNESS.*

Axiom 12 The primary condition of any universe is that two spaces, energies or objects must not occupy the same space. When this condition is violated (a perfect duplicate) the apparency of any universe or any part thereof is nulled.

Axiom 13 The cycle of action of the physical universe is create, survive (which is persist), destroy.

Axiom 14 Survival is accomplished by alter-isness and not-isness, by which is gained the persistency known as time.

Axiom 15 Creation is accomplished by the postulation of an as-isness.

Axiom 16 Complete destruction is accomplished by the postulation of the as-isness of any existence and the parts thereof.

Axiom 17 The static, having postulated as-isness, then practices alter-isness, and so achieves the apparency of isness and so obtains reality.

Axiom 18 The static, in practicing not-isness, brings about the persistence of unwanted existences, and so brings about unreality, which includes forgetfulness, unconsciousness and other undesirable states.

Axiom 19 Bringing the static to view as-is any condition devaluates that condition.

Axiom 20 Bringing the static to create a perfect duplicate causes the vanishment of any existence or part thereof.

A perfect duplicate is an additional creation of the object, its energy and space, in its own space, in its own time using its own energy. This violates the condition that two objects must not occupy the same space, and causes the vanishment of the object.

Axiom 21 Understanding is composed of affinity, reality and communication.

Axiom 22 The practice of not-isness reduces understanding.

Axiom 23 The static has the capability of total knowingness. Total knowingness would consist of total ARC.

Axiom 24 Total ARC would bring about the vanishment of all mechanical conditions of existence.

Axiom 25 Affinity is a scale of attitudes which falls away from the coexistence of static, through the interpositions of distance and energy, to create identity, down to close proximity but mystery.

By the practice of isness (beingness) and not-isness (refusal to be) individuation progresses from the knowingness of complete identification down through the introduction of more and more distance and less and less duplication, through lookingness, emotingness, effortingness, thinkingness, symbolizingness, eatingness, sexingness, and so through to not-knowingness (mystery). Until the point of mystery is reached, some communication is possible, but even at mystery an attempt to communicate continues. Here we have, in the case of an individual, a gradual falling away from the belief that one can assume a complete affinity down to the conviction that all is a complete mystery. Any individual is somewhere on this Know to Mystery Scale. The original Chart of Human Evaluation was the emotion section of this scale.

Axiom 26 Reality is the agreed-upon apparency of existence.

Axiom 27 An actuality can exist for one individually, but when it is agreed with by others it can be said to be a reality.

The anatomy of reality is contained in isness, which is composed of as-isness and alter-isness. An isness is an apparency, not an actuality. The actuality is as-isness altered so as to obtain a persistency.

Unreality is the consequence and apparency of the practice of not-isness.

Axiom 28 Communication is the consideration and action of impelling an impulse or particle from source-point across a distance to receipt-point, with the intention of bringing into being at the receipt-point a duplication and understanding of that which emanated from the source-point.

The formula of communication is: cause, distance, effect, with intention, attention, and duplication with understanding.

The component parts of communication are consideration, intention, attention, cause, source-point, distance, effect, receipt-point, duplication, understanding, the velocity of the impulse or particle, nothingness or somethingness.

A noncommunication consists of barriers. Barriers consist of space, interpositions (such as walls and screens of fast-moving particles) and time. A communication, by definition, does not need to be two-way. When a communication is returned, the formula is repeated, with the receipt-point now becoming a source-point and the former source-point now becoming a receipt-point.

Axiom 29 In order to cause an as-isness to persist, one must assign other authorship to the creation than his own. Otherwise, his view of it would cause its vanishment.

Any space, energy, form, object, individual or physical universe condition can exist only when an alteration has occurred of the original as-isness so as to prevent a casual view from vanishing it. In other words, anything which is persisting must contain a "lie" so that the original consideration is not completely duplicated.

Axiom 30 The general rule of auditing is that anything which is unwanted and yet persists must be thoroughly viewed, at which time it will vanish.

If only partially viewed, its intensity, at least, will decrease.

Axiom 31 Goodness and badness, beautifulness and ugliness are alike considerations and have no other basis than opinion.

Axiom 32 Anything which is not directly observed tends to persist.

Axiom 33 Any as-isness which is altered by not-isness (by force) tends to persist.

Axiom 34 Any isness, when altered by force, tends to persist.

Axiom 35 The ultimate truth is a static.

A static has no mass, meaning, mobility, no wavelength, no time, no location in space, no space. This has the technical name of "basic truth."

Axiom 36 A lie is a second postulate, statement or condition designed to mask a primary postulate which is permitted to remain.

EXAMPLES:

Neither truth nor a lie is a motion or alteration of a particle from one position to another.

A lie is a statement that a particle having moved did not move, or a statement that a particle, not having moved, did move.

The basic lie is that a consideration which was made was not made or that it was different.

Axiom **37** When a primary consideration is altered but still exists, persistence is achieved for the altering consideration.

All persistence depends on the basic truth, but the persistence is of the altering consideration, for the basic truth has neither persistence nor impersistence.

Axiom **38** 1. Stupidity is the unknownness of consideration.

2. Mechanical definition: Stupidity is the unknownness of time, place, form and event.

1. Truth is the exact consideration.

2. Truth is the exact time, place, form and event.

Thus we see that failure to discover truth brings about stupidity.

Thus we see that the discovery of truth would bring about an as-isness by actual experiment.

Thus we see that an ultimate truth would have no time, place, form or event.

Thus, then, we perceive that we can achieve a persistence only when we mask a truth.

Lying is an alteration of time, place, event or form.

Lying becomes alter-isness, becomes stupidity.

(The blackness of cases is an accumulation of the case's own or another's lies.)

Anything which persists must avoid as-isness. Thus, anything, to persist, must contain a lie.

Axiom **39** Life poses problems for its own solution.

Axiom **40** Any problem, to be a problem, must contain a lie. If it were truth, it would unmock.

An "unsolvable problem" would have the greatest persistence. It would also contain the greatest number of altered facts. To make a problem, one must introduce alter-isness.

Axiom **41** That into which alter-isness is introduced becomes a problem.

Axiom **42** Matter, energy, space and time persists because it is a problem.

It is a problem because it contains alter-isness.

Axiom **43** Time is the primary source of untruth.

Time states the untruth of consecutive considerations.

Axiom **44** Theta, the static, has no location in matter, energy, space or time, but is capable of consideration.

Axiom **45** Theta can consider itself to be placed, at which moment it becomes placed, and to that degree a problem.

Axiom **46** Theta can become a problem by its considerations, but then becomes MEST.

MEST *is that form of theta which is a problem.*

Axiom **47** Theta can resolve problems.

Axiom **48** Life is a game wherein theta as the static solves the problems of theta as MEST.

Axiom **49** To solve any problem it is only necessary to become theta, the solver, rather than theta, the problem.

Axiom **50** Theta as MEST must contain considerations which are lies.

Axiom **51** Postulates and live communication not being MEST and being senior to MEST can accomplish change in MEST without bringing about a persistence of MEST. Thus auditing can occur.

Axiom **52** MEST persists and solidifies to the degree that it is not granted life.

Axiom **53** A stable datum is necessary to the alignment of data.

Axiom **54** A tolerance of confusion and an agreed-upon stable datum on which to align the data in a confusion are at once necessary for a sane reaction on the eight dynamics. (This defines sanity.)

Axiom **55** The cycle of action is a consideration. Create, survive, destroy, the cycle of action accepted by the genetic entity, is only a consideration which can be changed by the thetan making a new consideration or different action cycles.

Axiom **56** Theta brings order to chaos.

COROLLARY: *Chaos brings disorder to theta.*

Axiom **57** Order manifests when communication, control and havingness are available to theta.

DEFINITIONS:
Communication: the interchange of ideas across space.

Control: positive postulating, which is intention, and the execution thereof.

Havingness: that which permits the experience of mass and pressure.

Axiom **58** Intelligence and judgment are measured by the ability to evaluate relative importances.

COROLLARY: *The ability to evaluate importances and unimportances is the highest faculty of logic.*

COROLLARY: *Identification is a monotone assignment of importance.*

COROLLARY: *Identification is the inability to evaluate differences in time, location, form, composition or importance.*

The above is a summary of states of being which can be used to create, cause to persist, or destroy.

Having agreed to the mechanics and retaining the agreements, the thetan can yet make innumerable postulates which by their contradiction and complexity, create, cause to persist, and destroy human behavior.

Scientology

■

An Analysis and Comparison of its Religious Systems and Doctrines

Bryan R. Wilson, Ph.D.

Emeritus Fellow
Oxford University
England

i. THE DIVERSITY OF RELIGIONS AND THE PROBLEMS OF DEFINITION

i.i. Elements of the Definition of Religion

There is no one definitive definition of religion that is generally accepted by scholars. Among the many definitions that have been advanced there are, however, a number of elements that are frequently invoked. These elements appear in various combinations. They include:

(a) Beliefs, practices, relationships and institutions relative to:

1) supernatural forces, beings, or goals;

2) higher unseen power or powers;

3) man's ultimate concern;

4) sacred things (things set apart and forbidden);

5) an object of spiritual devotion;

6) an agency that controls man's destiny;

7) the ground of being;

8) a source of transcendent knowledge and wisdom;

(b) Practices which constitute obedience, reverence or worship;

(c) The collective or group character of religious life.

Although causes are rarely included in definitions of religion, "an experiential encounter with the spiritual" is sometimes indicated. The consequences and functions of religion are indicated as:

(a) maintenance of a moral community;

(b) the conferment of group and/or individual identity;

(c) a framework of orientation;

(d) a humanly constructed universe of meaning;

(e) reassurance and comfort respecting prospects of help and salvation.

Religion is always normative, but since each religion differs from others, modern specialists in the sociology of religion and comparative religion seek to discuss the normative without themselves becoming committed to it.

Such is the diversity of patterns of belief, ritual, and organization, however, that any definition of religion is strained in attempting to encompass all the manifestations of religion that are known.

i.ii. The Original Use of the Concept

The concept "religion" was formerly often identified with actual concrete manifestations of beliefs and practices in Western society. Apart from Christians, Jews and Muslims, it was generally held that other peoples had no religion in the proper sense. They were "heathens". Theologians who used the term "religion" tended to mean by it Christianity, and in England reference to "Christianity" was often taken to mean that faith as purveyed specifically by the Church of England. That restricted usage has steadily receded as more has become known of oriental belief-systems, and as the study of religion has transcended the narrow normative prescriptive restraints of traditional Christian theology. Religion has become an object of study for academic disciplines — in particular the social sciences — which approach that subject objectively and neutrally and without any implication of adherence to any one particular religion, or a preference for one above another.

i.iii. Cultural Bias and the Definition of Religion

The development of a thoroughgoing neutrality in the study of religion was achieved only slowly, however. Some contemporary studies in comparative religion still manifest evident bias. Even in the social sciences, explicitly committed to value-free enquiry, certain prejudices are apparent in work done in the inter-war years. In particular, it was often gratuitously assumed that there had occurred a process of religious evolution analogous to that of biological evolution and that the religion of the most advanced nations was necessarily "higher" than that of other peoples. For some (conspicuously Sir James Frazer) it was believed that religion was an evolutionary step on the road from magic to science.

i.iv. Contemporary Usage

Today social scientists and increasingly theologians employ the concept as a neutral expression, no longer implying any *a priori* assumptions about the greater truth of one religion over another. It is not now assumed that belief in one deity is necessarily a higher form of religion than belief in several deities or in none. It is recognized that a religion may postulate an anthropomorphic god, some other form of deity, a supreme being, a plurality of spirits or ancestors, a universal principle or law, or some other expression of ultimate belief. Some Christian theologians such as Bultmann, Tillich, van Buren and Robinson have abandoned traditional depictions of deity, and prefer to refer to "the ground of being" or "ultimate concern".

i.v. Extension of the Concept

As anthropologists came to maintain that there was no clear instance of a society that lacked all forms of supernatural beliefs and institutions that supported such beliefs, so they concluded that, in the wider sense of the term, there was no society without religion. The concept "religion" came to connote phenomena that had family resemblance rather than shared identity, and religion ceased to be defined in terms specific to one particular tradition. The concrete items that pertained to Christianity, and which had been regarded as essential to the definition of religion, were now seen to be merely examples of what a definition might include. The specification of such concrete elements was superseded by more abstract formulations which embraced a variety of types of beliefs, practices and institutions which, although far from intrinsically identical, could be regarded as functional equivalents. Every society was perceived to have beliefs that, although diverse, transcended known empirical reality and had practices designed to bring men into contact or rapport with the supernatural. In most societies, there were people who undertook the special functions associated with respect to this goal. Together, these elements came to be recognized as constituting religion.

i.vi. Religious Diversity in Simple Societies

In relatively small, tribal societies there are often rites and myths of considerable complexity which do not usually constitute one consistent, internally integrated and coherent system. Religion undergoes change, and accretion occurs in both myth and ritual as a society experiences contact with neighbouring or invading peoples. Different rites and beliefs may be attached to different situations (e.g., to induce rain, to ensure fertility in crops, animals and women; to provide protection; to cement alliances; to initiate age-groups or individuals, etc.). All such activities are directed towards supernatural agencies (however defined) and they are recognized by scholars as religious.

i.vii. Religious Diversity in Advanced Societies

The codes of religious belief and practice in technically more advanced societies are generally more elaborately articulated and display greater internal coherence and stability, but even in advanced systems, elements of diversity persist. No theological system or schematization of beliefs pertaining to the supernatural, in any of the world's great religions, is wholly coherent. There are always unexplained residues. There are also remnants of earlier religious orientations such as folk religious elements which persist among the general populace. The sacred scriptures of all major religions manifest internal contradictions and inconsistencies. These and other sources give rise to differences among religious specialists who embrace different and at times irreconcilable interpretative schemes and exegetical principles, which feed different traditions even within what is broadly acknowledged to be orthodoxy.

i.viii. Development of Religious Pluralism

In advanced societies, deliberate and conscious dissent from orthodoxy must be regarded as a normal phenomenon. Christians, Jews and Muslims are divided, not only within orthodoxy, but by dissentient groups which reject all forms of orthodoxy and which follow a divergent pattern of religious practice (or who reject religion altogether). Dissent is most conspicuous in contexts in which religious exclusivity prevails: that is to say, in which the individual is required, if adhering to one religion, to renounce allegiance to all others — a pattern of commitment rigorously required in the Judaeo-Christian-Islamic traditions. As state governments have ceased to prescribe specific forms of religion, dissenting religious bodies have been both tolerated and granted certain general religious privileges in European countries, and have come in many cases to enjoy the general freedom of religion embraced constitutionally in the United States. The situation which obtains today of a large number of different denominations operating side-by-side is known as "religious pluralism".

i.ix. Normative and Neutral Approaches to Religion

A religion characteristically sets out certain stories (myths) and propositions respecting the supernatural which are expected to command belief. It prescribes ritual performances. It sustains institutions (in the broad sense of regulated relationships, whether at a rudimentary personal level or as a complex system of behaviour, procedures and property-maintenance). It sometimes also stipulates rules of moral conduct, although the rigour of such stipulation and the sanctions attached to morality vary considerably. But, at least, religion defines obligations and promises rewards for conformity in the shape of supernaturally provided benefits. Religion constitutes a normative system. Religious teachers ("theologians" in Christianity — but the term is inappropriate for some other religions) necessarily endorse and enjoin these norms. In contrast, social scientists regard the values which a religion canvasses merely as facts, neither endorsing nor denying their warrant or their worth. This approach resembles that of those formulations of the law which declare that the law does not discriminate among religions.

Because religion is normative and intellectually has been mainly the preserve of theologians, there is, in all advanced societies, an inheritance of learned language about religion which bears the normative stamp of religious commitment. It is deemed essential here to avoid the value-preference implicit in such language and to employ the neutral terminology of the social sciences, whilst seeking to maintain an appropriate sensitivity to those engaged in religious activity.

i.x. 'Borrowed' Nomenclature

Early definitions and descriptions of the essentials of religion frequently used terms borrowed from the religious traditions of those who formulated them. It is now recognized that the use of terms peculiar to one religion must distort the depiction of other religions, and may frequently involve false assumptions. Concepts evolved within one cultural and religious tradition will misrepresent the functionally equivalent but formally distinctive elements of religion in another. Instances of such inappropriate usage include reference to "the Buddhist church", "the Muslim priesthood" or, in reference to the Trinity, "Christian gods". Similarly, although acts of reverence, obeisance, contemplation, or dedication occur in all advanced religions, commentators have not always recognized them as worship because, in Western usage, that term has been heavily loaded with Christian preconceptions and prescriptions concerning appropriate attitudes and actions. For example, the functional equivalent of

If religions are to be accorded parity, it becomes necessary to adopt abstract definitive terms to encompass the diversity of religious phenomena.

Christian worship in cultivating the dispositions of worshippers occurs in Buddhism but its form is different and it is normally described by other terms. Thus, if religions are to be accorded parity, it becomes necessary to adopt abstract definitive terms to encompass the diversity of religious phenomena.

i.xi. The Inherent Deficiency of Abstract or Objective Analysis

This use of abstract language, which may be regarded as "clinical" in the sense of not being contaminated by the particular traditions of any one religion, will necessarily fail to capture all the intrinsic qualities of any specific faith but it is a necessity if an appraisal is to be achieved. It will exhaust neither the cognitive nor the emotional aspects of belief, ritual, symbolism and institutions. This social scientific approach makes possible objective comparison and explanation, but it does not, and does not pretend to, convey the whole substance of the inner meaning or emotional appeal that a religion has for its own adherents.

ii. THE INDICIA OF RELIGION

ii.i. The Principal Characteristics of Religion

In accordance with the foregoing considerations, we may now indicate, in abstract and general terms, the principal characteristics of religion. What follows does not purport to be a universally applicable definition so much as the enumeration of features and functions which are frequently found in religion, and which are identified as such.

These are:

(a) belief in an agency (or agencies) which transcend(s) normal sense perception and which may even include an entire postulated order of being;

(b) belief that such an agency not only affects the natural world and the social order, but operates directly upon it and may even have created it;

(c) the belief that at some times in the past explicit supernatural intervention in human affairs has occurred;

(d) supernatural agencies are held to have superintended human history and destiny: when these agencies are anthropomorphically depicted they are usually credited with definite purposes;

(e) the belief is maintained that man's fortune in this life and in afterlife (or lives) depends on relationships established with, or in accordance with, these transcendental agencies;

(f) it is often (but not invariably) believed that whilst transcendent agencies may arbitrarily dictate an individual's destiny, the individual may, by behaving in prescribed ways, influence his experience either in this life or in future life (lives) or both;

(g) there are prescribed actions for individual, collective or representative performances — namely, rituals;

(h) elements of placatory action persist (even in advanced religions) by which individuals or groups may supplicate for special assistance from supernatural sources;

(i) expressions of devotion, gratitude, obeisance or obedience are offered by, or in some cases, are required of believers, usually in the presence of symbolic representations of the supernatural agency(ies) of the faith;

(j) language, objects, places, edifices, or seasons that are particularly identified with the supernatural become sacralized and may themselves become objects of reverence;

(k) there are regular performances of ritual or exposition, expressions of devotion, celebration, fasting, collective penance, pilgrimage and re-enactments or commemorations of episodes in the earthly life of deities, prophets or great teachers;

(l) occasions of worship and exposition of teachings produce the experience of a sense of community and relationships of goodwill, fellowship and common identity;

(m) moral rules are often enjoined upon believers, although the area of their concern varies: they may be couched in legalistic and ritualistic terms, or they may be canvassed more as conformity with the spirit of a less specific, higher ethic;

(n) seriousness of purpose, sustained commitment and lifelong devotion are normative requirements;

(o) according to their performance, believers accumulate merit or demerit to which a moral economy of reward and punishment is attached. The precise nexus between action and consequence varies from automatic effects from given causes to the belief that personal demerit may be cancelled by devotional and ritual acts, by confession and repentance, or by special intercession from supernatural agents;

(p) there is usually a special class of religious functionaries who serve as custodians of sacred objects, scriptures, and places; specialists in doctrine, ritual and pastoral guidance;

(q) such specialists are usually paid for their services, whether by tribute, reward for specific services, or by instituted stipend;

(r) when specialists devote themselves to the systematization of doctrine, the claim is regularly made that religious knowledge provides solutions for all problems, and explains the meaning and purpose of life, often including purported explanations of the origin and operation of the physical universe and of human psychology;

(s) legitimacy is claimed for religious knowledge and institutions by reference to revelation and tradition: innovation is regularly justified as restoration; and

(t) claims to the truth of teaching and efficacy of ritual are not subjected to empirical test, since goals are ultimately transcendent and faith is demanded both for goals and for the

arbitrary means recommended for their attainment.

The foregoing items are not to be regarded as *sine qua non*, but as probabilities: they constitute phenomena frequently found empirically. It may be regarded as a probabilistic inventory.

ii.ii. Non-essential Characteristics of Religion

The foregoing inventory is set forth in terms of considerably abstract generalization, but actual religions are historical entities, not logical constructs. They encompass widely different organizing principles, codes of conduct and patterns of belief. At many points, generalization is not easy, and once the (often unconscious) prejudices of the Christian tradition are set aside, it becomes apparent that many of the concrete items which, on the basis of the Christian model, might be supposed to be the *sine qua non* of religion, are, in fact, not found in other systems. In the foregoing inventory, allusion to a supreme being is avoided, since for Theravada Buddhists (and for many Mahayana Buddhists), Jains and Taoists that concept has no validity. Worship, referred to above, has very different implications in Buddhism from those which it carries for worshippers in Christianity. The inventory makes no reference to creeds, which are of peculiar importance in the Christian tradition, but are not of such importance in other religions. It does not mention the soul, vital as is that concept in orthodox Christianity, because the doctrine of the soul is somewhat dubious in Judaism, and is explicitly denied by some Christian movements (e.g., the Seventh-day Adventists and Jehovah's Witnesses — each of which

bodies has millions of adherents throughout the world, and by Christadelphians and those Puritans, including Milton, who were known as moralists). There is no direct reference to hell in any sense of the idea developed in Christianity, since this item is lacking in Judaism. The afterlife is alluded to in the singular or the plural to accommodate the two variant Christian ideas of transmigration of the soul and of the resurrection, and the somewhat different accounts of reincarnation in Buddhism and Hinduism. None of these specific items can be considered essential to the definition of religion.

iii. SCIENTOLOGY BRIEFLY DELINEATED

iii.i. The Church of Scientology as a New Religion

Scientology is one of a number of new religious movements which embrace features which correspond in certain respects to some of the trends evident in the mainstream of Western religion. It employs language which is contemporary, colloquial and unmystical; and it presents its dogmas as matters of objective fact. Its conception of salvation has both a proximate and an ultimate dimension. The wide appeal which it has commanded among the public of the advanced countries of the Western world has made it a focus of attention among sociologists and other students of contemporary religion.

iii.ii. My Knowledge of Scientology

I began to read the literature produced by the Church of Scientology in 1968, and at one time even projected a study of the movement. Although I did not finally undertake that work, I continued to read Scientology literature. I have visited the Church's headquarters at Saint Hill Manor, East Grinstead and became acquainted with Scientologists. Since that time I have maintained contact with the movement in Britain, and have paid other visits to Saint Hill Manor and to a Scientology church in London. I have continued to take a close interest in the development of the religion as one among a number of contemporary religions which are objects of interest to me as a sociologist. I have read, among other material of a more ephemeral nature, the following works, all of them official publications, and most of them the writings of L. Ron Hubbard:

Scientology Handbook for Preclears
Scientology 8-80
Scientology 8-8008
The Book Introducing the E-Meter
Dianetics: The Original Thesis
*Dianetics: The Modern Science
   of Mental Health*
A Test of Whole Track Recall
The Problems of Work
Self-Analysis
The Creation of Human Ability
The Phoenix Lectures
The Axioms of Scientology
Advanced Procedure and Axioms
Scientology: A New Slant on Life
The Character of Scientology
*Ceremonies of the Founding
   Church of Scientology*
The Scientology Religion
Science of Survival
Introduction to Scientology Ethics
The Way to Happiness
Description of the Scientology Religion
What is Scientology?
The Scientology Handbook

In works that I have written on new religions, I have referred to Scientology on various occasions, and included a short account of this religion in my book, *Religious Sects* (London: Weidenfeld, 1970), and a longer discussion of the religious character of Scientology in my later book, *The Social Dimensions of Sectarianism* (Oxford: Clarendon Press, 1990). I have maintained my interest in the movement for the past twenty-six years.

iii.iii. Dianetics — the Genesis of Scientology

When, in May 1950, Mr. L. Ron Hubbard first set out the prospectus of Dianetics, from which Scientology later developed, there was no suggestion that he was putting forward a pattern of religious belief and practice. Dianetics, an abreaction therapy, was not set forth in the language of faith. There is no reason to suppose that, at that time, Hubbard envisaged that Dianetics would become a system of religious belief and practice, or that his following would come to describe and organize itself as a Church.

iii.iv. Mental Healing and Religion

Therapeutic practice, however, has often manifested a potential for acquiring metaphysical and religious affiliations, as, in different ways, may be seen from Christian Science, the New Thought movement, and yoga techniques. On the other side, established religions have at times developed specialist activities concerned with healing, particularly mental healing, and major churches sometimes have departments organized for this purpose. Dianetics invoked no religious principles at the outset, but as the theoretical legitimation for practice became elaborated, a metaphysical dimension was increasingly recognized and some of the ideas propounded came to be described in terms that were distinctly religious in their implication.

iii.v. How Religions Evolve

All religions are a product of evolution. No religion has come into being as a fully-fledged system of belief and practice at a given moment of time. In this, Scientology is no exception: from a body of therapeutic theory a religion developed. It would be quite impossible to say when Christianity itself became a religion, beginning, as it did, with a loose collection of ethical exhortations and occasional miracles; becoming a popular movement among Galileans; gradually becoming a Jewish sect; and then becoming a distinct religion. Even then, it took centuries for its doctrines to be fully articulated, and its ritual practice has continued to undergo frequent change. In movements of more recent times, the process of evolution into a religion is yet more clearly evident. The Seventh-Day Adventist Church traces its origins to the widely diffused belief in the very early advent of Jesus Christ which occurred among Baptists, Presbyterians, Methodists and others in upstate New York in the 1830s: the Church was formed only in 1860. Similarly, it took several decades after the first experience (of the Fox Sisters) of the "rappings" at Hydesville (purportedly messages from the "spirit world") before a Spiritualist church was formed. Similarly, Mary Baker Eddy had experimented for years with systems of mental healing before her "discovery" of her mind-cure in 1866, and even for some years after that date she thought her system would be taken into the major churches rather than becoming the basis for the Church of Christ, Scientist, which she founded in 1875. The Pentecostalists experienced the charismata of speech in unknown tongues, prophesying, healings and other "gifts" from the year 1900, but separate Pentecostal churches formed only very slowly in the course of the next two decades. None of these movements, all of which became separate religions, started as such. Neither did Scientology.

iii.vi. Scientology Doctrine — the Development of the Metaphysic

It is necessary, even at the cost of some possible repetition in what follows, to set out in broad terms a comprehensive statement of the major teachings of Scientology, and to indicate the extent to which these tenets of belief constitute a coherent religious system. Scientology grew out of a more narrowly focused therapeutic system, Dianetics. It has been suggested that this term was a combination of *dia* = "through" and *nous* = "mind or soul", and thus constituted, even if initially less than wholly consciously, a religious perspective. With the incorporation of Dianetics into the wider framework of Scientology, a much more extensive conception of an encompassing metaphysical system was articulated which made evident the fundamentally religious nature of this philosophy. Whilst the immediate application of Dianetics was — like that of Christ's teachings during his lifetime — in the sphere of mental healing, the purport of the subsequent teachings, which explained and promoted that therapeutic activity, implicated a growing apprehension of spiritual ideas and values.

iii.vii. Scientology Doctrine — the Thetan and the Reactive Mind

The basic postulate of Scientology is that man is, in fact, a spiritual entity, a *thetan* which successively occupies material human bodies. The thetan is an individual expression of *theta*, by which is understood life or the life source. Loosely defined, the thetan is the soul, but it is also the real person, the continuing and persisting identity which transcends the body which it inhabits. It is said to be immaterial and immortal, or at least to have the capacity to be immortal, and to have an infinite creative potential. It is not part of the physical universe — but it has the latent capacity to control that universe, which is comprised of Matter, Energy, Space and Time (MEST). Thetans are seen as having brought into being the material world largely for their own pleasure (as indeed might also be said of the creation of the world by the Christian God). It is held that, at sometime long past, thetans became victims of their own involvement with MEST, becoming entrapped by it and allowing their own creation to limit their own abilities and to circumscribe their sphere of operations. Thus, man's activities and achievements in the present material world fall far short of his potential: he is encumbered by innumerable past entanglements with MEST and these are recorded in a reactive mind which responds irrationally and emotionally to anything which recalls painful and traumatic past experiences (which he has suffered or caused to others). The reactive mind functions in defiance of that capacity for control which, were he able to recapture his true native spiritual abilities, he would be able to exercise over his body and his environment. Whilst man is regarded as fundamentally good, and both desirous and capable of survival, his past forfeiture of his abilities has rendered him an endangered species.

iii.viii. Scientology Doctrine
— Reincarnation and Karma

Thetans are believed to have occupied innumerable bodies over aeons of time. Thus, Scientology embraces a theory which, whilst differing in particulars, shares major assumptions with that theory of reincarnation as maintained in Hinduism and Buddhism. The Scientological emphasis on the importance of present (or future) consequence of past actions resembles the concept of karma. Untoward effects result from "overt acts" (harmful acts) which are an aspect of the entanglement with the material universe. The ideal for the thetan is to maintain rational action and to be "at cause" over phenomena: that is to say, to determine the course of events in the immediate environment. This idea has clear analogies with the Eastern concept of creating good karma for the future by wholesome deeds, although Scientologists do not use these terms or concepts. The events of past lives affect the present, but, by the techniques developed in Scientology, these events can be recalled, confronted, and the specific sources of present problems can be located in those events. It is this facility which provides the basis for spiritual healing — that is, it provides the opportunity for altering the "karmatic" effects of past actions.

iii.ix. Scientology Doctrine
— the Eight Dynamics

Existence, according to Scientology, may be recognized in eight different divisions in an ascending order of magnitude, each being designated as a dynamic. Briefly described these are: 1st, the self dynamic, the urge of the self for existence; 2nd, the sex dynamic, which incorporates both the sexual act and the family unit and the maintenance of the family; 3rd, the will to existence, which is found in a group or an association, such as the school, the town, or the nation; 4th, the dynamic will of mankind to maintain its existence; 5th, the existence and will to survive of the entire animal kingdom, which includes all living entities; 6th, the urge towards existence of the entire physical universe of matter, energy, space and time; 7th, "the urge towards existence as or of spirits", which includes all spiritual phenomena, with or without identity; and finally, the 8th dynamic: the urge towards existence as infinity. This dynamic is identified as the Supreme Being, which also can be called the "God dynamic". Scientology is concerned with survival, and the survival of each of these dynamics is seen as part of the goal of the practice of Scientology. Thus although much of the initial practice of Scientology is concerned more narrowly with more personal spiritual benefits for those (preclears) who seek Scientological assistance, ultimately the Scientologist must realize that his present life is but a fragment of his continuing existence as a thetan, and that the life of the individual is linked to each of these ascending levels described in the eight dynamics, and so ultimately to the existence and survival of the Supreme Being or infinity.

iii.x. Scientology Doctrine
— Therapy and Communication

As in other religions, the primary and initial preoccupation of many of those who are drawn to Scientology is proximate salvation from immediate suffering and travail; this is the appeal of the therapeutic element which is found in many religions — and conspicuously so in early

Christianity — alongside the more mystical, metaphysical, spiritual teachings which believers are expected to come to as they grow in the faith (see Hebrews, 5:12-14). Most Scientologists have first learned of the possibility of improving their everyday experience and of enhancing their intelligence (by gaining increasing control of the reactive mind). The possibility of achieving such results, through the process of auditing, is represented in the formulation known as A-R-C. A stands for Affinity, which represents the emotional experience of the individual and his sense of relationship to others through the emotions. R stands for Reality, which is represented as inter-subjective consensus about objective phenomena. C stands for Communication, and great importance is attached in Scientology to communication. When people have an affinity, when they agree about the nature of objective phenomena, then communication can occur very readily. Associated with this triadic concept of A-R-C, is the scale of human emotions, known to Scientologists as the "tone scale". As emotional tone descends, so communication becomes difficult, and reality becomes badly experienced. Communication itself is, however, an agency which seeks to increase understanding and, effectively and precisely used, it becomes the main therapeutic agency for releasing the individual from the entrapment he has experienced with the material world. The thetan can be enabled to communicate with its own past, recognize the nature of past traumatic experiences, and attain self-knowledge which permits him to escape from these encumbrances.

The basic postulate of Scientology is that man is, in fact, a spiritual entity, a thetan which successively occupies material human bodies.

iii.xi. Scientology Doctrine — Auditing as an Agency of Therapy

The Tone Scale is the first representation to the individual of the possibility of benefit from Scientology, indicating an ascent from chronic emotional tone, such as apathy, grief, and fear to enthusiasm (and, at more advanced levels, to exhilaration and serenity). It is to experience benefits of this kind that many are first drawn to Scientology. The technique for such progress is found in auditing, in which a trained Scientologist, by the use of carefully controlled questions, brings back to the awareness of the individual episodes from his own past which have left a traumatic imprint (an "engram") in his reactive mind and which prevent the individual from behaving rationally. Release from the effects of these impediments to rational thinking is thus the process by which an individual is raised on the "tone scale", so improving his competencies, but it is also — and herein lies its fuller religious significance — the method by which the thetan might achieve salvation, initially by eliminating the aberrations that it suffers as a consequence of entanglement with the material world, and eventually by gaining total freedom from the ill effects of the MEST universe. Scientologists refer to this condition as being "at cause". It has clear analogues with the mode of salvation that is offered in Eastern religions. Since they, too, see the individual as encumbered by the effects of past deeds (karma), the conception of salvation which they espouse is also through a process (enlightenment) by which the effect of karma can be broken, liberating the individual. The ultimate goal is for the individual, known as an Operating Thetan, to exist outside the body, to be in a condition described as "exterior" to all physicality. Such a condition is one which at least some Christians would acknowledge as the condition of the saved soul.

iii.xii. Scientology Doctrine — Rational Means for Salvation

The religious philosophy outlined above lies behind the practice of Scientology. Hubbard has himself regarded it as in some ways similar to the philosophy of Eastern religions. In particular, he has cited the Vedas, the hymns of creation which form part of the Hindu tradition, as containing a concept very similar to Scientology's "Cycle of Action". The Cycle of Action is the apparent order of life from birth, through growth, to decay and death, but through the knowledge which Scientology makes available, the baleful effects of the operation of this cycle might be avoided. The cycle can be amended from one of creation, survival and destruction, to one in which all elements can be creative acts: Scientology is committed to promoting and increasing creativity and conquering chaos and negativity. It recognizes a continuing "track" or line of descent of wisdom from the Vedas and Gautama Buddha to the Christian message, and claims some affinity with the teachings of all of these. But whereas the wisdom presented, for example in Buddhism, perhaps allowed occasional individuals to attain salvation in one lifetime, there was, then, no set of precise practices which

ensured that result; there was little possibility of replication. The attainment of salvation remained subject to random or uncontrolled factors. Salvation was attained by a few, here and there, now and then, if at all. What Hubbard claimed to do was to standardize, almost to routinize, religious practice, and to increase the predictability of soteriological results. Such application of technical methods to spiritual goals indicates the extent to which Scientology adopts modern techniques for the realisation of goals that were once reached only spasmodically and occasionally, if at all. This, then, is the attempt to introduce certainty and order into spiritual exercises and attainments. Scientology seeks to discipline and order the religious quest by the employment of rational procedures. In this sense, it has done in the technological age much of what Methodism sought to do at an earlier stage of social development, by trying to persuade people that the goal of salvation was to be sought in a controlled, disciplined, methodical way. Whilst the actual methods of the Methodists were still couched in the relatively conventional language of current Christianity, the methods advocated by Scientology bear the strong imprint of a society more fully committed to rational and technological procedures. The means which Scientology employs have been likened to the *upaya* ("right method") of the seventh stage of the Bodhisattva Way to salvation in Mahayana Buddhism. According to this version of Buddhism, at the seventh stage, the believer becomes a transcendental Bodhisattva who (like the Operating Thetan in Scientology) is no longer tied to a physical body.

iii.xiii. Scientology Doctrine — Auditing as Pastoral Counsel

The means which Scientology employs constitutes a form of pastoral counselling, most specifically organized into the techniques of *auditing* (from Latin *audire*, to listen). The specific techniques and apparatus of auditing are organized as a technology which constitutes the core part of Scientological religious practice. This pattern of practice is essential for all who would experience the saving benefits of the faith, and Hubbard's effort has been to reduce the process of spiritual enlightenment to a set of ordered procedures which systematically reach deeper levels of consciousness. This method, like that of affirmation in Christian Science, is claimed to eliminate both the sense of sin and the effects of past suffering and wrongdoing.

iii.xiv. Scientology Doctrine — Stages of Salvation

The two principal stages in this healing and soteriological process are the conditions described respectively as Clear and Operating Thetan. The pre-clear who first encounters Scientology is troubled by the mental impedimenta of past painful and emotional experiences. Auditing seeks to bring these items to consciousness, to make the individual communicate with his past, to confront those events which have given rise to emotional discharge, and thereby to bring the individual to a point at which he transcends that discharge and can review these hitherto forgotten disturbances with total equanimity and rational awareness. The baleful effects of such items are thereby dissipated.

Mental blocks, feelings of guilt and inadequacy, fixation with past traumas or incidental occasions of emotional upset are overcome. The individual is brought up "to present time", that is, he is freed from the disabling effects of events that have occurred on the "time track" of the thetan's earlier present life or past lives. By improving communication, auditing brings the thetan into a condition where past hindrances have been eliminated. He is defined as a Clear, a being who no longer has his own reactive mind, who is self-determined, at least with respect to his own being. The Operating Thetan is at a higher level of the same process, since he has also acquired control over his environment. He is no longer dependent on the body which, for the time being, he occupies: he is said, indeed, to be no longer in a body. In other words, it might be said that the Operating Thetan is a being who has realized his full spiritual potential, who has achieved salvation. The current work, *What is Scientology?* (p. 222, 1992 edition) affirms "at the level of Operating Thetan one deals with the individual's own immortality as a spiritual being. One deals with the thetan himself in relation to eternity... there are states higher than that of mortal man".

iii.xv. Religious Roles in Scientology — the Auditor

Religious ministrations are available in Scientology through four related agents, whose roles both complement each other and to some extent overlap. These functionaries are the auditor, the case supervisor, the course supervisor, and the chaplain. The auditor's role is fundamental:

auditing is the vital technique for the acquisition ultimately of that form of enlightenment by which the individual is saved. The auditor is trained in skills with which he helps others, and helps them to help themselves. "All Scientology auditors are required to become ordained ministers" [*What is Scientology?* p. 557, 1992 edition] and every auditor has taken training courses which fit him for ministry, even though he might not actually take up that role. The auditor learns to deal with the pre-clear who seeks his help as neutrally and clinically as possible. Unlike the confessor in the Roman Catholic Church, the auditor does not proceed according to his own spiritual apprehensions and on his own personal assessment of the preclear's needs; rather, he follows in detail the prescribed procedures. The whole thrust of Scientology is towards the elimination of incidental, adventitious, and idiosyncratic elements from its therapeutic and spiritual ministrations. Every effort is made to ensure that auditor emotion does not disturb the standardized procedures and techniques of auditing. Pastoral counselling is thus seen, particularly in the auditing situation *per se*, as a much more exact technique than it has generally been considered in conventional churches, and much greater and more precise attention is paid to it. For Scientologists, pastoral counselling is not the purveyance of random advice given at the personal discretion or variable competence of one individual to another, but a systematic and controlled endeavour to promote self-enlightenment and spiritual knowledge.

For Scientologists, pastoral counseling is… a systematic and controlled endeavour to promote self-enlightenment and spiritual knowledge.

iii.xvi. Religious Roles in Scientology — the Case Supervisor

Responsibility for the correct application of auditing procedures lies with the case supervisor. One of the case supervisor's most important functions is to review carefully the notes the auditor has taken of the auditing session in question. These notes are highly technical, incomprehensible except to a trained auditor — and consist of notations concerning the auditing procedures applied, the responses indicated by the E-Meter and how the preclear fared. The notes must be sufficiently complete to show that the preclear's spiritual progress is in accordance with the soteriology of Scientology. The case supervisor is able to understand these technical notes since he himself is a highly trained auditor who has undergone additional specialised training as a case supervisor. He checks that the auditing has conformed to prescribed standards, the techniques have been correctly applied, and that the preclear is making appropriate progress. Should any error have occurred in auditing the case supervisor detects and corrects it. He may require an erring auditor to re-study the misapplied materials and practise the correct procedure to ensure that errors are not repeated. After each session he specifies the next stage of auditing. Since people differ, each case is reviewed individually to determine the appropriate processes to be applied and to ensure that the preclear is making due spiritual progress. The case supervisor's role thus ensures that Scientology auditing is properly conducted and controlled.

iii.xvii. Religious Roles in Scientology — the Course Supervisor

The course supervisor is even more fundamental to the practice of Scientology than the auditor. It is the course supervisor who trains auditors to the exacting standards set forth by Hubbard. The course supervisor is an expert in the techniques of study developed by Hubbard. He is trained to identify any obstacles to understanding and to resolve any difficulties that the student of Scientological literature might encounter. The course supervisor ensures that a Scientology student grasps Scientology theory and by practising drills and exercises, masters its application. Unlike other classroom supervisors, the course supervisor does not lecture, nor does he in any way offer his own interpretation of the subject. This point is important because Scientologists believe that the results obtained in Scientology come only from closely following Scientology scripture exactly as written by Hubbard. Verbal expositions passed on from teacher to student would, no matter how unintentional, inevitably involve alteration of the original material. Thus, the course supervisor is necessarily an expert in recognising the situation when a student encounters a problem, and in directing him to the place where, by his own endeavours, he can find its resolution.

iii.xviii. Religious Roles in Scientology — the Chaplain

Scientology churches and missions each have a chaplain. He is a trained auditor, and the ministerial course is an essential part of his training. That course presents Scientology as a religion, as an agency by which men may attain salvation. It includes an introduction to the teachings of the world's great religions; training in conducting services and ceremonies; study of the Creed and codes of Scientology; and instruction in ethics and auditing technology. Perhaps the major aspect of the chaplain's role is that of pastoral counselling, not in the general sense in which such counselling is provided in the course of auditing, but rather in the more diffuse sense, in listening to problems and difficulties encountered by Scientologists in mastering the teachings and techniques of the faith. Chaplains seek to smooth organizational operations, and, if called upon, seek to interpret moral and even family matters in accordance with Scientological principles. In their functioning within a particular Scientology organisation, they act much as does a bishop's chaplain in the established church. The chaplain serves as celebrant in the rites of passage performed in the Church (naming, wedding and funeral rites). In weekly services (held, for general convenience, on Sundays), the chaplain orders the service, about which he exercises some general discretion. Within the service, he also fulfils a preaching role, much like that of a Nonconformist minister, and here his function is as an expositor (rather than as an orator). His discourse is always closely concerned with the teachings and application of the principles of the faith.

iii.xix. Technical Means to Spiritual Goals — a Religion not a Science

To understand the operation of Scientology and of its religious professionals, it is necessary to recognise that Scientology conjoins technical means to spiritual goals. Its emphasis on technique, its use of technical language, and its insistence on systematic procedure and detailed order should not obscure the spiritual and soteriological nature of its ultimate concerns. Scientology is a religion that emerged in a period dominated by science; its methods bear the imprint of the age in which it came into being. Part of its fundamental commitment is to the idea that man needs to think rationally, and to control his own powerful but disturbing emotions. Only in this way will man attain the complete free-will and self-determination which Scientologists believe is his right and his necessity. To attain salvation, the individual must make a consistent and stable application of well-articulated formulae. Like Christian Science, Scientology seeks to deal in certainties. Scientology's ultimate goals would seem to transcend empirical proof, and the beliefs of its followers are transcendental, metaphysical, and spiritual even though the religion emphasizes personal experience as the route to personal conviction or certainty. The scientific style of Scientological discourse does not derogate from its religious status and concerns.

iv. A Sociological Analysis of the Evolution of the Church of Scientology

iv.i. The Evolution of Scientological Ideas — Past Lives

From mid-1950, Hubbard had already perceived that past lives might be of importance in explaining man's problems. The foundation that he set up in Elizabeth, New Jersey, was devoting itself at that time to a study of possible benefits of "recalling" "the circumstances of

deaths in previous incarnations" [Joseph A. Winter, *A Doctor's Report on Dianetics: Theory and Therapy*, New York: 1951, p. 189]. This interest developed into a positive commitment to the view that deleterious experiences in past lives (as well as in early life) created "engrams" (impressions or mental image pictures which form the reactive mind, which are associated with pain and unconsciousness, and which cause illnesses, inhibitions and hence irrational behaviour). Dianetics and Scientology had thus to be extended to eliminate these engrams as well as those created by early experiences in the individual's present life.

iv.ii. The Evolution of Scientological Ideas — From Dianetics to Scientology

This disruption of mental life was expressed, at another level, as theta, the universe of thought, having become "enturbulated" by MEST. Auditing was intended to free theta from this encumbrance. The concept of theta also underwent refinement in 1951, being recognized as "life-force, elan vital, the spirit, the soul" [in *Science of Survival*, I, p. 4]. At this point, Hubbard's belief system may be said to have become a system for the cure of souls. This development became more explicit when, in 1952, Hubbard launched Scientology, and this new, expanded, and more encompassing belief-system subsumed Dianetics, providing it with a more fully-articulated metaphysical rationale. *Theta* now became the *thetan*, a more explicit analogue of the soul, and the religious dimension of the system now became explicit. The thetan was perceived as the essential identity of the individual, the person himself (that which is aware of being aware) and the Scientological theory now provided the metaphysical justification for the soteriological task of freeing the thetan from the ill-effects of previous lives (previous occupations of human bodies).

iv.iii. The Evolution of Scientological Ideas — Thetan and Body

The individual cannot talk about "my thetan" since in essence the individual *is* the thetan occupying a body; in this sense, the thetan is seen as even more important than the soul in conventional Christian interpretation. The thetan enters a body (at, after, or even before birth) seeking identity. In this sense, Scientology has some similarity to the concepts embraced in the Buddhist theory of reincarnation. Hubbard is, however, more definite and precise in his characterisation of the reallocation of thetans to bodies than anything found in Buddhist scriptures.

iv.iv. Proximate and Ultimate Salvation

The initial goal of Scientology auditing is to release the thetan from the confines of the reactive mind: the ultimate goal is to rehabilitate the thetan so that he achieves a stable state where he no longer has a reactive mind. He moves from preoccupation with the proximate and immediate goal of his own survival (the 1st dynamic) to an increasingly expanded recognition of the possibilities of salvation, as he identifies progressively with the family, associations, mankind, the animal world, the universe, spiritual states, and infinity or

God. Thus, the ultimate goal of the thetan working through the eight dynamics is the attainment of something of a god-like condition which Scientologists refer to as "Full OT" or "Native State."

iv.v. The Soteriology of Scientology

This scheme is in itself a soteriology, a doctrine of salvation. If the final condition appears to exceed the salvation normally posited in Christian religion, that is because soteriologists often deal with proximate rather than with ultimate salvation. Christianity, too, has concepts of man as joint-heir with Christ, although the more limited prospect of the soul finally reaching heaven has frequently satisfied both the Church and the laity. Even so, in some movements — Mormonism is one example — the idea of man attaining the status of god is explicitly acknowledged. The terms in which salvation is to be accomplished differ in Scientology, but the long-term idea of saving the soul is easily recognized in its teachings. In its practice, the proximate ends of salvaging the individual's sanity, curing his psychic distress, and helping him to overcome depression are emphasised, but they are justified by reference to the soteriology outlined above.

iv.vi. Similarities to Buddhism and the Sankhya School

The mechanics of life as characterised by Scientology have considerable similarity to those embraced by both Buddhism and the Sankhya school of Hinduism. The accumulation of a reactive bank in the mind bears some similarity to the idea of karma. The concept of past lives has much in common with the theories of reincarnation in Eastern religions. The idea of acquiring access to levels of consciousness is found in Yoga (the Yoga school is closely related to that of Sankhya) and the yogin is believed to be able to attain supernatural power.

iv.vii. Salvation as a Global and as an Individual Possibility

The ultimate prospect of salvation for the thetan embraces the idea of survival for mankind and the animal and material universes, through the agency of Scientology. This element of concern for society and the cosmos certainly exists in Scientology. The idea of "clearing the planet" (producing "Clears" — people who have become entirely clear of the reactive mind) has been put forward as a goal. Hubbard, however, at times, shifted the emphasis and wrote, "Scientology is interested not in saving the world but in making able individuals more able by exact technological address to the individual himself, which is the spirit." [*Character of Scientology*, 1968, p. 5]. However, what may be being emphasised here is that world salvation is itself contingent on the salvation of individual thetans — a typical evangelical emphasis.

iv.viii. Morality in Scientology

It is sometimes suggested that it is a characteristic of religion to prescribe a moral code, though religions vary considerably in the extent to which they are committed to a specific code of morality. Scientology began with the general goals

of enhancing the individual's potential. In its emphasis on freedom, it adopted a more permissive approach to morality than that expressed by traditional Christian churches. However, from the very early exposition of Dianetics, Hubbard made clear that the individual was responsible for his own limitations, that a thetan was basically good and would diminish his own power were he to commit further harmful acts. The emphasis of auditing is also to demand that the individual should confront problems and take responsibility for his own well-being. He must acknowledge the "overt acts" (harmful acts) that he has committed in both his present and his past lives.

In an important publication, *Introduction to Scientology Ethics*, L. Ron Hubbard set out the ethical standards required of a Scientologist, and made it clear that a commitment to ethics was fundamental to the faith. The individual's goal is survival — that is, survival on all eight dynamics, from concern for the self and the family up to concern for the urge towards existence as infinity, the so-called God dynamic [see paragraph iii.ix]. Survival, as a Scientological concept, conforms to the general concern of all religion — salvation. Ethical action is deemed to be rational behaviour conducive to that end. Thus Hubbard laid stress on the individual's need to apply ethical standards to his conduct and to behave rationally if he was to achieve his own salvation and facilitate that of all mankind. Thus, in ways analogous to the Buddhist's self-interested commitment to good actions as a way of improving his future karma, so the Scientologist is enjoined to behave rationally — that is, ethically — towards the attainment of survival, for himself and for the widening constituencies embraced by the eight dynamics. Hubbard wrote, "Ethics are the actions the individual takes on himself in order to accomplish optimum survival for himself and others on all dynamics. Ethical actions are survival actions. Without a use of ethics we will not survive" [p. 17]. Survival is not mere survival. It is rather survival in a felicitous condition. "Survival is measured in pleasure" [p. 32]. Thus, as in Christianity, salvation entails a state of happiness. But "a clean heart and clean hands are the only way to achieve happiness and survival" [p. 29]; thus, in practice, achieving survival demands the maintenance of moral standards. Hubbard wrote, "As for ideals, as for honesty, as for one's love for one's fellow man, one cannot find good survival for one or for many where these things are absent" [p. 23]. Scientology ethics subsumes moral codes, but goes further in affirming the essential rationality of Scientological ethics, the application of which is seen as the only way in which the deteriorating condition of contemporary morality and the activities of anti-social personalities can be redressed and mankind redeemed.

In 1981, Hubbard formulated a set of moral precepts, said to be based on common sense. He described the booklet in which they were presented as "an individual work ... not part of any religious doctrine" and intended they be widely disseminated as a solution to the declining moral standards of modern society; however, Scientologists adopted this moral code as part of the religion. This code echoes in considerable measure

Survival, as a Scientological concept, conforms to the general concern of all religion — salvation. Ethical action is deemed to be rational behaviour conducive to that end.

both the Decalogue and other precepts of Christian morality, expressed in modern language and with the addition of social, functional, and pragmatic justification for many of the principles that are put forward. The code interdicts murder; theft; untruthfulness; all illegal acts; the infliction of harm on people of goodwill; and it enjoins, *inter alia*, faithfulness to sexual partners; respect for parents; assistance to children; temperateness; support for just government; fulfilment of obligations; respect for the religious beliefs of others; care for health and for the environment; industry; and competence. It contains, in both negative and positive terms, a version of the golden rule that is frequently rendered in Christian traditions as: "Do not unto others that which you would not that others should do unto you." The booklet urges its readers to present copies to all others for whose happiness and survival the reader is concerned.

iv.ix. The Religious Claims of Scientology

Despite the various elements described above which pertain to religion, Scientology was not initially claimed as religion. Even when, in 1954, three churches were incorporated for Scientology (with somewhat different titles), the religious implications of Scientology were still not fully explored. However, Hubbard affirmed that Scientology had religious aims. He wrote "Scientology has accomplished the goal of religion expressed in Man's written history, the freeing of the soul by wisdom. It is a far more intellectual religion than that known to the West as late as 1950. If we, without therapy, simply taught our truths we would bring civilisation to a barbaric West" [*Creation of Human Ability*, 1954, 1968, p.180]. Certainly, Hubbard regarded Christianity as in some respects less advanced than Buddhism, referring to the Christian day of judgment as "... a barbaric interpretation of what Gautama Buddha was talking about, the emancipation of the soul from the cycle of births and deaths" [*Phoenix Lectures*, 1968, pp. 29-30]. Scientology itself was a religion "in the oldest and fullest sense" [*ibid*, p. 35]. In *The Character of Scientology*, 1968, Hubbard reiterated some of these earlier points, and claimed that the background of Scientology included the Vedas, the Tao, Buddha, the Hebrews and Jesus, as well as a number of philosophers. Scientology had "brought the first religious technology to overcome the overwhelming backlog of spiritual neglect" [p. 10], and this he saw as combining the honesty and precision of the Gautama Buddha with the urgent productive practicality of Henry Ford [p. 12]. He saw the auditor as someone trained in auditing technology, and Scientological training as religious education.

iv.x. L. Ron Hubbard as Religious Leader

The claim is often made (by their followers if not by themselves) that the founders of religious movements are special agents of revelation through whom a supreme being expresses himself. This prophetic mode of religious leadership is characteristic of movements in the general Judaeo-Christian-Islamic tradition, but in the Hindu-Buddhist tradition, the

religious leader is more typically seen as a master who benefits his followers by indicating to them the path to enlightenment which he has himself trodden. Hubbard conforms much more fully to this latter model. He is represented as a teacher who, rather than having had religious truths revealed to him, is said to have discovered by scientific research facts which indicate certain therapeutic practices and a metaphysical body of knowledge which explains man's higher being and ultimate destiny. Contemporary Scientological works build up an image of Hubbard, who is readily described as a genius, very much in the style of eulogistic biographies produced to enhance the reputation and acclaim the unique experience of prophets, gurus, and founders of religious movements [for example, *What Is Scientology?* pp. 83-137]. In the Christian tradition, religious leaders whose roles and acclaimed reputations have most closely approximated that of Hubbard in Scientology are Mary Baker Eddy, founder of Christian Science, and the leaders of the various New Thought movements of the late nineteenth and early twentieth centuries.

iv.xi. Religion and Church Organization

It is not by any means necessary for a religion or a religious system to organize as a church. The spiritual elements within the Scientological scheme were in evidence before the movement registered church organizations, and these elements, taken together, certainly justify the designation of the belief system of Scientology as a religion. But even if the organisation as a church were the criterion of a religion, Scientology meets this test. The Church was incorporated and a creed was promulgated in the 1950s, and the form of certain ceremonies was prescribed. The Creed and the ceremonies formalised institutionally the commitments implicit in the belief system of Scientology. The ecclesiastical structure of Scientology is hierarchical, reflecting the graduated system of learning and spiritual enlightenment required to master its teachings. Lower-order organisations are conducted as missions conceived as evangelistic agencies. The lower-echelon churches undertake what may be designated as elementary training of ministers leading towards ordination, and serve local congregations of "parish" members. This tier of church organisation constitutes the core of the system. Above this level there are higher church organisational echelons engaged in advanced auditor training and auditing. The higher level organisations provide guidance for lower-level institutions. Analogous to this structure, the Church has developed a volunteer ministry of lay people who undergo training for social and community work. The ministry itself is hierarchically organised, each grade being marked by the completion of certificated training courses. At the lower levels of qualification, the volunteer ministers undertake, *inter alia*, prison and hospital visiting, while higher level ministers seek, where numbers warrant it, to bring into being congregations of Scientologists. The formal overall ecclesiastical structure bears some resemblance to that of Christian denominations, different as teaching and practices may be. The volunteer ministry has some loose parallels with the lay diaconate of the Anglican and other churches.

iv.xii. The Creed of Scientology

In a work, *Ceremonies of the Founding Church of Scientology*, 1966, it was explained that "in a Scientology church service, we do not use prayers, attitudes of piety, or threats of damnation. We use the facts, the truths, the understandings that have been discovered in the science of Scientology" [p. 7]. The Creed of the Church of Scientology devotes much attention to human rights. It affirms the belief that men were created equal, and have rights to their own religious practices and performances; to their own lives, sanity, defence and to "conceive, choose and assist or support their own organisations, churches, and governments," and "to think freely, to talk freely, to write freely their own opinions...." It also affirms the belief that "the study of the mind and the healing of mentally caused ills should not be alienated from religion or condoned in non-religious fields." It is maintained "that man is basically good; that he is seeking to survive; that his survival depends upon himself and upon his fellows; and his attainment of brotherhood with the universe." It is also affirmed that "... we of the Church believe that the laws of God forbid Man to destroy his own kind; to destroy the sanity of another; to destroy or enslave another's soul; to destroy or reduce the survival of one's companions or one's group. And we of the Church believe that the spirit can be saved and that the spirit alone may save or heal the body."

iv.xiii. Scientology Ceremonies

The wedding and funeral ceremonies prescribed for the Church, whilst somewhat unconventional, do not depart radically from the general practice of Western society. The christening ceremony, referred to as a "naming ceremony" is more explicitly committed to the principles of the Scientological belief-system. Its purpose is to assist the thetan who has recently come to acquire this particular body. At the time of his acquisition of a new body, the thetan is believed to be unaware of his identity, and this naming ceremony is a way of helping the thetan to learn the identity of his new body, of the parents of that body, and the god-parents who will assist the new being. This ceremony is, therefore, a type of orientation process, fully in accordance with Scientological metaphysics.

v. CONCEPTIONS OF WORSHIP AND SALVATION

v.i. Worship — a Changing Concept

Theistic religions — traditional Christianity among them — attach importance to worship, which constitutes formalized expression of reverence and veneration of a deity, humility, submission to that deity, prayer (communication with the deity), proclamations in his praise, and thanksgiving for his benefits. (Older conceptions of worship also involve sacrifice — animal or human — and acts of propitiation of a vengeful or jealous deity. But concepts of worship have changed, and older forms of worship, once regarded as indispensable, would now be regarded as against the law. The idea of worship is changing in our own times, both within the traditional churches and among new movements.) The traditional conception of worship is generally associated with the postulation of a deity (or deities) or a personage who is

the object of worshipful attitudes and actions. This definition of worship, which accords with those employed in recent court cases in England, is narrowly based on the model of historic Judaeo-Christian-Islamic practice. As empirical evidence makes clear, however, worship in this sense does not occur in all religions, and where it occurs it manifests significant variations, some of which are instanced below.

v.ii. Variations in Worship — Theravada Buddhism

First: Theravada Buddhism — in its pure form — and some other religions posit, not a supreme deity, but an ultimate law or principle which neither demands nor depends upon the reverence, praise, or worship of believers. It is generally accepted that a deity is not a *sine qua non* of religion, thus — if the concept is to be retained — a definition of worship broader than that prescribed in the Christian tradition must be adopted.

v.iii. Variations in Worship — Nichiren Buddhism

Second: There are religious movements, found for example in Nichiren Buddhism, which deny supreme beings but which require the worship of an object. The Soka Gakkai Buddhists, a movement which has about 15 million adherents, with about six thousand in Britain, worships the Gohonzon, a mandala on which is inscribed the vital symbols or formulae of ultimate truth. In worshipping the Gohonzon, these Buddhists expect benisons from it. Thus, something resembling the concept of worship as understood in Christian contexts may occur even when a supreme being is explicitly denied.

v.iv. Variations in Worship — Quakers

Third: Even within the broad Christian tradition, attitudes of reverence and humility need not imply specific forms of behaviour such as are to be observed in Orthodox, Roman Catholic or High Church Anglican services, in which believers may bow, kneel or prostrate themselves, pronounce words of praise, thanksgiving, blessing, and seek, by supplication, blessings in return. Within Christianity there are many movements which follow different practices: The Quakers provide a cogent example. Quakers meet in a spirit of reverence, but do not engage in formal acts of worship such as set or spoken prayers, the singing of hymns or chanting of psalms: often they conduct their entire meeting in silence.

v.v. Variations in Worship — Christian Science

Fourth: Within Christianity, there has been a tendency both within the old-established churches and in a variety of relatively recently arisen groups for the idea of God to be expressed in increasingly abstract terms. Since some major modern theologians have re-defined conceptions of God, often eliminating the idea of God as a person (see above, paragraph iv.iii) older conceptions of worship appear to some to be anachronistic. Opinion polls reveal that a steadily increasing proportion of those who believe in God none the less do not believe that God is a person, they aver rather that God is a force. In newly arisen religious movements, there are sometimes forms of "worship" adapted to these more modern, abstract apprehensions of deity. One example is Christian Science. Since that movement, which pre-dates Scientology by over seventy years, has many characteristics in common with Scientology, and since Christian Science has long been recognised as a religion, the attitude to worship in that movement is explored more fully. In Christian Science, God is defined as "Principle," "Life," "Truth," "Love," "Mind," "Spirit," "Soul." These impersonal abstractions do not require manifestations of submission and veneration, and such dispositions are accorded only limited expression in Christian Science church services. The opinions of Mary Baker Eddy (founder of Christian Science) on worship are represented in these quotations from her textbook, *Science and Health with Key to the Scriptures*:

Audible prayers can never do the works of spiritual understanding .... Long prayers, superstitions, and creeds, clip the strong pinions of love and clothe religion in human forms. Whatever materializes worship hinders man's spiritual growth and keeps him from demonstrating his power over error. [pp. 4-5]

Dost thou 'Love thy Lord God with all thy heart, and with all thy soul and with all thy mind'? This command includes much, even the surrender of all merely material sensation, affection, and worship. [p. 9]

Jesus' history made a new calendar, which we call the Christian era; but he established no ritualistic worship." [p. 20]

It is sad that the phrase divine service has come so generally to mean public worship instead of daily deeds. [p. 40]

We worship spiritually only as we cease to worship materially. Spiritual devoutness is the soul of Christianity. Worshipping through the medium of matter is paganism. Judaic and other rituals are the types and shadows of true worship." [p. 140]

The Israelites centered their thought on the material in their attempted worship of the spiritual. To them matter was a substance and Spirit was shadow. They thought to worship Spirit from a material standpoint, but this was impossible. They might appeal to Jehovah but their prayer brought down no proof that it was heard because they did not sufficiently understand God to be able to demonstrate his power to heal. [p. 351]

Although Christian Scientists use the Lord's Prayer congregationally, that prayer is translated into a number of affirmations in accordance with Eddy's teachings. Silent prayer in Christian Science is affirmation of "truths" not supplication, God is a "Principle" to be demonstrated, not a "Being" to be placated or propitiated. Hence worship in Christian Science is different in form, mood and expression from worship in traditional churches.

v.vi. Worship Defined by Its Objectives, not by Its Forms

The foregoing comments on the variations in worship indicate the need — if all the appropriate empirical evidence is to be taken into account — for a much broader definition of worship than that which is confined to, and dependent upon, the assumptions of one specific tradition. The forms traditional in Christian churches do not exhaust all the variant modes in which worship can and does occur (even within Christian churches).

A distinction must be made between the external forms of worship (which may be particular, local, regional, or national) and the aims of worship, which we may represent as universal. The aim of worship is to establish rapport between the votary and the supernatural ultimate (being, object, law, principle, dimension, "ground of being," or "concern") in whatever way that ultimate is conceived by the religious body to which the votary belongs, with a view to his ultimate attainment of salvation or enlightenment. To emphasise that the defining characteristic of worship lies in its purpose makes apparent the cultural relativity of the various forms that worship assumes. Once worship is defined by reference to its objectives, we can comprehend diverse conceptions of the ultimate, extending from idols to transcendental laws. Thus, an idol is worshipped as a despotic entity who confers favours or inflicts injuries; the worship of an anthropomorphic deity emphasizes rather a relationship, of trust, but also of dependence; worship of more sophisticated conceptions of a supreme being places less emphasis on the emotional volatility of the deity, and stresses the search for harmony of dispositions in accordance with more general ethical principles; worship of an entirely abstract ultimate verity, law, or dimension, tends to be concerned with the diffusion of knowledge, the attainment of enlightenment, and the realisation of full human potential. All of these variously specified goals may be seen as part of man's search for salvation, however differently salvation itself may be conceived. Reverence for the ultimate, for man's "ground of being," however depicted, is a general attribute of the respect and concern for life, which does not depend on any specific culture-bound behavioural forms or norms.

v.vii. The Decline of the Poetic Mode of Worship

In multi-religious societies, the concept of what constitutes worship must be stated in abstract terms if the diversity of religion is to be duly acknowledged. The recent and continuing trends in religion are towards abstract and more readily universalized expression. This is true not only of major theologians and among the clergy, but is also evident among many new religious movements. In a scientific and technological age, men's conception of deity, or of the ultimate, tends to be understood in terms which are themselves more concordant with scientific and technical experience, even though this type of language and conceptualization stands in contrast with traditional poetic imagery which was once typical of religious expression. The poetic mode is steadily abandoned not only in new movements, but also in the so-called traditional churches, as may be seen by the liturgical reforms in the Roman Catholic Church since Vatican II, and in the replacement of the Book of Common Prayer in the Church of England by more prosaic, vernacular and colloquial forms of expression. Outside these churches, in movements without the obligation to even vestigial respect for tradition, the creation of new language and new liturgical forms has enjoyed even greater freedom. Among these movements is Scientology.

Scientology is a movement which incorporates people from diverse religious backgrounds, which emphasizes new conceptions of creation, the meaning of life, and salvation.

v.viii. Communication as Worship

Scientology presents a thoroughly abstract conception of the Supreme Being, as the Eighth Dynamic. Scientologists seek to expand their awareness and comprehension to embrace all dimensions of being, with the objective of aiding, and being part of, the survival of the Supreme Being or Infinity. Scientologists venerate life, and recognize God as an ultimate ground of being, but this recognition does not entail specific forms of behaviour that at all closely approximate those acts that are considered to be "worship" in traditional Christian churches. Scientology is a movement which incorporates people from diverse religious backgrounds; which emphasizes new conceptions of creation, the meaning of life, and salvation; and its teachings draw on more than one of the great religious traditions as well as on broad scientific orientations. It is therefore entirely appropriate that Scientology should present its theories in abstract and universal terms, and its conception of worship accommodates these perspectives. The general position has been expressed as follows: "In Scientology we worship in terms of communication. Who would worship effectively would be he who considered himself capable of reaching the distance to communicate with the Supreme Being" [*Scientology as a Religion*, p. 30].

The essence of Scientology is understanding through communication — communication with the thetan's own past and with the environment, and in that sense it may be likened to the communication that takes place in Christian worship, the communication which the individual seeks with the deity in prayer and in the eucharistic service, when, indeed, he behaves, as the traditional churches phrase it, as a "communicant." The purpose is in large part the same — the purification of the individual, the rehabilitation of his soul as part of the longer-term process of salvation. In Scientology there are two fundamental forms of such communication — auditing and training. Auditing, occurring as private communication by the individual with his (the thetan's) past, is mediated by the auditor and the E-meter, but it is essentially a process of bringing the individual into better rapport with his true and original self, and in this sense seeks to put him in contact with a basic spiritual reality.

Training in the Scientology Scripture is communication with the fundamental truths and ground of existence. Through increased understanding the individual seeks greater communication with his basic self, with others and with all life. These activities, too, share elements characteristic of worship, even if such aspects as adoration (of a deity), antiquated concern for his propitiation, and the ancient procedures of supplication are, in this modern context, superseded.

v.ix. The Scientology Goal of Survival

The key term which reveals the purpose of the services that are conducted in a Scientology chapel is "survival," a concept recurrently emphasized in Scientological literature. "Survival" is, however, merely a modern synonym for the old religious concept, "salvation," and salvation is the primary objective of worship in all religions,

the establishment of rapport between powerful deity and dependent votary which will result in the diminution or elimination of untoward and evil experiences, and the multiplication of benefits culminating in the final benefit of continuing life. Scientology is concerned with the salvation of the thetan, its liberation from the encumbrance of matter, energy, space and time, and, in the more proximate instance, with its capacity to overcome bodily disabilities and the vicissitudes of daily life. The thetan, as the trans-human essence, or soul, existed before the physical body and has prospect of surviving it. That survival is ultimately linked to the survival of the Eighth Dynamic, the Supreme Being, and the Scientology services of auditing and training to enhance the consciousness of this ultimate reality. The practice is thus an occasion for participants to renew and reinforce their recognition of the supernatural. In the wide sense that we have explored above, this is an occasion for worship and enlightenment.

v.x. Auditing and Training

The core activities of Scientology are auditing and training. These are the agencies of spiritual salvation. Only by these means can the thetan — that is the individual — be liberated and achieve the spiritual state of being "at cause" over life and the material world. Auditing, in which the individual confronts his own past pain and traumas, helps him to establish control of his life and frees him from the irrational impulses of there active mind. Thus, in being audited, the preclear may be said to be embarking on a spiritual quest for salvation, the benefits of which are accretive, and which lead ultimately to a condition in which the thetan ceases to be "enturbulated" with material conditions (MEST). Such a spiritual quest, with salvation as its ultimate end, divergent as may be the outward forms and doctrinal specifications, is the central overriding concern of all the world's advanced religions. Training is directed to communicating wisdom to anyone who is seeking enlightenment as well as to those who engage in helping others in their endeavour to attain salvation. Implicit in these processes is the demand that the individual face up to his own painful past experiences and overcome the tendency to transfer blame to others for his own failings. Training to this end is achieved through a series of hierarchically graduated courses in which the student learns and perfects the techniques of auditing which, once the appropriate standard is attained, is believed to be effective in application to any preclear. Training is organised as an intensive programme, and anyone who has witnessed the concentrated dedication of those undergoing training courses, as I have on visits to the Church of Scientology at Saint Hill Manor, could not but be impressed by the single-mindedness and seriousness of purpose uniformly manifested by the students, which is, of course, a religious commitment.

vi. SCIENTOLOGY AND OTHER FAITHS

vi.i. Some Similarities of Scientology and Other Faiths

Scientology differs radically from traditional Christian churches and dissenting sects in matters of ideology, practice, and organisation. Yet, taking the broad view which, in a multi-cultural and multi-religious society must prevail, it is evident that in all essentials, Scientology occupies a position very close to that of other movements that are indisputably religions. Ideologically, it has significant resemblances to the Sankhya school of Hinduism. In its congregational activities, which are, however, far less central to it than is the case with Nonconformist movements, there are, none the less, points of emphasis not dissimilar to those of some Nonconformist bodies. Its soteriological goals are emphatically metaphysical, and resemble in some respects those of Christian Science.

vi.ii. Dual Membership

A distinctive feature of Scientology is that members are not required to abandon other religious beliefs and affiliations on taking up Scientology. It might be inferred from this feature that Scientology contented itself with being a merely additional or supplementary set of beliefs and practices, but such an inference would be unwarranted. I have spoken with senior Church officials as well as individual Scientologists on this aspect of Scientology and their response was that while exclusivity is not required, it comes about as a matter of practice. According to them, as one becomes more involved with Scientology, one inevitably discards one's prior faith. For example, my experience is that a Jew who becomes a Scientologist might remain affiliated with Judaism for cultural reasons and might celebrate Jewish holidays with family and friends, but he or she would not practise and would not believe in Jewish theology. From my view as a scholar this explanation seems correct. Scientologists regard their faith as a complete religion demanding dedication of its members.

Further, while it is a characteristic of the Judaeo-Christian-Muslim tradition that religious commitment be exclusive and that dual or multiple membership is not tolerated, this principle is far from universal among religions. It is not demanded in most branches of Hinduism and Buddhism. The Buddha did not prohibit the worship of local gods. Hinduism is tolerant in respect of plural allegiances. In Japan, large numbers of people count themselves as both Buddhists and Shintoists. The symbiosis of religions is a well-known phenomenon and in certain respects it has occurred in Christianity (for example, in the tolerance of Spiritualism or Pentecostalism by certain Anglican Bishops, even though these belief-systems were not specifically accommodated by official doctrine). The fact that Scientology adopts a different position respecting dual or multiple affiliations from that conventionally assumed in western Christianity is not a valid ground for denying it the status of a religion.

vi.iii. Exoteric and Esoteric Elements of Scientology

The public image of Scientology does not conform to general stereotypes of religion. Its literature may be divided into a widely circulated exoteric literature, and an esoteric literature. The exoteric literature is concerned principally with the basic principles of Scientology metaphysics and their practical application in helping people to cope with their problems of communication, relationships, and the maintenance of intelligence, rational, and positive orientations to life. The restricted corpus of esoteric literature, which is made available only to advanced students of Scientology, presents both a fuller account of the metaphysics of the religion and more advanced techniques of auditing. It sets out in further detail the theory of the

theta (primal thought of spirit); its deterioration by becoming involved in the material universe of matter, energy, space, and time in the process of past lives; and indicates the way in which man can acquire — strictly said, regain — supernatural abilities. Only Scientologists who are well-advanced are considered capable of grasping the import of this exposition of the belief-system and of fully comprehending the higher levels of auditing procedures set out in the esoteric literature.

In distinguishing between exoteric and esoteric teachings, Scientology is by no means unique among religions. On the principle enunciated by Jesus "I have many things to say unto you, but ye cannot bear them now" (John 16:12) and by Paul in distinguishing strong meat for seasoned believers from milk for babes (I Cor. 3:1-3; and Hebrews 5:12-14), various Christian movements have maintained a distinction between elementary and advanced doctrines and practices. The general gnostic tradition at the fringes of Christianity was explicitly committed to the preservation of esoteric doctrines, and contemporary movements sometimes categorized by scholars as "gnostic-type" sects commonly make such distinctions. An example is Christian Science, the general teachings of which are augmented by subjects taught to those aspiring to become recognized practitioners by designated teachers in special classes, the content of which is confidential. Apart from these cases, The Church of Jesus Christ of Latter-day Saints admits to its special ceremonies only those Mormons who are in good standing and receive a permit from their bishop: that indicates, *inter alia*, that they have been fulfilling their commitment to tithe 10 percent of their earnings to the church: no others are allowed to see these rituals.

Close to the Protestant mainstream, Pentecostalists often disclose the full significance of their teaching and practice of "the gifts of the Spirit" only at designated services and not at those meetings designed to attract the non-Pentecostal public. The justification for such differentiation is also an educational principle — advanced material is available only to those who have undergone earlier and more elementary instruction which enables them to assimilate higher levels of instruction. This is the position taken by Scientology, the teachings of which require concentrated and systematized endeavour from students.

vii. INDICIA OF RELIGION APPLIED TO SCIENTOLOGY

vii.i. The Elimination of Cultural Bias

There are various distinct difficulties in appraising new religious movements. One is that there are, in most societies, unspoken assumptions concerning religion that put a premium on antiquity and tradition. Religious usage and expression is frequently legitimized by specific reference to tradition. Innovation in matters of religion is not easily promoted or accepted. A second problem is the strong normative stance of orthodoxy (particularly in the Judaeo-Christian-Islamic tradition) which proscribes deviations and which uses a heavily pejorative language to describe them ("sect," "cult," "nonconformity," "dissent," etc.). A third problem is alluded to in foregoing paragraphs, namely, that it is peculiarly difficult for those acculturated in one society and brought up in one religious tradition to understand the belief-system of others, to empathize with their religious aspirations, and to acknowledge the legitimacy of their means of expression. Religious ideas encapsulate certain cultural biases and blinker vision. But, in seeking to interpret a movement like Scientology, it is indispensable that these obstacles be recognized and transcended. This does not imply that to understand a set of religious ideas one must accept them as true, but a certain rapport must be established if the convictions of those of other faiths are to be given appropriate respect.

vii.ii. The Case Thus Far

The foregoing discussion is necessarily wide-ranging and discursive, involving *en passant* comparisons with other religious movements, and a review of literature produced by Scientologists and literature about Scientology by academic commentators. The history, doctrines, practices, and religious organization and moral implications of Scientology have been briefly surveyed with particular attention to those facets most at issue in the present appraisal of the religious status of the movement. Such an assessment, in which many pertinent considerations have been brought forward, satisfies the contention that Scientology is a religion. However, since we have attempted (paragraph ii.i above) to set out in terms of abstract generalization those features and functions which are of wide distribution, and hence of high probability, in religious systems, it is now appropriate to bring this model into deliberate use as a bench-marker for Scientology's claim to be a religion. There are wide divergences between the terminology used in Scientology and in the specifications of the model, but this might, at least to some extent, be the case for many — perhaps all — religious movements. None the less, allowing for the generality of the abstract concepts employed, it should be possible to perceive, without undue difficulty or potential for disagreement, the extent to which Scientology meets the desiderata of the inventory we have produced.

vii.iii. Scientology in Light of the Indicia of a Religion

We now compare the attributes of Scientology with the probabilistic inventory of the features and functions of religion set out in para ii.i, above. We note those items in which Scientology agrees, as Accord or Qualified Accord; those in which it does not correspond, as Non-Accord, or Qualified Non-Accord and other cases as Indeterminate.

(a) Thetans are agencies which transcend normal sense perception. It is also noted that Scientology affirms the existence of a supreme being. Accord. (b) Scientology postulates that thetans created the natural order. Accord. (c) Thetans occupy human bodies, which amounts to continuous intervention in the material world. Accord. (d) Thetans operated before the course of human history, and are said to have created the physical universe and occupy bodies for their own pleasure, identity and the playing of a game. This is, however, an indefinite purpose and the Supreme Being in Scientology is not represented as having definite purposes. Qualified Accord. (e) The activity of thetans and the activity of human beings are identical. The future lives of the thetan will be profoundly affected insofar as he gains release from the reactive mind, in addition to being profoundly affected by the same process in his present lifetime. Accord. (f) Auditing and

It is clear to me that Scientology is a bona fide religion and should be considered as such.

training are means by which an individual can influence his destiny, certainly in this life and in the lives of the bodies which he may later occupy. Accord. (g) Rituals as symbolism in the traditional sense of worship (e.g., Catholic Mass) are minimal and rudimentary in Scientology, as they are among Quakers, but they do exist. Nonetheless, to adopt a conservative position, we may regard this item as Indeterminate. (h) Placatory action (e.g., sacrifice or penance) is absent from Scientology. The individual seeks wisdom and spiritual enlightenment. Non-Accord. (i) Expressions of devotion, gratitude, obeisance and obedience to supernatural agencies are virtually absent, except in the rites of passage prescribed in Scientology. Non-Accord. (j) Although Scientology has a distinctive language which provides a means of reinforcement of values internal to the group, and the Scripture or teachings of L. Ron Hubbard are held sacred in the popular connotation of the term, this cannot be said to conform to the technical sense of sacred, as "things set apart and forbidden." Non-Accord. (k) Performances for celebration or collective penance are not a strong feature of Scientology, but in recent years the movement has developed a number of commemorative occasions, including the celebration of the anniversary of Hubbard's birth, the date of the founding of the International Association of Scientologists, and a date celebrating auditors for their dedication. Qualified Accord. (l) Scientologists engage in relatively few collective rites, but the movement's teachings do provide a total Weltanschauung, and so do draw members into a sense of fellowship and common identity. Qualified Accord. (m) Scientology is not a highly moralistic religion, but concern for moral propriety has grown as the full implications of its metaphysical premises have been realized. Since 1981, the moral expectations of Scientologists have been clearly articulated: these resemble the commandments of the Decalogue, and make more explicit the long-maintained concern to reduce "overt acts" (harmful acts). The doctrines of the reactive mind and reincarnation embrace ethical orientations similar to those of Buddhism. Accord. (n) Scientology places strong emphasis on seriousness of purpose, sustained commitment and loyalty to the organization and its members. Accord. (o) The teachings of transmigration in Scientology meets this criterion fully. The accumulative reactive mind corresponds to demerit for the thetan, and such demerit can be reduced by the application of Scientological techniques. Accord. (p) Scientology has functionaries who serve primarily as "confessors" (auditors), some of whom are also chaplains whose tasks are primarily expository and pastoral. Auditors, course supervisors, and chaplains (in fact all staff members) seek to preserve Scientology theory and practice from contamination, and in this sense are custodians. Accord. (q) Auditors, course supervisors and chaplains are paid. Accord. (r) Scientology has a body of metaphysical doctrine which offers an explanation for the meaning of life and its purpose, and an elaborate theory of human psychology, as well as an account of the origin and of the operation of the physical universe. Accord. (s) The legitimacy of Scientology is in a form of revelation by L. Ron Hubbard. Hubbard's own sources include mention of the ancient wisdom of the Orient, but are claimed to be almost exclusively the results of research. This mixture of appeal to tradition, charisma, and science has been found in other modern religious movements, conspicuously, Christian Science. Qualified Accord. (t) Claims to the truth of some of Scientology's doctrines are beyond empirical test, but the efficacy of auditing is said to be provable pragmatically.

The goals of Scientology depend on faith in the metaphysical aspects of the doctrine, however, even if the means are claimed to be susceptible to empirical test. Qualified Accord.

vii.iv. The Comparison Reviewed

The foregoing appraisal of Scientology in the light of the probabilistic inventory of religion results in eleven items in which there is accord; five items on which there is qualified accord; three items on which there is no accord; and one item which is indeterminate. It cannot be assumed that these various features and functions of religion have equal weight of course, and the numerical count should not produce an unduly mechanistic basis for assessment. Some items — for example, the existence of a paid body of specialists — although common to religions, are not confined to religions, and may therefore be deemed to be of less import than some other items. Similarly, the placatory element that is common in religion might be held to be merely a residual feature of earlier patterns of quasi-magical dependence from which more recently instituted religious organisations may have freed themselves. Whilst most traditional religions would meet most of these probabilities, many well-recognized denominations would be out of accord with some of them. We have noted this of Quakers with respect to worship, and of Christian Science with respect to legitimation. Unitarians would fall short on a number of items — worship, sacralization, traditional concepts of sin and virtue, and perhaps on the significance of metaphysical teaching. Neither Christadelphians nor Quakers would meet the criteria relating to religious specialists or their payment.

vii.v. Scientologists Perceive Their Beliefs as a Religion

The use of the foregoing inventory should not be allowed to create an impression that the findings set forth in this opinion rely on formal or abstract reasoning alone. The inventory is a basis against which empirical evidence — that is observed behaviour — is assessed. Many Scientologists have a strong sense of their own religious commitment. They perceive their beliefs and practices as a religion, and many bring to them levels of commitment which exceed those normally found among believers in the traditional churches. In this respect, many Scientologists behave like members of Christian sects, who are generally more intensely committed to their religion than are the vast majority of believers in the old-established churches and denominations. As a sociologist, I see Scientology as a genuine system of religious belief and practice which evokes from its votaries deep and earnest commitment.

vii.vi. Contemporary Change in Religion

We have noted that all religions have undergone a process of evolution: they change over time. It is also the case that religion *per se* undergoes change. As a social

product, religion takes on much of the colour and character of the society in which it functions, and newer movements reveal characteristics that were not found in older movements (at least at the time of their origin). Today, new developments in religion make it apparent that there is much less concern with a posited objective reality "out there," and more interest in subjective experience and psychological well-being; less concern, therefore, with traditional forms of worship, and more with the acquisition of assurance (which is itself a type of salvation) from other sources than the supposed comfort afforded by a remote saviour-god. We must, therefore, expect this emphasis to become apparent in the inventory that we have used as a model. The model reflects a great deal that remains extant in religion but which derives from ancient practice. Newer religions — even religions as old as the major Protestant denominations — will not find accord with all these elements: they reflect the characteristics of the evolutionary stage at which they came into being. We must, therefore, allow that modern movements will not be in accord with all items in our (relatively timeless) model. Taking all of this into account, it is clear to me that Scientology is a bona fide religion and should be considered as such.

Bryan Ronald Wilson

About the Author

Bryan Ronald Wilson is Reader Emeritus in Sociology, University of Oxford. From 1963 to 1993 he was also a Fellow of All Souls College and in 1993 was elected an Emeritus Fellow.

For more than forty years he has conducted research into minority religious movements in Britain and in the United States, Ghana, Kenya, Belgium and Japan and other countries. His work has involved reading publications of these movements, and wherever possible, associating with their members in the meetings, services and homes. It has also entailed sustained attention to, and critical appraisal of, the works of other scholars.

He holds the degrees of B.Sc (Econ) and Ph.D. of the University of London and the M.A. of the University of Oxford. In 1984, the University of Oxford recognized the value of his published work by conferring upon him the degree of D. Litt. In 1992, The Catholic University of Louvain, Belgium, awarded him the degree of Doctor Honoris Causa. In 1994, he was elected a Fellow of the British Academy.

Scientology

∎

The Marks of Religion

Frank K. Flinn, Ph.D.

Adjunct Professor in Religious Studies
Washington University
Saint Louis, Missouri, U.S.A.

i. INTRODUCTION

I am currently self-employed as a writer, editor, lecturer and consultant in the fields of theology and religion. I also serve as Adjunct Professor in Religious Studies at Washington University, St. Louis, Missouri.

I hold a Bachelor of Arts degree in Philosophy (1962) from Quincy University, Quincy, Illinois; a Bachelor of Divinity degree (1966), *magna cum laude*, from Harvard Divinity School, Cambridge, Massachusetts; and a Ph.D. in Special Religious Studies (1981) from the University of St. Michael's College, Toronto School of Theology, Toronto, Ontario. I have also done advanced study at Harvard University, the University of Heidelberg, Germany, and the University of Pennsylvania. At the University of Heidelberg, I was a Fulbright Fellow in Philosophy and Ancient Near Eastern Religions, 1966-67.

At the University of Pennsylvania, I was a National Defense Foreign Language Fellow, Title VI, in Semitic languages, 1968-69.

Since 1962 I have devoted intense study to religious sectarian movements, ancient and modern. A portion of my doctoral studies was focused specifically on the rise of new religious movements in the United States and abroad since World War II. That study included the investigation of new religions in terms of their belief systems, lifestyles, use of religious language, leadership, motivation and sincerity, and the material conditions of their existence. At Washington University I regularly teach a course entitled *The North American Religious Experience*, which contains a section on new religious movements. Besides a scholarly interest in religions I have had long-standing personal experience with the religious life. From 1958 to 1964 I was a member of the Order of Friars Minor, popularly known as the Franciscans. During this period I lived under solemn vows of poverty, chastity, and obedience and, thus, experienced many of the disciplines typical of the religious life.

Prior to my present position, I taught at Maryville College, St. Louis, Missouri, 1980-81; St. Louis University, St. Louis, Missouri, 1977-79, where I was Graduate Director of the Masters Program in Religion and Education; the University of Toronto, Ontario, 1976-77, where I was Tutor in Comparative Religion; St. John's College, Santa Fe, New Mexico, 1970-75, where I was Tutor in the Great Books Program; LaSalle College, Philadelphia, Pennsylvania, Summers 1969-73, where I was Lecturer in Biblical Studies and the Anthropology of Religion; Boston College, Boston, Massachusetts, 1967-68, where I was Lecturer in Biblical Studies; and Newton College of the Sacred Heart, Newton, Massachusetts, where I was Lecturer in Biblical Studies.

I am a member in good standing of the American Academy of Religion. I am a practicing Roman Catholic at All Saints Church, University City, Missouri.

Since 1968 I have lectured and written about various new religious movements which have arisen in the 19th and 20th centuries in North America and elsewhere. In my lecture courses Anthropology of Religion (LaSalle College), Comparative Religion (University of Toronto), The American Religious Experience (St. Louis University) and The North American Religious Experience (Washington University), I have dealt with such religious phenomena as the Great Awakening, Shakerism, Mormon, Seventh-day Adventism, Jehovah's Witness, New Harmony, Oneida, Brook Farm, Unification, Scientology, Hare Krishna and others.

I have published several articles and been general editor of books on the topic of new religions. It is my policy not to testify about a living religious group unless I have long-term, first-hand knowledge of that group. I have testified on various aspects of the new religions before the U.S. Congress, the Ohio Legislature, the New York Assembly, the Illinois Legislature, and the Kansas Legislature. I have delivered lectures on the topic of the new religions at colleges, universities and conferences in the United States, Canada, Japan, the Republic of China and Europe.

I have studied the Church of Scientology in depth since 1976. I have sufficiently sampled the vast literature of Scientology (its scriptures) to help form the opinions expressed herein.

I have visited Scientology Churches in Toronto; St. Louis; Portland, Oregon; Clearwater, Florida; Los Angeles and Paris, where I have familiarized myself with the day-to-day workings of the Church. I have also conducted numerous interviews with members of the Church of Scientology. I am also familiar with most of the literature written about Scientology, ranging from objective scholarship to journalistic accounts, both favorable and unfavorable.

As a comparative scholar of religion, I maintain that for a movement to be a religion and for a group to constitute a church, it needs to manifest three characteristics, or marks, which are discernible in religions around the world. Below, I define these three characteristics:

(a) First, a religion must possess a system of beliefs or doctrines which relate the believers to the ultimate meaning of life (God, the Supreme Being, the Inner Light, the Infinite, etc.).

(b) Secondly, the system of beliefs must issue into religious practices which can be divided into 1) norms for behavior (positive commands and negative prohibitions or taboos) and 2) rites and ceremonies, acts and other observances (sacraments, initiations, ordinations, sermons, prayers, funerals for the dead, marriages,

meditation, purifications, scriptural study, blessings, etc.).

(c) Thirdly, the system of beliefs and practices must unite a body of believers or members so as to constitute an identifiable *community* which is either hierarchical or congregational in polity and which possesses a spiritual way of life in harmony with the ultimate meaning of life as perceived by the adherents. Not all religions will emphasize each of these characteristics to the same degree or in the same manner, but all will possess them in a perceptible way.

On the basis of these three markers and of my research into the Church of Scientology, I can state without hesitation that the Church of Scientology constitutes a bona fide religion. It possesses all the essential marks of religions known around the world: (1) a well-defined belief system, (2) which issues into religious practices (positive and negative norms for behavior, religious rites and ceremonies, acts and observances) and (3) which sustain a body of believers in an identifiable religious community, distinguishable from other religious communities.

ii. SYSTEM OF BELIEFS

In terms of the Scientology belief system, there exists a vast amount of religious material through which the scholar must wend her or his way. Furthermore, the scholar needs to be sensitive to the fact that Scientology, like every other religious tradition in history, is organic and has undergone and is undergoing an evolution. One can mention such key scriptures by L. Ron Hubbard as *Dianetics: The Modern Science of Mental Health*, *Scientology: The Fundamentals of Thought*, *The Phoenix Lectures*, plus the voluminous training and management manuals, but this would only be the tip of the iceberg of Scientology scriptures. Central to everything are the writings of L. Ron Hubbard, who is the sole source of inspiration for all Scientology doctrines pertaining to auditing and training. My interviews with Scientologists and my study of its scriptures have shown that members of the Church adhere to a basic creed, in which they confess that mankind is basically good, that the spirit can be saved and that the healing of both physical and spiritual ills proceeds from the spirit. In full, the Scientology creed states:

We of the Church believe:

That all men of whatever race, color or creed were created with equal rights;

That all men have inalienable rights to their own religious practices and their performance;

That all men have inalienable rights to their own lives;

That all men have inalienable rights to their sanity;

That all men have inalienable rights to their own defense;

That all men have inalienable rights to conceive, choose, assist or support their own organizations, churches and governments;

That all men have inalienable rights to think freely, to talk freely, to write freely their own opinions and to counter or utter or write upon the opinions of others;

That all men have inalienable rights to the creation of their own kind;

That the souls of men have the rights of men;

That the study of the mind and the healing of mentally caused ills should not be alienated from religion or condoned in non-religious fields;

And that no agency less than God has the power to suspend or set aside these rights, overtly or covertly.

And we of the Church believe:

That man is basically good;

That he is seeking to survive;

That his survival depends upon himself and upon his fellows and his attainment of brotherhood with the universe.

And we of the Church believe that the laws of God forbid Man:

To destroy his own kind;

To destroy the sanity of another;

To destroy or enslave another's soul;

To destroy or reduce the survival of one's companions or one's group.

And we of the Church believe that the spirit can be saved and that the spirit alone may save or heal the body.

This creed elaborates on and complements the Scientology teaching on the Eight Dynamics. A "dynamic" is an urge, drive or impulse to survival at the levels of the self, sex (including procreation as a family), group, all of mankind, all living things, all the physical universe, spirit and, finally, Infinity or God. Contrary to some popular presentations of Scientology, the Church has always maintained a belief in the spiritual dimension and, specifically, a Supreme Being. The earliest editions of *Scientology: The Fundamentals of Thought* explicitly state: "The Eighth Dynamic — is the urge toward existence as Infinity. This is also identified as the Supreme Being." (*Scientology: The Fundamentals of Thought*. Los Angeles: The Church of Scientology of California, 1956, page

38.) The average believer is expected during his or her adherence to Scientology to realize the self as fully as possible on all eight dynamics and thus develop an understanding of a Supreme Being, or, as the Scientologists prefer to say, Infinity.

Scientologists define the spiritual essence of humanity as the "thetan," which is equivalent to the traditional notion of the soul. They believe that this thetan is immortal and has assumed various bodies in past lives. The Scientology doctrine of past lives has many affinities with the Buddhist teaching on *samsara*, or the transmigration of the soul. More will be said about the soul under para. iii (a).

Scientologists define the spiritual essence of humanity as the thetan, *which is equivalent to the traditional notion of the soul.*

The Creed of Scientology can be compared with the classic Christian creeds of Nicaea (325 C.E.), the Lutheran Augsburg Confession (1530 C.E.), and the Presbyterian Westminster Confession (1646 C.E.) because, like these earlier creeds, it defines the ultimate meaning of life for the believer, shapes and determines codes of conduct and worship in conformity with that creed, and defines a body of adherents who subscribe to that creed. Like the classic creeds, the Creed of the Church of Scientology gives meaning to transcendental realities: the soul, spiritual aberrancy or sin, salvation, healing by means of the spirit, the freedom of the believer and the spiritual equality of all. Following their creed, Scientologists distinguish between the "reactive" or passive (unconscious) mind

and the "analytical" or active mind. The reactive mind records what adherents call "engrams," which are spiritual traces of pain, injury or impact. The reactive mind is believed to retain engrams that go back to the fetal state and reach further back even into past lives. The theological notion of "engrams" bears close resemblance to the Buddhist doctrine of the "threads of entanglement" which are held over from previous incarnations and which impede the attainment of enlightenment. Scientologists believe that unless one is freed from these engrams, one's survival ability on the levels of the eight dynamics, happiness, intelligence and spiritual well-being will be severely impaired. It is on the basis of this belief or spiritual knowledge that adherents are motivated to go through the many levels of auditing and training, which constitute the central religious practices of Scientology. I will discuss auditing and training in greater detail in section iii. A neophyte or beginner in the auditing/training process is called a preclear and one who has removed all engrams is called a Clear. This distinction can be compared with the Christian distinction between sin and grace and the Buddhist distinction between unenlightenment (Sanskrit, avidya) and enlightenment (bodhi).

Scientologists do not speak of "Clearing" simply in terms of individual well-being. Their belief is that auditing and training have a beneficial effect on the person's family, group, environment and sphere of influence. In other words, the beneficial effect takes place on all eight levels of the "dynamics." Scientologists also believe that they should take responsibility for bettering the world around them and that they should help others attain the state of Clear. They believe that when enough people have attained the Clear state, the central aim of Scientology, as enunciated by L. Ron Hubbard, will have been achieved: "A civilization without insanity, without criminals and without war, where the able can prosper and honest beings have rights, and where man is free to rise to greater heights." (L. Ron Hubbard, *Scientology: The Fundamentals of Thought.* Los Angeles: The Church of Scientology of California, 1956, page 112.) In this quest to remove the conditions leading to mistrust, war and self-destruction, Scientology is no different than all the other missionary or evangelical religions, namely, Buddhism, Judaism, Christianity and Islam.

Three aspects of Scientology's goal to "Clear the planet" so as to bring about a new civilization demonstrate that the belief system of the Church accords fully with the pattern of the great historic religions, past and present. Those three aspects are (a) its missionary character, (b) its universality, and (c) its quality of ultimate concern and commitment.

(a) First, Scientology's religious quest is envisioned in terms of a sacred mission, addressed and available to one and all. Thus, the prophets of the Bible such as Amos, Isaiah and Jeremiah, received revelations that they had a mission to address the nations far and wide about peace, justice and love. Thus, too, the Buddhist missionaries of the second century B.C.E. onward sensed a calling to spread the message of the Buddha throughout the Far East, including China, Indochina, Indonesia, Korea and Japan. Today, Japanese Buddhist missionaries are spreading their message to Europe and the Americas. So also, Jesus of Nazareth saw his gospel as having a missionary goal; hence he sent his disciples unto all the nations. The missionary aspect of Islam is so strong that today it is the fastest growing historic religion in the world, especially in Africa and East Asia. In its dedication to "Clear" the planet in order to bring about a new civilization, Scientology's missionary efforts conform entirely to the pattern of the great historic religions.

(b) Secondly, Scientology sees its mission in universal terms. As a result, it has set out to open mission centers in all parts of the world in order to make the auditing and training technology universally available. The most obvious historic parallel to traditional historic religion is Jesus' commission to his disciples: "Go ye therefore and teach all nations, baptizing them in the name of the Father, and of the Son, and of the Holy Spirit" (Matthew 28:19). In the eighth century B.C.E., the Jewish prophet Amos was called to bring God's word not only to Judah and Israel but also to Damascus, Gaza, Ashkelon, Tyre, Sidon and Edom, all of which were "pagan" Canaanitic city-states that did not share Israel's belief in the God of the Fathers (Amos, chaps. 1-2). Today, Muslims are establishing full-scale mosques in cities including London, Los Angeles, Toronto and even Seoul because they believe in the universal value of the Word of the Prophet Muhammed.

Likewise, Buddhist and Hindu Vedanta spiritual leaders are bringing their sacred teachings and forms of life to our shores because they are convinced that their teachings have a universal application. Again, in this respect, Scientology follows the pattern of the historic religions in the worldwide spread of its auditing and training technology, which Scientology missionaries believe will benefit all of humankind.

(c) Thirdly, the dedicated aim of Scientology is to assist enough people to attain the status of "Clear" so that the tide of civilization may turn to the better. This aim has the character of an ultimate concern and commitment. Each of the great historic religions has a central core of teaching which provides its followers a compelling motivation to fulfill its religious mission on a worldwide scale and with a sense of urgency and ultimacy.

For the Buddhist that core teaching is summed up in the religious notion of "release" (*moksa*) from the entangling bonds of craving and the bestowal of bliss in egoless thought (*nirvana*). The Buddhist scripture, *The Dhammapada*, has the Buddha declare: "All the rafters [of my old house] are broken, shattered the roof-beam; my thoughts are purified of illusion; the extinction of craving has been won" (section 154). The ultimacy of this awakening is what motivated and motivates every Buddhist monk and missionary.

As I have noted above, the Scientology belief in past lives is closely related to the Buddhist idea of *samsara*; likewise, the Scientology notion of "Clearing" has close affinities with the Buddhist belief in *moksa*. As Buddhist missionaries in the past sought to make available to all sentient beings "release" from the cravings of existence, so also the Scientologist missionary strives to make available to one

and all the opportunity to be rid of engrams which impede universal survival, peace and abundance by becoming "Clear."

Zen Buddhists in Japan seek to attain *satori*, or "sudden enlightenment," for all humanity, and the strength of this belief has led them to establish monasteries in the Americas and Europe. The Muslim conviction in the ultimacy of the word of the Prophet Muhammed — summed up in the great shahada: "There is no God but Allah, and Muhammed is his prophet" — gives the missionaries of Islam the strength of conviction to seek converts on a worldwide scale. In the Biblical tradition, the most compelling core belief which motivated and still motivates missionary activity is the firm trust that God desires the ultimate salvation and universal redemption of all humankind. Thus the biblical prophet Isaiah saw God's salvation of all the nations as the new creation of a heavenly Jerusalem on earth in which all flesh would worship the one, true God (Isaiah 66:22-23).

In the New Testament the redemption wrought by God in Jesus the Christ is viewed by the Apostle Paul not simply as the salvation of Christians, or even of all humanity, but as the pledge of universal liberation, restoration and re-creation of the cosmos itself (Romans 8:19-23). In this context the Scientology belief in the mission of "Clearing the planet" to bring about a renewed civilization corresponds in like kind to the ultimacy of conviction which characterizes the motivation and faith of the world's great historic religions.

iii. Religious Practices

In terms of religious practices, Scientology possesses the typical ceremonial religious forms which are found among the world's religions, namely, initiation or baptism (which is called "naming" by Scientologists), marriage, funerals, etc. However, a central religious practice unique to Scientology is *auditing*, which can be compared to the progressive levels of meditation among Roman Catholics, Buddhists and Hindu Vedantists. Concomitant with auditing is Scientology *training*, which I will discuss at greater length in para. iii (b).

(a) Auditing is a religious instructional type of process by which spiritual guides (trained Scientology ministers) lead adherents through the states of spiritual enlightenment. Scientologists believe that by actively going through this gradated auditing process, they help to free the soul, or "thetan," from its entangling afflictions or "engrams." The stages of auditing are called "grades" or "levels," and these are shown on the Scientology "Classification, Gradation and Awareness Chart." This chart depicts metaphorically the span between the lower and higher levels of spiritual existence. Scientologists call the chart "The Bridge to Total Freedom" or, simply, "The Bridge." The Bridge details the spiritual continuum, ranging from negative "unexistence," through middle level "communication," "enlightenment," "ability," and finally to "Clearing," "source," and ultimately "power on all 8 dynamics." The vast bulk of Scientology religious practice is devoted to auditing and training courses for enlightenment and the training of *auditors*, who are the Church's spiritual counselors. These gradated stages are remarkably like the stages and levels of religious and spiritual illumination in the noted Christian treatises *Journey of the Mind into God* by the medieval Franciscan theologian St. Bonaventure, and the *Spiritual Exercises* by St. Ignatius of Loyola, founder of the Jesuits. The spiritual goal of auditing is first to become "Clear" of harmful "engrams" and then to become a full "Operating Thetan" (OT) so that one is "at cause," over "life, thought, matter, energy, space and time." While not opposed to consulting physicians for physical ailments, Scientologists are firmly against the use of psychotropic drugs which they believe impede rather than assist the attainment of mental and spiritual healing of the soul.

(b) The other central religious practice of Scientology is *training*, which involves intensive study of the Church's scriptures. Although one important aspect of training is the education of individual auditors capable of ministering auditing to parishioners, auditor training has an equally important individual, spiritual component as well. As discussed below, this spiritual element is in keeping with the emphasis of Scientology and Eastern religions on meditative and instructional worship rather than on celebratory worship which prevails in most Western religions. Scientology doctrine states that training provides fully one-half of the spiritual benefit parishioners receive in moving up The Bridge.

iv. CHURCH COMMUNITY

As with every religion known to me, Scientology has a communal life and ecclesiastical organization which function both to preserve and express the belief system and to foster the religious practices. In ecclesiastical terms, the Church of Scientology is hierarchical rather than congregational in organization. Congregational religions exercise authority by locally electing ministers of churches, voting on reformulations of belief systems (creeds) and religious practices, as well as church polity. Most Protestant denominations in the United States are congregational in their polity. They exercise authority from the bottom up, so to speak. Hierarchical religions, on the other hand, exercise authority by appointment and delegation from the top down, either from a central religious figure such as the Supreme Pontiff (Pope) in Roman Catholicism and the Dalai Lama in Tibetan Buddhism, or from a central executive body such as a synod of bishops or council of elders. My study of the Church of Scientology showed me that it follows the classic hierarchical type of church polity.

I will here give a brief summary of the organization of the Church of Scientology. L. Ron Hubbard, who died in 1986, was and remains the sole source of Scientology religious doctrine and technology, including the upper OT levels. The highest ecclesiastical authority in the Church of Scientology is exercised by Church of Scientology International (CSI) and Religious Technology Center (RTC). CSI is the mother church and has the chief responsibility to propagate the Scientology creed around the world. The all-important function of RTC is to preserve, maintain and protect the purity of Scientology technology and to insure its proper and ethical delivery in accord with the tenets of the faith. RTC functions very much like the Congregation for the Doctrine of the Faith in Roman Catholicism.

Scientology Missions International (SMI) functions as the mother church to the mission churches around the world. This structure is very similar to the First Church of Christian Science in Boston, which also serves as the mother church to all other Christian Science churches. In all doctrinal disputes, RTC is the ultimate and final court of appeal in Scientology, just as the Vatican and its congregations are the final courts of appeal in Roman Catholicism.

I need also to mention here the Sea Organization. The Sea Org is composed of Church of Scientology members who take vows of service "for a billion years," signifying their commitment to serve the Church in this life and in countless lives to come. The Sea Org has become to Scientology what Jesuits are to Roman Catholicism. From the ranks of the Sea Org have come almost all the Church's leadership.

Scientology sometimes describes itself as "an applied religious philosophy." Some have used this phrase to argue that Scientology is not a religion. But as noted above, my research into the teachings of the Church and interviews with its members show that Scientology possesses all the marks which are common to religions around the world and throughout history: a well-formed belief system, sustained religious practices, and a hierarchical ecclesiastical polity. Furthermore, the word "philosophy" can have several meanings and is not at all incompatible with the word "religion." Literally, the word philosophy means "love of wisdom" and every religion known to humankind preaches some sort of "wisdom" or insight into ultimate truth. My interviews with Scientologists showed that adherents consider the word "philosophy" to refer to the ultimate meaning of life and the universe in the religious sense of the term. Scientology's "philosophy" is dependent upon the belief that the soul is immortal and has an eternal destiny. In making use of philosophical concepts and in stressing the application of its teachings, Scientology is certainly no different from any other religion known to me. Religion always links up with philosophy. In his great work the *Summa Theologica*, St. Thomas Aquinas, the greatest theologian in the history of Roman Catholicism, makes use of countless philosophical ideas, terms and constructs borrowed from the Greek philosopher Aristotle and urges the moral application of these "philosophical" notions, yet no one would classify the *Summa* as anything but a religious treatise of the highest order. The phrase "an applied religious philosophy" in no way detracts from Scientology being a bona fide religious faith in the fullest sense of the term.

Western religions — specifically, Judaism, Christianity and Islam — traditionally have been exclusivistic in nature. Each faith claims to be the one true faith by virtue of its own unique

My research into the teachings of the Church and interviews with its members show that Scientology possesses all the marks which are common to religions around the world...

religious law, savior, prophet, path to salvation or interpretation of the ultimate meaning of life and truth. This exclusivistic trait is, on the whole, absent in Eastern religions such as Hinduism, Buddhism, Confucianism, Shintoism and Taoism. In the East, one and the same person can be initiated into life as a Shintoist, doubly married in Shinto and Christian rites, and finally buried in a Buddhist rite, without having to "choose" which religion is the "right" one. Today even Western Christianity is losing some it its exclusivistic character, as evidenced by various denominations deeply engaged in interreligious theological dialogue and intercommunal religious worship. Such pluridenominationality is not at all surprising and is fully understandable to scholars of religion who study current practices firsthand. Although Scientology has close affinities to both the Hindu and Buddhist traditions, it is not purely non-exclusivistic nor, for that matter, purely exclusivistic. Scientology does not require members to renounce prior religious beliefs or membership in other churches or religious orders. This is in keeping with the pluridenominational temper of our times. Nonetheless, as a practical matter, Scientologists usually become fully involved with the Scientology religion to the exclusion of any other faith. In any event, openness to persons from other religious traditions in no way detracts from Scientology's specific religious identity.

v. SCIENTOLOGY WORSHIP

There is no hard-and-fast definition of worship which can be applied to all forms of religion with complete impartiality. At the end of section ii above, on the marks of religion, I noted that every religion will have all three marks (a system of beliefs, religious practices, and religious community) in some way, but no two religions will have them in the precise same degree or in the same manner. These variations are what make religions unique. Roman Catholicism, Eastern Orthodoxy, and high Anglicanism place an enormous stress on elaborate rituals, including vestments, processions, candles, hymns, icons, holy water, incense and so forth. On the other hand, in many strict Protestant denominations such as the Brethren, such ornate ceremonial forms are considered slightly superstitious if not outrightly idolatrous. In the branches of Christianity, worship is pared down to the preaching of the Word, maybe a few hymns and prayer. Among the Religious Society of Friends — commonly known as the Quakers — the Meeting for Worship consists of no external acts at all but is a gathering in silence during which members may or may not share a brief word of inspiration. Likewise, the central act of worship in Buddhist monasteries is totally silent meditation for great periods of time centered not on revering a Supreme Deity but on the extinction of the self and release from the entanglements of existence.

The impossibility of discovering any absolutely rigid and fixed definition of worship necessitates keeping a flexible notion for comparative study. Most dictionary definitions face this problem by including several ideas under the concept of worship. First, worship can include ideas of "rites" and "ceremonies." Some scholars of religion see rites and rituals as being transformative. In the Christian rite of baptism, for example, an initiate is transformed from one state (sin) to another (grace). In primal societies, the rites of passage transform neophytes from childhood to adulthood. The Scientology auditing process of passing from the state of "preclear" to "Clear" would be transformative in this sense. Conversely, ceremonies are seen as confirmatory; that is, they affirm and confirm the status quo. Various forms of Sabbath and Sunday services are often ceremonies in this sense. Ceremonies confirm to the believing community its status as a worshipping body and its identity as a denomination. Often, but not necessarily always, accoutrements including vestments, rites and ceremonies are accompanied by elaborate dancing, music, sacred sprinklings and purifications, sacrifices of animals or food, gestures such as blessings, and so forth.

Secondly, scholars of religion universally recognize that rites and ceremonies cannot be the end-all and be-all of worship. Hence, most definitions include further notions such as "practices," "acts" and "observances." These further notions are included in common definitions for good reasons. One person's worship may be another's superstition. And what may appear to be a meaningless act to one believer—for example, making the sign of the Cross, to a Protestant—may be an act of devotion to another. Thus scholars are compelled to see religious acts in the context of the specific religion as a whole, that is, in terms of the ultimate goals and intentions of the body of believers. The scholar does not have to believe what the believer believes, but if he or she is seriously attempting to understand religious phenomena, that scholar must take a step in the direction of believing as the believer believes. It is only from this stance that the scholar can determine which acts, practices and observances constitute worship in a given religious community.

Under the broader definition of religious worship (acts, practices, observances) we can include such topics as the study of sacred texts, the training of others in the study and recitation of these texts and various forms of religious instruction. Some religions even imbue these kinds of acts with sacred ceremony. In Japanese Zen monasteries, I have observed Zen novices ceremonially carrying copies of the Lotus Sutra and solemnly committing it to memory through ritualized chanting. The study of the Talmud in Jewish yeshivas takes on a similar ritual character.

In the many varieties of religious worship the scholar can detect two fundamental orientations: One strand of worship is more celebratory and ritual-centered; the other is more instructional and meditation-centered.

The question of whether auditing and training can be forms of worship may naturally arise in the minds of adherents of the mainline religions of the West, namely, Judaism, Christianity and Islam. In those religions, worship is chiefly, but not exclusively, centered on public celebrations, feast days, sermons, hymn singing, Sabbath or Sunday worship and various devotions. Although one can find this form of worship plentifully represented in Eastern religion, there is a fundamental undertone in many strands of Eastern piety which places greater stress on meditation and instruction. As already

noted, in Vedanta Hinduism and Zen Buddhism, worship is centered not on celebration but on meditation and the study of *sutras*, spiritual textbooks. In Zen this spiritual study is often accompanied by meditation on *koans*, short, pithy and often contradictory sayings which aid the devotee in cracking the shell of ordinary consciousness so that he or she may attain *satori*, sudden enlightenment.

While the discovery and codification of the technology of auditing belongs exclusively to L. Ron Hubbard, the Church of Scientology and L. Ron Hubbard himself have always recognized that Scientology has affinities with certain aspects of Hinduism and especially Buddhism. Scientology shares with both religious traditions a common belief that the central process of salvation is the passage from ignorance to enlightenment, from entanglement to freedom, and from obfuscation and confusion to clarity and light. A number of years ago I published an article on Scientology's relation to Buddhism: Frank K. Flinn, "Scientology as Technological Buddhism" in Joseph H. Fichter, editor, *Alternatives to American Mainline Churches*, New York: Paragon House, 1983, pages 89-110. In consonance with these Eastern traditions, Scientology quite logically sees worship not so much in the mode of celebration and devotion but in the mode of meditation and instruction, which stresses awareness, enlightenment or, to use the Scientology term, "Clearing."

As an important side-note, one would not want to say that the meditational and instructional form of worship is absent in the West. The pious Orthodox Jew believes that the devout study of the Torah or Law is a form, if not *the* form, of worship.

Hence, Orthodox Jews set up yeshivas, which are dedicated to the worshipful study of the Torah and the Talmud. A yeshiva is not simply a place for ordinary education; it is also a place of worship. Likewise, Muslims have set up *kuttabs* and *madrassas* for the devout study of the Qur'an. Similarly, many Roman Catholic monastic religious orders, most notably the Cistercians and Trappists, devote the greater part of their worship to silent study and meditation on sacred texts.

On the whole, however, meditation, sacred study and instruction are not perceived as much to be forms of worship in the West as they are in the East. In India, it is a common practice for people in later life to sell all their worldly goods, go to a sacred site, such as Varanasi (Benares) on the Ganges, and spend the rest of their lives, occasionally performing *pujas* or ritual offerings but mostly meditating on divine things. To the ordinary Hindu, such meditation is the highest form of worship possible.

Aside from these discussions, it is abundantly clear that Scientology has both the typical forms of ceremonial and celebratory worship and its own unique form of spiritual life: auditing and training. By way of comparison and contrast, the Roman Catholic church considers all of its seven sacraments as forms of worship. That is why all the sacraments are administered principally in its churches by ordained clergy. Sacraments are administered outside church premises only under special circumstances such as ministering to the sick. The sacraments include baptism, confirmation, confession, reconciliation or confession, the Eucharist, marriage, holy orders and the anointing of the sick and infirm. But the "sacrament of all sacraments" for Roman Catholics is the Eucharist, commonly called the Mass, which celebrates the death and resurrection of Jesus Christ and his presence in the believing community.

So also the Church of Scientology has, so-to-speak, its "sacrament of all sacraments," namely, auditing and training. The chief religious aim of all practicing Scientologists is to become Clear and attain the status of being an Operating Thetan who has mastery over "life, thought, matter, energy, space and time." The central religious means to these ends are the complex levels and grades of auditing and training. What the Eucharist is in religious importance to the Roman Catholic, auditing and training is to the Scientologist. As Roman Catholics consider the seven sacraments as the chief means for the salvation of the world, so also Scientologists consider auditing and training the central means of salvation, which they describe as optimum survival on all dynamics.

As a scholar of comparative religion, I would answer the question, "Where do Roman Catholics have places of worship?" with the answer, "Where the seven sacraments are ministered to adherents as a matter of course." To the question "Where do Scientologists have places of worship?" I would answer, "Where auditing and training in Scientology scripture are ministered to parishioners as a matter of course." Hubbard's works on Dianetics and Scientology constitute the sacred scriptures of the Church of Scientology. The vast majority of these works is devoted to what Scientologists call *auditing technology* and the management and delivery of auditing and training to the membership. The sheer preponderance of the emphasis on auditing in Hubbard's works will convince any scholar of religion that auditing and training are the central religious practices and chief forms of worship of the Church of Scientology.

As a scholar of comparative religion I can assert without hesitation that auditing and training are central forms of worship in the belief system of the Scientologist. Secondly, the places where auditing and training are ministered to adherents are unequivocally Scientology houses of worship.

Frank K. Flinn

About the Author

Frank K. Flinn serves as Adjunct Professor in Religious Studies at Washington University in St. Louis, Missouri. He holds a Bachelor of Arts degree in Philosophy from Quincy University, Quincy, Illinois; a Bachelor of Divinity degree *magna cum laude*, from Harvard Divinity School, Cambridge, Massachusetts; and a Ph.D. in Special Religious Studies from the University of St. Michael's College,

Toronto School of Theology, Toronto, Ontario. He has done advanced study at Harvard University, the University of Pennsylvania and the University of Heidelberg, Germany, where he was a Fulbright Fellow in Philosophy and Ancient Near Eastern Religions.

Since 1968, Mr. Flinn has written and lectured about new religious movements which have arisen in the 19th and 20th centuries and is a member in good standing of the American Academy of Religion.

Scientology

■

Its Cosmology, Anthropology, System of Ethics & Methodologies

Régis Dericquebourg

Professor, Sociology of Religion
University of Lille III
Lille, France

The purpose of this consultation is to take stock of Scientology from a sociological viewpoint.

The question is: Is Scientology a religion and if so, which type of religion? We will try to provide elements of answers in this paper.

We will also describe some aspects of Scientology as it appears to us today. Our presentation is neither polemic nor apologetic.

i. Is Scientology a Religion?

i.i. What Do We Mean By Religion?

This consultation cannot give rise to a basic discussion on the definition of religion. We may nevertheless have an operational viewpoint and agree on a minimum number of characteristics found in most religions. We are aware that this view provisionally ignores the discussion on the definition of religion imposed by new forms of religion. With Bryan Wilson we can agree that a religion includes:

• A cosmology in which the universe takes on a meaning regarding one or more supernatural forces. The conception of Man exceeds the boundaries of his terrestrial existence. There is a before and an after. The finite character of Man is not accepted.

• A moral which stems from this cosmology. It supplies directives and guidelines in accordance with the suggested meaning of the universe.

• Tools which put human beings in contact with the supernatural principle: prayer, religious ceremonies, techniques of meditation.

• A community of followers, however small, which is capable of maintaining and reproducing the beliefs and of managing the benefits of salvation.

The combination of these elements makes it possible to distinguish religions:

(1) from deist philosophies, which provide a cosmology and a meaning for existence but which are not intended to link human beings with supernatural powers;

(2) from individual magic, intended to obtain empirical results through the use of empirical techniques;

(3) from deist organizations such as *Freemasonry*, which acknowledge the existence of the Grand Architect of the Universe but whose ceremonies are not directed to putting Man in relation with Him.

i.ii. The Contents of Scientology

Scientology contains a cosmology, an anthropology, ethics, religious ceremonies, an auditing method, a method for purifying the body, training methods, a theory of communication.

The Cosmology: The Supernatural in Scientology

The founder, L. Ron Hubbard (1911-86), renews the thesis of primordial spirits. He asserts that before the birth of the universe, spirits existed, which he calls *thetans*. They were non-material, massless beings without temporal limits, occupying no space, omniscient, omnipotent, indestructible, immortal and capable of creating anything. These intangible beings, along with the Supreme Being, created the universe. In doing so, they got caught in their own trap and got stuck in their creation—and especially in Man—i.e., in matter, energy, space and time (MEST, the physical universe), even forgetting that they were the creators. Thus they lost their power and omniscience and became vulnerable human beings. Since that time, they have returned, life after life, inhabiting different bodies. Today, thetans have forgotten their true spiritual identity and believe they are human bodies. Hence, Man has a spiritual origin: he is altogether a body, a mind and a thetan.

This is a gnostic version of the fall of perfect man into imperfection and a transposition of Greek drama, where the Gods interfere in human affairs and are trapped.

A liberation must put an end to the succession of lifetimes. Scientology wants to bring man close to the state of original thetan.

The Dynamics and Ethics

Scientology deals with the driving force of the universe and the meaning of existence.

The universe is motivated by a dynamic urge which is a force at the service of survival, the very principle of existence. It varies among individuals and races. It depends on physiology, environment and experience. It influences the persistence of Man towards life and the activity of intelligence considered as the ability of an individual, a group or a race to solve problems related to survival.

The morality of an individual is judged with regard to the actions which he accomplishes for survival. In such a perspective, goodness is what is constructive, badness what is against survival. One can see that Scientology ethics are not a set of recommendations (the Bergsonian idea of closed morals). They are the result of an understanding and interiorization of the meaning of life which acts as a personal compass. It would be an open moral system.

In Scientology as in spiritualist groups there is no "sin." There are mistakes which are destructive actions against Man, family, society, God. Part of ethics is to spot and repair faults.

The dynamic drive becomes more complex as the organism becomes more complex. In a "normal" (unaberrated) man, it breaks down into eight areas, corresponding to objectives:

(1) The dynamic of self consists in a dynamic urge to survive as an individual, to obtain pleasure and to avoid pain. It deals with food, clothing, housing, personal ambition and the general objectives of the individual.

(2) The sex dynamic guides procreation.

(3) The group dynamic governs social life. It stimulates the conduct intended to maintain the survival of the group to which the individual belongs.

(4) The dynamic of humanity encompasses the survival of the species.

(5) The dynamic of life pushes the person to work for life in itself — i.e., all living things, both plant and animal.

(6) The dynamic of the physical universe is the individual drive to increase survival of matter, energy, space and time.

(7) The dynamic of thought is the individual urge to survive as thought and spiritual beings.

(8) The dynamic of universal thought is the urge to survive for the creator or Supreme Being. The first four dynamics are connected with Dianetics. The others, added in the early 1950s, of metaphysical nature, are dealt with in Scientology (cf., difference below).

The follower is invited to be in accordance with all dynamics. Checklists of self-exploration enable him to take stock of his condition on each. With the help of a minister, he looks for means to remedy defective conditions.

The Anthropology of Scientology

L. Ron Hubbard's teachings include a concept of the individual in which the body and the mind are intimately linked.

Based on his research into the mind and human nature, L. Ron Hubbard wrote *Dianetics: The Modern Science of Mental Health* in 1950 which became an immediate bestseller and resulted in the founding of Dianetics organizations. At that time Dianetics was addressed solely to the mind as a means of unburdening or releasing an individual from mental trauma. However, Mr. Hubbard continued his research and in the early 1950s entered the spiritual realm with the discovery that Man is an immortal spirit who has lived countless lives and transcends the physical dimension. The first Church of Scientology was founded in 1954.

Through auditing, Man gains a greater understanding of his spirituality and his relationship with the Supreme Being.

In Scientology the mind may be likened to a computer with two main divisions: the analytical mind and the reactive mind.

The first would represent intelligence, an unfaulty faculty supposed to be the awareness center of the individual (the "I" or basic personality). This analyzer is analogous to a computer working with perceptions (stimuli from the outside world), the imagination and memories contained in the standard memory bank. This memory receives, from birth to death, whether awake or asleep, information transmitted by the various senses, which it stores in full, in chronological sequence, in various files (auditory, visual, tactile, etc.) which it keeps at the disposal of the analytical mind. This mind thinks permanently. It continually receives copies of stored facsimiles, evaluates them, compares them, in order to supply correct answers to the problems encountered by the individual. To accomplish routine tasks such as walking, typing, etc. without having useless information, it sets up ready-to-work circuits that regulate acquired functions. In principle, the analytical mind is a sort of rational, unfaulty computer which does not create psychic or psychosomatic disorders.

Aberrated conduct is due to the reactive mind, which is a deposit of engrams. The latter are not exactly memories. They are complete recordings in all details of all perceptions received by the individual during a moment of pain and total or partial unconsciousness, such as fainting or anesthesia.

a. Auditing

The primary Scientology religious practice is known as *auditing*. For Scientologists, auditing is a methodical spiritual path. What is it?

Auditing permits an individual to recover all events in this life as well as in past lives — on the time track. The most significant events found are the traumatizing events in which a quantity of energy has been alienated that reduces capacity by blocking action and rational thinking. The recall of these events and the running of them releases, by abreaction, the energy linked to the incidents, which is thus made available. This produces a feeling of well-being. Moreover, past incidents are considered sources of physical or psychic diseases. Their recognition and the work that the audited person does on them are supposed to erase them. For example, someone in pain may discover in auditing that he has been strangled in an earlier life. Running the traumatic incident, he releases the pain accompanying the past incident. This reminds one of the construction of a personal myth in the shamanic cure as discussed by Levi-Strauss in his book *Anthropologie structurale*.

In Hubbardian terminology, Scientology auditing uses the capacities of the analytical mind to empty the reactive mind of its damaging engrams, which hamper the ability to recover the power of the incarnated thetan.

Auditing produces two things: (1) through exploration of the past, it quickly shows the adept that he is an all-powerful incarnated spirit limited by his human condition; (2) the erasure of engrams leads to the state of "Clear."

The elimination of engrams helps to regenerate the being. It shows in an increase of the life force, with a greater capacity to survive, with a feeling of power and with better abilities which can be measured on a tone scale.

For Scientologists, auditing is a form of pastoral counseling. Bryan Wilson shares those views (in "Scientology," 1994) by considering that Scientology manifests the systematization of the relationships with spirituality, an orientation that one finds in "methodism." For us it is a form of rationalization of religious life.

To Scientologists, auditing is first and foremost a spiritual adventure which gives one access to the spiritual, immortal part of Man, as in oriental religions.

It is through auditing that the thetan becomes certain of its immortality and is able to grow spiritually. Through auditing, Man gains a greater understanding of his spirituality and his relationship with the Supreme Being. Auditing also enables Man to become more understanding and capable along all eight dynamics.

Some detractors of the religion have compared Scientology to a form of psychotherapy. However, the methods and rituals are not the same, and they have totally different goals: psychotherapy deals with the mind; the goal of Scientology, on the other hand, is salvation of the spirit. 1) The audited person comes to understand the duality of Man and, through the discovery of past lives, understands the permanence of a single principle throughout all lives; 2) Scientology also deals with the thetan. By unburdening the thetan of the mental and corporal masses he recovers his initial power; the individual that the thetan represents would become "freed-alive" (*jivan mukti*).

b. Religious Training

The other core religious practice in Scientology is called *training*, which is the intensive study of Scientology Scripture both for spiritual enlightenment and for training as Scientology clergy.

Scientologists consider that they must use their quality of spiritual awareness in all conditions of life. They find this path through their study of Scientology Scripture. This is similar to study for enlightenment found in other religions such as the study of the Talmud in Judaism, study of the teachings of Buddha and study of esoteric scripture. Moreover, according to them, auditing and training go together. One must raise at the same time one's abilities, one's responsibilities and one's knowledge. One discovers that one can act with the power of the incarnated thetan and that one can communicate with other spiritual beings. For instance, in training, Scientologists also learn how to "audit" to discover the process of spiritualization in others and to exercise their responsibilities of believers.

c. Ceremonies

The Church of Scientology observes a number of religious ceremonies which are traditionally found in mainstream religions: naming ceremonies, Sunday services, weddings and funerals.

d. Organization

The Church of Scientology has the complex organization typical of modern civilization, based on a large number of organizations. Each religion borrows its form of organization from the era in which it arises. More recently, the Jehovah's Witnesses borrowed organizational methods from the industrial era, while Scientology has adopted the organization style of the post-industrial era.

The purpose of the organization is to administer and reproduce the benefits of salvation. It is in the service of international expansion.

e. Pastoral Counseling

Scientology has a body of ordained ministers who celebrate ceremonies and practice auditing.

ii. WHO ARE THE SCIENTOLOGISTS?

In their studies on the Church of Scientology, Roy Wallis and Roland Chagnon have tried to outline a profile of the followers. On a good number of points their results agree.

In France, we have tried to gather data of the same type from 285 followers chosen randomly. The profile which emerges shows that two-thirds are men, that most are between 26 and 41 years old. Most are married and have one or two children.

Usually, the Scientologists were born and lived in an urban zone up to the age of 18. They are well-integrated in society; their professional level is high (intermediary businesses, senior executives, businessmen, craftsmen, shopkeepers). Forty-two percent have gone up to secondary level education, and specialized in technical fields, art, trade or literature.

French Scientologists are mainly from Catholic backgrounds, but had fallen from it; 16 percent say they were atheists. Of those who agreed to talk about their present attitude towards their original religion, a bit more than half stated that they still belong to it, and several wanted to say that they understand it better and that they live it more spiritually. It is of note that the Scientology practice does not necessarily lead to a dismissal of the original religion, although as a practical matter Scientology is a complete religion and Scientologists generally retain affiliation with their prior religions solely for social and familial reasons.

iii. How Do Scientologists Validate Their Creeds?

Scientological writings provide some arguments to validate (legitimize) the Scientology religious doctrine of L. Ron Hubbard, which is called an "applied religious philosophy." A reading of the argumentation shows that integration exists between Scientology and the ideals and practices of contemporary occidental society.

Scientology doctrine — which is not conceived as a revealed morality but rather as the result of the right use of human reason — takes on the ideals and values of liberal society: individual success, a morality of competition between individuals in order to avoid savage behaviour, the rise of economic power and science and technology which provide improvements in personal well-being, faith in the continuous progress of civilization, in Man and his potential, in the possibility of harmony between personal aims and those of civilization as a whole. Faith in these ideals is justified by the nature of Man: Man is good and, consequently, aspires to that which is good, i.e., optimum survival. If he fails to become more powerful or to practice a morality which encourages progress in civilization, this is because he suffers from aberrations which can be cured by means of certain techniques.

To summarize, Man may return to the omniscience and omnipotence of the primordial spirits and produce a human race like that in the beginning of the world. This is a kind of regressive utopia which spiritualizes progress by making it a pilgrimage towards a world of perfect people which existed at one stage in the past. The Scientology doctrine appeals to Man's responsibility and offers him a choice between an increasingly savage society if they do not change and a powerful society without war or violence if they agree to treat their aberrations. We can see that L. Ron Hubbard proposes an ethos of personal responsibility, a way to happiness, efficiency, prosperity and personal development which is not far from the philosophy of the Enlightenment which dominates our highly developed societies.

Therefore, we can see how the Scientology doctrine corresponds to empirical reality as far as the content of Western capitalist societies is concerned. It also corresponds in its means of acquisition and structure. The method of religious training conforms to the learning methods used in most systems of education: lessons, courses, practical exercises. Scientology's doctrinal edifice resembles the knowledge adherents have already acquired: the members think it is rational (it is presented like a scientific proof with concepts, hypotheses and axioms) and scientific (there is a collection of thick books documenting the discoveries of L. Ron Hubbard together with his various experiments, mistakes, problems and results). The system also allows each person to acquire techniques which they can immediately put into practice according to a clear order of precedence with predictable results. This type of training is similar in form to the training that Scientologists received in their earlier school or university system.

Many Scientologists are managers, company directors, professional people, sportsmen and show business personnel. They have usually reached at least A-level in their general education, often higher. The characteristics of Scientology which we have just described allow the members to feel at home because of the education they have already received. We can add that Scientology also speaks to the fears common in contemporary society — violence, wars, nuclear threat, pollution, etc.

On the other hand, the life force required to achieve these goals is identified with God, which gives the movement spiritual legitimacy. During the Sunday services the chaplain announces that "the ascension to Survival is in itself an ascension to God." We can find here an energetic vision of the divine common to many different metaphysical movements.

Secondly, to Scientologists, the validity of Scientology comes from the workability of its technology. Scientology holds that the man who applies the ethics technology and uses Scientology will inevitably have a better life and increased well-being and healing which indicate success. An instance of the absence of positive results does not discredit the technology. Rather, any apparent failure invites the user to examine his own resistances, his relationship problems within society or his faulty use of the technology. In either case, he is invited to persevere because Scientologists believe there is always a technical solution to any problem. Scientology works if followed correctly. Standard technology can be consulted in Scientology texts. The application of the technology is strictly standardized; one need only follow the instructions step by step to achieve the desired result, learned by training in the religion. Certainty of the validity arises from experiencing the techniques.

Success proves the legitimacy of the technology and therefore also the applied religious philosophy and the spiritual concepts which go with it.

We wanted to know if the legitimation of Scientology as it is described in the official literature was the same as that used by the members. For this reason we interviewed 15 Scientologists. We asked them why they thought Scientology was true. The members interviewed had been in the movement for between five and 20 years. They were all highly educated. Their arguments can be divided into several categories.

iii.i. Pragmatic Legitimacy

The Scientologists questioned thought that their beliefs were valid because they brought tangible improvements in their lives, sometimes changing their situation completely. They claim that their health has improved, that their family life is more harmonious. They continued in the movement because they saw definite results right from the start. For the members, Scientology is a *useful* religion.

iii.ii. Probability in Belief

Personal verification of the validity of Scientology principles leaves an "unverified" realm. Many Scientologists admit that they have not personally verified all of L. Ron Hubbard's doctrine for themselves and that there remain some zones of hypothetical belief.

Belief in God is much discussed. For some, the existence of a Supreme Being is not in doubt. They speak of an inner conviction, evidence of God's existence which made them make up their differences with the "God of the Catholics" of their childhood. Others have been marked by contact with their past lives during auditing which led them to the idea of an infinite being. For example, "To start with I wasn't aware of it, but as the auditing went on I realised that there really was an eighth dynamic which is infinite and which exists; at first I didn't know about it, but now I know it exists." However, for most of them, God (in their vocabulary — the eighth dynamic) needs to be verified in the same way as the other beliefs. At the same time, they consider God a probable hypothesis: for one thing, if they have checked a part of L. Ron Hubbard's teaching, there is no reason why the rest should not be true. For example: "I know that there is a creator of all things, of the universe... I believe that there is a Supreme Being, it's just a question of time. Does he still exist? At the stage I've reached now I have no means of knowing. It's partly faith and partly *knowing,* because when you've verified for yourself 70 percent of a subject, you think the rest is probably true." — Scientologist of 20 years, age 47. Still others think that if Scientologists at higher levels have found God, then he must exist.

At the same time, they admit that they are on a search which may not end for them with the same discovery. For many Scientologists "the eighth dynamic" remains a world which must be explored personally to be fully believed. For the moment they are waiting. God is probably there. This can be called faith in probability.

iii.iii. Relative Truth

Where personal exploration dominates, truth is always relative to the stage reached along the Scientologist's path of spiritual development. Two truths mentioned by one of those questioned illustrate this relativity: the one which is beyond time and words and the truth of "here and now."

iii.iv. Relevance

Scientologists state that their belief is relevant to reality. One spoke about being in tune with reality, while at the same time admitting that he created it himself and that it had become natural for him. For example, one of them perceived Scientology ethics as adequate for understandings with others and for dealing with them. Another believer said that she had found a satisfactory method of social reform. Before her involvement with Scientology she had been a militant socialist. She felt that she had found in Scientology technology the tools she needed to "thoroughly reform society."

iii.v. The Meaning of Life

Members claim to have found a meaning for their lives. One of them described himself as a sailor drifting on the ocean under a cloudy sky with no compass and no landmarks to guide him when he found a map and all the navigational equipment he needed. Scientologists think they have found the meaning of life and the way to go forward. One of them, who gave up studying medicine, admits that he could not see the point of all the effort he was making, because the comfortable, middle-class existence he was heading for seemed to be inconsistent with what he felt was the meaning of life, meaning he said he had found in Scientology.

iii.vi. References to Science

In our interviews we found no references to accredited sciences as proofs for the doctrine or the technology of the Scientologists. This is in direct contrast with:

a. The expert knowledge required by leadership and mentioned above.

b. L. Ron Hubbard's statement that "I have to face up to the fact that we have come to the point where science and religion meet, and from now on we should stop pretending to have exclusively material aims. We cannot treat the human soul if we close our eyes to this fact."

We can form the hypothesis that:

a. Compatibility with the accredited sciences is an official doctrine considered as an accepted fact and which Scientologists do not feel the need to justify. Or,

b. The legitimation of this belief is a question of personal experience rather than attachment to an official position.

c. That Scientological technology replaces science.

We should also note that the Church of Scientology has changed from its formative years. It describes itself as a specific religious movement; the legitimacy that the Church seeks nowadays is less positioned on a scientific level than before.

iii.vii. The Importance of Scientological Technology

Scientology is not so much believed as practiced. The phrase "doing Scientology" was used several times. In an earlier series of interviews on the subject of defining what is Scientology, the members stressed *application* of the technology. During the current series of interviews, validity relied on the workability of the technology.

Scientology appears to be a practical religion.

iii.viii. Reference to a Religious Tradition

Those questioned only talked about religious traditions to point out their shortcomings. No one mentioned the link between Buddhism and Scientology although it is asserted by L. Ron Hubbard. He underlined their common points but lamented Buddhism's lack of effectiveness in the world.

This omission accompanies the omission of science. The faithful do not seek to legitimize their beliefs by referring to external factors. That which they have confirmed for themselves seems to suffice. They do not feel the need to support their beliefs to others in theological terms, nor to place themselves in a tradition of religious thought, even if L. Ron Hubbard perceived similarities between Scientology, Buddhism and various ancient wisdom religions.

The legitimation of Scientology by some members differs slightly from official documents. The "science based on certainty" is rather a "science based on certainties," which are only accepted after being confirmed by personal experience. It follows that faith is based on probability and is relative to the stage reached by the member on the spiritual scale. On the other hand, doctrinal affirmations with regard to the technology of the movement are accepted. We are not dealing with discernible proof of the truth which leads to a form of behaviour as in cases of conversion in religions with a doctrine of salvation. In those religions, believers pray because they accept the belief structure which recommends prayer. The Scientologist adds one certainty to another until he obtains sufficient evidence for the truth. One Scientologist told me that he preferred to talk about "continuous conversion."

It also appears that their faith is a *fides efficax* as the believers claim to have found in Scientology a means of understanding society and to transform both it and the whole world.

iv. CONCLUSIONS

Scientology has the characteristics of a religion. It has a theology, a set of exercises making it possible to reach the spiritual part in every human being, a "very bureaucratized" church structure, and religious rites. Several authors before us, even the most critical, have not doubted of its religious nature: Michel de Certeau, Roy Wallis, Bryan Wilson, Harriet Whitehead, Lonnie D. Kliever, Frank K. Flinn.

We find the following characteristics:

(1) It has techniques which are meant to make a path towards freedom as "a healthy spirit in a healthy body." L. Ron Hubbard and Scientologists carry very far the rationalization of religious life and its instrumentalization. Most often it has been rightly compared to Buddhism. Some have described it as a "technological Buddhism." Others have seen a resemblance with Methodism due to the systematic character of auditing (pastoral counseling).

(2) It enables the follower to give sense to cosmic, historical and personal events; it offers the believer the conviction that he holds the solution to personal and group salvation; it enables the individual to be at cause in his life and not the effect of external causes.

(3) L. Ron Hubbard is not a prophet who claimed a salvation path stemming from a revelation; he appeared as a spiritual researcher who progressively set up a salvation method, which is a path to "achievement."

(4) It rests on a personal experience, somewhat mystical, which enables one to contact his own spiritual nature. It implies a "religious virtuosity," i.e., an important self-commitment, and thus it is not a religion of mass worship.

(5) Scientology has the character of a "this world" religion reminiscent of Soka Gakkai where business success honestly obtained is seen as a sign of positive spiritual evolution. We can also draw a parallel between the ethics of Scientology and those of traditional Protestantism. In the latter case, success in worldly affairs testifies to a state of grace, and in the former it is the outward manifestation of the person's work on his own personality, of a personal religious and moral code made up principally of psychological liberation techniques that free the individual spiritually, and the application of a very concrete system of morality.

(6) It is not a sect —it is not exclusive, and the follower is not obliged to renounce his former religion, although most practice Scientology exclusively.

(7) The religious character of the Church of Scientology has been asserted since the early 1950s, according to the brochure the Church of Scientology International published on the occasion of its 40th anniversary in 1994. The Church of Scientology International, headquartered in Los Angeles, is described as the Mother Church (as the one of Boston for Christian Scientists). There is reference to the parishioners and religious brotherhood, pastoral services and church-affiliated charitable works. Moreover, during the recent interviews of Scientologists that we have done, the religious dimension was more and more emphasized. By increasingly proclaiming its religious nature, Scientology attracts people in search of religion, whereas in its beginnings it attracted people seeking to solve personal problems. As Scientology developed, Dianetics became integrated into progress of the whole.

(8) Scientology includes utopian elements: L. Ron Hubbard has conceived a utopian project of "Clearing the planet," which envisions a society free of insanity, criminals and war where the able can prosper, honest beings have rights and man is free to rise to greater heights. Ethics, spontaneously applied (open Bergsonian morals), will eliminate all the wrongnesses of existence and through theta being recovered, will be increased. The world should improve as the number of Scientologists grows.

(9) Scientology is born in a modern context. It gets from it certain elements (technicity, well-asserted methodical approach, importance of communication, well-being, understanding of organization, personal experience) which it has mixed with ancient spiritualistic traditions.

L. Ron Hubbard and Scientologists extend the use of instruments of rationality in the service of a mystical path, a self-transformation and a transformation of the world. It is probably for that reason that it appears unique among the religions.

Régis Dericquebourg

About the Author

Regis Dericquebourg is a Professor of Sociology of Religion at the University of Lille III, Lille, France. He holds a degree in psychology from the University of Paris and Doctorate in Sociology from the University of Sorbonne and currently works with the National Center of Scientific Research.

Since 1972, Professor Dericquebourg has devoted himself to the study of minority religions, a project which he began by spending three years with the Jehovah's Witnesses as an observer.

Scientology

■

An Analysis and Review of a New Religion

M. Darrol Bryant, Ph.D.

Professor of Religion and Culture
Renison College, University of Waterloo
Waterloo, Ontario, Canada

i. PROFESSIONAL BACKGROUND

I received my B.A. cum laude (1964) in philosophy and political science from Concordia College, Moorhead, Minnesota, USA. My S.T.B. cum laude (1967) in theology is from Harvard Divinity School, Harvard University, Cambridge, Massachusetts, USA. My M.A. (1972) and Ph.D. *distinction* (1976) in Special Religious Studies are from the Institute of Christian Thought, University of St. Michael's College in the University of Toronto, in Ontario, Canada. My dissertation was entitled "History and Eschatology in Jonathan Edwards: A Critique of the Heimert Thesis."

I have taught at Concordia College, Moorhead, Minnesota (Summer, 1966), Waterloo Lutheran University, Waterloo, Ontario (1967-1969), University of Windsor, Windsor, Ontario (Summer, 1972,

1973), University of Toronto, Extension, Toronto, Ontario (1972), and Renison College, University of Waterloo, Waterloo, Ontario, since 1973. I hold an appointment as a Professor of Religion and Culture at Renison College, University of Waterloo, where I am also an Associate Professor of Social Development Studies. Since 1982 I have been part of the Supporting Faculty for the Consortium in Reformation History of the University of Waterloo and the University of Guelph. I served as the Chair of the Department of Religious Studies at the University of Waterloo (1987-1993) and I am currently the Graduate Officer for the M.A. in Religious Studies at the University of Waterloo.

I have also been a Visiting Scholar at Cambridge University, Cambridge, U.K., (1980), the Indian Institute of Islamic Studies, New Delhi, India (1986), the Dr. S. Radhakrishnan Institute for Advanced Studies in Philosophy, University of Madras, Madras, India (1987), Hamdard University, New Delhi, India (1993), and Nairobi University, Nairobi, Kenya (1994). I have lectured at numerous universities in Asia, Africa, Latin America and Europe.

I am the author of four volumes in the study of religion: *To Whom It May Concern: Poverty, Humanity, Community* (Philadelphia, 1969), *A World Broken By Unshared Bread* (Geneva, 1970), *Religion in a New Key* (New Delhi, 1992) and *Jonathan Edwards' Grammar of Time, Self and Society* (Lewiston, NY, 1993). I have also edited (singly or jointly) twelve fur-

ther volumes in the field of religious studies including *Exploring Unification Theology* (New York, 1978), *God: The Contemporary Discussion* (New York, 1982), *The Many Faces of Religion and Society* (New York, 1985), *Eugen Rosenstock-Huessy: Studies in His Life and Thought* (Lewiston, NY, 1986), *Interreligious Dialogue: Voices for a New Frontier* (New York, 1989) and *Pluralism, Tolerance and Dialogue* (Waterloo, 1989). I have compiled with Doris Jakobsh *A Canadian Interfaith Directory* (Waterloo, 1993). I have published more than forty scholarly articles including "Faith and History in Grant's Lament," "Media Ethics," "Cinema, Religion and Popular Culture," "Sin and Society," "The Consolations of Philosophy," "New Religions: Issues and Questions," "Towards a Grammar of the Spirit in Society," "Interreligious Dialogue and Understanding," "The Purposes of Christ: Towards the Recovery of a Trinitarian Perspective," "From 'De' to 'Re' or Does the 'Future of Ontotheology' Require the Recovery of the Experience/Sense of Transcendence?", "The Kumbha Mela: A Festival of Renewal," and "To Hear the Stars Speak: Ontology in the Study of Religion." My publications range across the broad area of religion and culture but can be broken down into the following areas: I. Theology and Ethics, II. Religion in North America, III. New Religious Movements, and IV. Interreligious Dialogue.

I have been teaching in Religious Studies for more than twenty-five years. At Renison College, University of Waterloo, I regularly teach courses on the Religious Quest, The Study of Religion,

The History of Christian Thought and Interreligious Encounter and Dialogue that employ the comparative, historical and sociological methods common to the academic study of religion. I also teach courses from time to time on Religion and Politics, Religion and Literature, Religion and Film and I have lectured in the course on Sects, Cults and New Religious Movements. I have also taught graduate courses on Christianity and World Religions.

I am a long-standing member of the Canadian Society for the Study of Religion, the American Academy of Religion, the Canadian Theological Society, the Society for Values in Higher Education, the Royal Asiatic Society and the Society for Buddhist Christian Studies. I have served as a Consultant to major international and interreligious conferences including the Assembly of the World's Religions (1985, 1990, 1992).

As a scholar of religion and culture, I have been engaged in the study of new religious movements since the mid-1970s. I have been interested to understand the origins, beliefs, practices and the relationships of these new movements to the wider culture. (Many of the new religions are not "new" in any profound sense, but are simply new to North American society.) I have also been interested in, and somewhat amused by, the intense, often hysterical, reaction of sectors of the public to the new religious movements. I have done extensive field work with several new religious communities in Canada, the United States and India.

In relation to the Church of Scientology, I first became aware of this new religious community in the mid-1970s. Then I met members of the Church of Scientology in Toronto and Kitchener,

Ontario. I was able to participate in some meetings in the late 1970s and early 1980s that brought together members of the Church of Scientology and scholars of religion to discuss the basic beliefs and practices of Scientology. I have met some members of American and British branches of the Church. I have had extended conversations with church members concerning their experience of Scientology and its impact on their lives. I have maintained a limited contact with some Canadian church members down to the present day. I have visited Scientology Centers in Kitchener and on Yonge Street in Toronto. Since the mid-1970s I have read many of the major publications of the Church of Scientology including *Dianetics: The Modern Science of Mental Health*, *The Volunteer Minister's Handbook*, *What Is Scientology?*, and *The Scientology Religion*. I have also read Church publications that address current social issues including drug abuse, mental health practices and religious liberty. I have read scholarly articles and books, mainly by sociologists of religion, on the Church of Scientology.

ii. THE ASSIGNMENT

I have been asked to share my opinion, as a scholar of religion, on two questions. 1. Is Scientology a "religion?" and 2. Are Scientology churches "places of worship?" It is further my understanding that these questions are germane to questions pertaining to the exemption of Church of Scientology organizations from taxation in certain jurisdictions. In approaching these questions, I provide some background in the study of new religious movements and then turn to directly address the above questions. My analysis and response to the questions are based only on my status as a scholar of religion and not on any expertise in any legal or administrative field.

iii. THE "NEW RELIGIONS" AND THE STUDY OF RELIGION

The second half of this century has seen the emergence of a host of "new religions" in North America and Europe. In the public media they were often called "the cults" and included such groups as Hare Krishna, 3HO, the Unification Church, Transcendental Meditation and Scientology. When the "new religions" attracted the attention of the public media it was usually in relation to sensational claims that members of the new religious communities were not there by choice but had been "programmed" or "brainwashed." Such claims have been the subject of scholarly investigation (Eileen Barker, *The Making of a Moonie*, Oxford, 1984) as well as a number of governmental inquiries (Hill Report on "Mind-Development Groups, Sects and Cults in Ontario," 1980). Such responsible scholarly and governmental inquiries have found no grounds for such charges, but such prejudicial images still persist.

When scholars of religion turned to the study of the "new religious communities" in the 1960s and 70s, they made several observations that are worth noting here. These studies continued into the 1980s and 90s and extended the investigations to other parts of the world.

Many of the "new religions" were not really "new" but just new to North America. For example, the Hare Krishna movement is often regarded as a "new religion/cult," but it was in fact only "new" in North America. It is a community of long standing in India and has its origins in the life and work of the 15th century Hindu reformer, Caitanya. It has been a continuous presence in India since that time, but only came to North America in the 1960s. The same is the case for a number of other new religious movements that have their origins in Eastern Hindu, Buddhist and Sikh traditions.

A smaller number of the "new religions" have their origins in the recovery of forgotten or neglected aspects of older religious traditions, often the mystical and meditative dimensions of the Muslim, Jewish and Christian faiths. For example, Canada's first "deprogramming" case involved a young woman, a graduate of the University of Waterloo, who had joined a Catholic charismatic community in Orangeville, Ontario.

Many of the "new religions" have emerged from the encounter of missionary Christianity or missionary Islam with indigenous traditions in Africa and Asia. When these groups have come to propagate their faith in North America, this has been viewed with alarm since many of the beliefs of the newer communities are considered "heretical" to the older denominations.

Some of these synthetic movements, like the Unification Church, have their origins in the Christian missionary world but incorporate elements of the indigenous or traditional religions as well as "new revelations." An analogous case is the Bahai tradition which emerges out of the Islamic tradition but incorporates a "new revelation."

Some of the new religions were generally "new," for example, Scientology and the Prosperos. (See Robert Ellwood, Jr., *Religious and Spiritual Groups in Modern America*, Englewood Cliffs, NJ, 1973.) Yet we find, even in these cases, a rejection of absolute novelty when, for example, L. Ron Hubbard declares that Scientology is "a direct extension of the work of Gautama Siddhartha Buddha" (*Volunteer Minister's Handbook*). Thus, even in these cases, there are elements of belief, practice, inspiration or ritual that have antecedents or parallels in older and/or other traditions.

Historians of religion remind us that "new religious movements" are always emerging. For example, historians pointed to 19th century America as a century in which "new religious movements" sprang up all across the country or to 20th century Japan especially after WW II where a similar phenomenon was observed. Most of the 19th century American cases were variant readings of Christianity, but "new" nonetheless. (See Mary Farrell Bednarowski, *New Religions and the Theological Imagination in America*, Bloomington, IN, 1989.) There were Shakers and Quakers, Mormons and New Lights, Oneidians and New Harmonians and a thousand others. In the Japanese case, most of the new religious movements had their roots in Buddhism, the most well known is Sokka Gakkai. This led these same historians to make the following correlations: (i) that while new religious movements are continually emerging, they generally have a very short life. Emerging around a charismatic or prophetic or revelatory figure, they often disappeared within 2-3 years. And (ii) the some few that did endure came to be

recognized as fully legitimate religious traditions. Consider, for example, the Mormons, Church of Christ, Scientists and Seventh-Day Adventists, all of whom were widely attacked when they emerged in the 19th century, but are now considered "legitimate" religious communities. The Bahai community is a non-North American example of this same phenomenon as is Sokka Gakkai in Japan with its Buddhist roots.

Sociologists of religion also made an important observation when they observed that one of the differences between earlier new religious movements and those of the later 20th century in North America was their social location. New religious movements typically emerge among the most marginalized and disadvantaged sectors of society. This phenomenon one would easily recognize if one were to walk through the ghettos of urban America (or the favelas of Latin America or the squatter towns that ring the cities of Africa) or visit the rural poor: there one would discover a host of religious groupings that are not familiar. But in these social locations, not much attention is given to them. The new element in the religious movements of the late 20th century is that they attracted a different social class: youth from middle and upper-middle classes. (See Bryan Wilson, *The Social Impact of New Religious Movements*, New York, 1981.) It is easy to imagine middle or upper-class parents becoming distressed when they learned that their 25-year-old son who had graduated from Harvard was now following a Korean messiah or that their 24-year-old daughter who had graduated from the University of Toronto was now singing and chanting "Hare Krishnan" at the airport. But we know historically — e.g.,

St. Thomas' parents held him captive for a year when he wanted to become a Dominican, then a new religious order — that such responses often occurred when adult children embrace new or unconventional religious traditions. The young adults attracted to the popular new religions of the 1960s and 70s were neither poor nor marginalized. They were from the middle and upper-middle classes. Moreover, these movements were usually much smaller than media accounts suggested. In Canada, for example, memberships in many of the new religious communities numbered in the hundreds or thousands rather than the tens or hundreds of thousands often alleged by opponents of these newer communities. Some groups in Canada, however, had larger memberships.

The "new religions" presented phenomena to the scholar of religion that challenged some conventional academic notions, but no scholar of religion, to my knowledge, had any doubt that in the "new religions" we were dealing with religious phenomena. Whether or not it was "good religion" or "bad religion" was often a matter of considerable public debate, but scholars of religion never doubted that it was religious phenomena that we were encountering here. (See J. Gordon Melton, *Encyclopedic Handbook of Cults in America*, New York, 1986 and *The Encyclopedia of America Religions*, Detroit, 1989, which includes the "new religions.")

The "new religions" presented phenomena to the scholar of religion that challenged some conventional academic notions, but no scholar of religion, to my knowledge, had any doubt that in the "new religions" we were dealing with religious phenomena.

iv. Is Scientology a Religion?

The modern academic study of religion that emerged in the 19th and 20th centuries must be distinguished from the classical disciplines of theology. While the task of theology was the exposition of the faith of a particular community (Christian, Jewish, Muslim, Hindu, etc.) — this most commonly meant the Christian faith in the West — the academic study of religion was concerned to offer a scientific description and analysis of all religious phenomena. Thus one of the first tasks of the modern discipline of the study of religion was to free the definition of religion from its typical identification with Christianity. Standard dictionary definitions of religion still reflect this tendency to identify religion in general with the characteristics of especially Christianity and other monotheistic faiths. Those definitions often indicate that the sole or central characteristic of religion is "belief in a Supreme Being." But scholars of religion knew of great and ancient religions that had no such "belief in a Supreme Being." The principal examples were Buddhism, especially in its Theravadin forms where such a belief was explicitly rejected, and Jainism, which also explicitly rejected this belief. Yet these religions were more than 2,000 years old. Moreover, the Confucian traditions minimized the emphasis on the Transcendent and maximized emphasis on proper human relations. And in Hinduism one encountered many gods and goddesses and not just a single "Supreme Being." Moreover, the very mystical traditions of the monotheistic faiths of the West were often critical of the very notion of God as a "Supreme Being" and insisted that the Reality of God transcended such conceptions. Thus it was seen as essential to have a definition or understanding of religion that was adequate to the wide variety of religious traditions found among human beings throughout history.

At the same time, there was a recognition that in the religious traditions of humankind there was a dimension that transcended the mundane. However, that dimension or reality was named in a wide variety of ways. While Christians might strive for "union with God," or Muslims seek "submission to Allah," Buddhists were more bent on achieving "inner enlightenment or satori," Hindus more directed to realizing the "eternal atman or Self," and Jains strove to cultivate a "good mind." Thus the definition of religion that emerged in the modern study of religion included some recognition of "a Beyond" understood broadly enough to include those religions that either did not have a notion of a "Supreme Being" or explicitly rejected such an idea in the name of another conception of the Ultimate. While every religion identifies a *sacred* dimension of life, not every religion identifies the sacred with a "Supreme Being."

While Western Protestant Christianity may have especially emphasized *belief* as central to religion, other strands of religious life, Christian and non-Christian, put more emphasis on *practice*. In Buddhism, for example, the issue is practice: the practice of the Eight-Fold Path as the Way to overcome suffering. In Hinduism one encounters a whole Way to the Ultimate where the whole life is one of practice (*rajyoga*) or work (*karmayoga*). But practice is not just meditation or contemplation or action, it is also prayer, ethical behaviour, familial relations and a host of other practices. In all religious traditions, though in varying degrees, there is a whole life that is to be lived in conformity to the ideal of the religion and that is a life exemplified in practice. Thus, practice in conformity to the ideals and the ethical guidelines of a given religious way was seen as a further dimension to the understanding of what religion is. Moreover, the practice we observe in religious communities and traditions is often ritual practice.

Thus, the modern study of religion was led to acknowledge a further dimension of religious life, namely, the ritual dimension. Rites and rituals are structured acts of the religious community to facilitate communion with the Ultimate dimensions of life. In some of the Chinese traditions, rites were considered essential to maintain the order of the cosmos and were elaborate events spreading over several days. Some religious traditions downplay the role of ritual, e.g., Quaker Christians, but even here they would consider the "gathering in silence" to be essential to their community. Though the ritual dimension varies greatly from tradition to tradition — and even within a given tradition as is witnessed in the ritual splendor of Orthodox Christianity and the ritual simplicity of the Mennonite meeting house — it is a dimension present to the religious life of humankind.

These elements of belief, practice and ritual do not stand in splendid isolation but come together in the life of religious community to create its distinctive *way of life* or *culture*. Hindus, then, are people who share a complex of beliefs, practices and rites that serve to facilitate their way of life, a way that has both mundane and supramundane dimensions. The Latin root of the term religion, religare, means "to bind together," and here we can see the two-fold meaning of that "binding together." There is the "binding together" of "the human and the divine" through a religion, and the "binding together" of human beings in a religious community.

It is in the light of these considerations that there has emerged in the modern study of religion an understanding of religion as a *community of men and women bound together by a complex of beliefs, practices, behaviours and rituals that seek, through this Way, to relate human to sacred/divine life*. It is essential, however, to understand that each dimension of this definition of religion — community, belief, practice, behaviour, ritual, Way and divine — will be understood (a) within the specific terms of a given religious tradition and (b) with relatively more emphasis to some rather than other elements in a given tradition. Thus, for example, the "community" dimension of religion might receive more emphasis in Orthodox Judaism than it does in Taoism or even in other strands of Judaism. Likewise, the divine might be understood as a Transcendent Reality as in Judaism or as an immanent, though unrealized, Self, as it is in many Hindu schools. But such variations do not invalidate the definition of religion, but simply reflect the variety of religious phenomena that must be covered by a modern academic account of religion.

It is in the light of the above that we can then ask whether or not Scientology is a religion. The brief answer is "yes, it is." We can make this clearer if we now take the above understanding of religion and look at the case of Scientology.

In the Church of Scientology, do we encounter a distinctive set of religious beliefs concerning the meaning and ultimate end of human life? Even the most cursory familiarity with the Scientology community and its literature will lead one to answer in the affirmative.

According to their own literature, Scientology is "an applied religious philosophy and technology resolving problems of the spirit, life and thought." Those "problems of the spirit, life and thought" are not permanent but can be overcome, according to Scientology. That overcoming of the "problems of the spirit, life and thought" is centered, in Scientology, in awareness and knowledge. Central to that awareness and knowledge are the *thetan* and the *Eight Dynamics*. Each requires a brief clarification in order to indicate some central aspects of Scientology belief.

According to Scientology, our humanity is composed of different parts: the body, the mind and the *thetan*. The thetan in Scientology is analogous to the soul in Christianity and the spirit in Hinduism. Part of the problem of life is that human beings have lost an awareness of their true nature. In Scientology, this means an awareness of themselves as thetans. Yet awareness and knowledge of oneself as a thetan is essential to well-being and survival. Human beings often confuse their deepest reality with the body or the mind, or see themselves as only body and/or mind. But for Scientology it is essential that human beings recover and recognize their spiritual nature, that, in the language of Scientology, "one is a thetan." As thetans, human beings are "spiritual, immortal and 'virtually indestructable.'"

Since the awareness of oneself as thetan has been obscured by "engrams" or lost in the confusions of thetan with the body and/or the mind, a chief religious task is to recover one's spirituality. It is essential since "the thetan is the source of all creation and is life itself." This awareness then is the first stage in the practice of a religious way that will lead us to become, in Scientology terms, *Clear*. As human beings become aware of their true nature, according to Scientology, and of the concentric circles of reality, then, Scientologists believe, they can proceed, freely and creatively, through life's *Eight Dynamics*. (See *What Is Scientology?*, 1992 edition.)

The basic message of life, according to Scientology, is survival across the Eight Dynamics. The First Dynamic is "Self," or the dynamic of life to survive as an individual. This First Dynamic exists within ever larger circles of existence that extend to the Eighth Dynamic or Infinity. Since the delineation of the Eight Dynamics is fundamental to Scientology, it is appropriate to outline each "dynamic" briefly. As indicated, the Dynamics begin with the individual existence or "Self" and its drive to survive and proceed through the Second Dynamic which Scientology calls "creativity" or "making things for the future," and includes the family and the rearing of children. The Third Dynamic is "Group Survival," that compartment of life that involves voluntary communities,

friends, companies, nations and races. The Fourth Dynamic is "the species of humankind" or the "urge toward survival through humankind and as all humankind." The Fifth Dynamic is "life forms" or the "urge of all living things" towards survival. The Sixth Dynamic is the "physical universe." The Seventh Dynamic is the "spiritual dynamic" or the urge "for life itself to survive." The Eighth Dynamic is "the urge toward existence as Infinity," or what others call "a Supreme Being or Creator." "A knowledge of the Dynamics allows one to more easily inspect and understand any aspect of life." (*What Is Scientology?* 1992 edition, p. 149.) It is within life as a whole, or across the Eight Dynamics in Scientology terms, that the religious journey and task unfolds.

It is particularly within the Eighth Dynamic that one encounters the Scientology affirmation of "what others call" the Supreme Being or Creator. But Scientology prefers the term "Infinity" to speak of "the allness of all." The reticence of Scientology in relation to "Infinity" has its parallels in other traditions. Before the Ultimate Mystery, mystics of all traditions counsel restraint, even silence.

Scientology beliefs concerning the thetan have parallels in other religious traditions, as does their belief in the Eight Dynamics and the ultimate spiritual nature of things. The religious quest in Scientology is more analogous to Eastern processes of enlightenment and realization than it is to Western versions of the religious quest which tend to emphasize conformity to the Divine Will. Some scholars even suggest that in Scientology we have a version of "technologized Buddhism" (See F. Flinn in J. Fichter, ed., *Alternatives to American Mainline Churches*, New York,

1983), while others emphasize its parallels to Eastern mind development practices. But one can also see in their belief in the Eight Dynamics a parallel with the medieval vision of the Soul's Journey to God which culminates in identification with the Ultimate Mystery, God.

Like some other religious traditions, Scientology sees the religious quest in largely religio-therapeutic terms, that is, the process of addressing the human problem is a process of actualizing a lost or hidden human spiritual power or dimension of life. In Buddhism the problem and process is to move from unenlightened to enlightened and in Christianity from sinful to redeemed, while in Scientology, it is to move from "preclear" to "Clear" and beyond. Here the state of Clear is understood as an awareness of one's spiritual nature and realized spiritual freedom, freed from the burdens of past experiences and capable of living a rational, moral existence. This in Scientology is the nature of the religious quest, the goal of religious striving. This quest does not end in the state of Clear, however, but continues on to higher levels of spiritual awareness and ability on the upper or "Operating Thetan" levels. At these upper levels of achievement, one is able to control oneself and environment, or, as Scientology doctrine puts it, to be "at cause over life, thought, matter, energy, space and time."

Coupled then with the beliefs outlined above is a religious practice and way. This dimension of Scientology is often described in their terms as "technology," or the methods of applying the principles. Central to the religious practice in Scientology is the phenomenon of *auditing*, regarded as a

sacrament by Scientologists. This is a process by which one becomes aware of the hidden spiritual barriers that keep one from becoming aware of one's essential spiritual nature as a thetan and from properly exercising that nature. These obstacles to a fully functioning or realized life are called "engrams." A religious artifact known as the "E-meter" is used in auditing to assist parishioners or Scientology adherents to recognize and overcome these negative blocks on the way to Clear. (See L. Ron Hubbard, *The Volunteer Minister's Handbook*, Los Angeles, 1976.) The auditing process unfolds between a religious specialist — an *auditor* who is a minister or minister-in-training in the Church of Scientology — and a person receiving auditing, a *preclear*. Following set procedures and questions, the auditing process is designed to enable the preclear to become aware of what he or she is and to develop their abilities to live more effectively. Scientologists believe that such a practice will allow a person to move from "a condition of spiritual blindness to the brilliant joy of spiritual existence."

Such practices have parallels in the spiritual disciplines of other traditions that likewise seek to awaken one's inner spiritual nature. While the technology of the E-meter in Scientology is unique to our century, the idea behind it is not. It is analogous to the roles of mandalas in some Buddhist traditions, or meditation with the aid of external means in other Eastern traditions.

Moreover, it is precisely the belief of Scientologists that L. Ron Hubbard has both achieved insight into the nature of reality and a practical technology for the recovery of humanity's true nature. The writings of Hubbard serve as authoritative texts within the Scientology community in ways analogous to the sacred literatures of other traditions: the Vedas in Hinduism, the Sutras of Buddhism, etc. But the insights of Hubbard are not, Scientologists claim, a matter of mere belief, since they are open to confirmation in experience through the practice of the religious way that Hubbard has devised. This also echoes the ancient Buddhist wisdom which gives priority to experience.

The practice of Scientologists extends beyond this central religious technology and way since, as one moves towards the state of Clear and beyond, all one's action becomes more free, dynamic, and significant. On the way to that end, Scientologists read their texts, test their beliefs, act in the wider society, develop their inner life, marry, and in all their actions and behaviour seek to realize the ideals of their faith. In Scientology literature one finds numerous references to "Codes of Conduct" and other ethical guidelines that should shape the life of Scientologists.

Religion is not just a set of beliefs, rites, and practices, it is also a community of people joined together by such beliefs, practices, and rites. In Scientology we also find this dimension of religious life. In many parts of the world we find groups of Scientologists regularly gathering as a religious community. There one finds sermons, reading from Scientology Scripture, listening to L. Ron Hubbard's recorded lectures, etc., acts meant to deepen one's commitment to the faith and to extend knowledge of that faith to others. The community is composed of those who

have found in Scientology answers and technologies that address the fundamental questions of life. (See Eileen Barker, *New Religious Movements, A Practical Introduction*, London, 1989.)

Conclusion: In the light of this review of Scientology in relation to the elements of the modern scientific definition of religion, it is apparent that Scientology is a religion. It has its own distinctive beliefs in and account of an unseen, spiritual order, its own distinctive religious practice and ritual life, it has its own authoritative texts and community-building activity.

v. IS SCIENTOLOGY A WORSHIPPING COMMUNITY?

Just as the modern academic definition of religion has found it necessary to open its definition to include types of religious behaviour, practice and belief that move beyond the boundaries of the Western monotheistic traditions, so too in its understanding of "worship," modern academic definitions have had to move beyond the Western context and include the practices of Eastern traditions of religious and spiritual life.

Viewed historically and globally, the student of religion encounters a wide range of "worshipping behaviour and action." Cosmic religious traditions of indigenous peoples tuned their worshipping activities to the cosmic rhythms of nature and the Creator. Virtually every act of the community — from hunting to planting, from birth to death — was preceded by ritual or worshipping activity. In the historical religious traditions of the West, prayer and ritual were central acts of the worshipping community. Here worship ranged from remembering Allah in five daily acts of prayer, to recalling the Covenant with Yahweh on the holy days, and elevating the "Body of Christ" in the daily masses of the Roman Catholic faith. In the traditions of the East, worship might be the act of silent meditation of a yogi in the solitude of the Himalayas or the repetitious chanting of sky-clad Jains before the image of a "realized soul" or the elaborate Shinto rituals in the presence of the "kami" that are present to every drop of water or leaf on a tree, or the week-long services of "chant and prayer" by Tibetan Buddhists who reject the notion of a Creator god. Worship, in general, came to be seen, by modern students of religion, as religious actions that facilitate communion with, or alignment to, the unseen Sacred. Viewed globally and historically, it involves a wide range of action and behaviour.

Within the Church of Scientology we find a wide range of worshipping activity, actions designed to facilitate communion with, and alignment with, the Sacred. It is to be found in their auditing activity (described above) and in their *training*. Auditing is the practice that moves one from "preclear" to "Clear" and beyond; it is the Scientology way of facilitating awareness of oneself as an immortal spiritual being, the "thetan," that unseen dimen-

In the light of this review of Scientology in relation to the elements of the modern scientific definition of religion, it is apparent that Scientology is a religion.

sion that is the subject of the religious life. But of equal importance in Scientology is the practice of training. In auditing, one becomes free; through training, one *stays* free and learns "to accomplish the purpose of improving conditions in life."

As we already indicated, the forms of worship within a given religious tradition accord with their experience of what is sacred and/or ultimate. For Scientology, training is the activity which enables one to move through the Eight Dynamics towards the Eighth Dynamic, Infinity. Training is neither random nor mere "learning" in Scientology. It is rather a moving through a precise sequence — at one's own speed and according to a "checksheet" — in order to acquire essential knowledge and the ability to apply that knowledge in everyday life. There are a variety of training courses offered in Scientology, ranging from introductory to those that contain "knowledge about the ultimate capabilities of the thetan."

More familiar forms of worshipping activity are to be found in the communal rituals that occur when Scientologists gather for rites and observances. The literature of Scientology contains rites and rituals that mark major events in the life cycle: birth, naming, marriage, and death. These rites and rituals link these life events to the sacred depths of life as seen by the Scientology community. (See L. Ron

Hubbard, *The Scientology Religion*, London, 1950 for descriptions of some of the rites and rituals.) These life-cycle rituals of Scientology find their analogs in virtually every other religious tradition. Such rituals enact the conviction that human life is linked to unseen, spiritual dimensions that must be recognized and acknowledged if human life is to achieve its wholeness and fulfillment.

Acts of worship can be individual as well as communal. This is probably most obvious in relation to prayer, but it is also true in relation to meditational acts and spiritual disciplines. Whether it is a Sufi praying alone or joined with others in a whirling dance prayer, one is engaged in worshipping activity. Whether it is the Buddhist alone on the hillside deep in meditation or joined with others in chanting a *sutra*, one is encountering acts of worship.

[I]n Scientology, like the realization traditions of the East, individual effort is central. This process of realization or movement towards total spiritual freedom involves auditing and training within Scientology.

In Scientology one encounters both the individual and communal acts of worship. But in Scientology, like the realization traditions of the East, individual effort is central. This process of realization or movement towards total spiritual freedom involves auditing and training within Scientology. The analogy is the "guru-disciple" relationship within Eastern traditions. In the "guru-disciple" relationship the principal acts of worship are interior acts which facilitate, in Hinduism, movements towards the realization of *atman*, the soul, which is also the Ultimate.

These inward movements may be linked with certain outward actions like yogic postures or breathing techniques or even certain inward actions like visualizing an image. These inward spiritual movements can unfold over shorter or longer periods of time and are part of the worshipping activity of the devotee.

In many Eastern traditions, the ascetic and meditative acts of training and discipline of an individual for growth in the spiritual life may unfold over many months or years or in essential solitude once direction is given by the master. Though the practice is carried out in solitude, it is still linked to the life of a community through shared convictions, beliefs, and shared acts. In Scientology, this is the proper context for auditing and training where the relationship between the religious counselor and the individual initiate is pivotal. Again, the analog is there with the spiritual director in Christian monastic traditions, the pastor in the Protestant traditions, the guru in the Hindu traditions, the Lama in Tibetan Buddhist traditions.

In Scientology, these inward and spiritual acts associated with auditing and training to facilitate the unfolding of one's spiritual nature are also linked with growth in religious knowledge and education. In the Scientology context this means primarily the study of the writings and recorded lectures of L. Ron Hubbard on Dianetics and Scientology. (But it also includes the courses which he constructed and films that he wrote and directed.) Again, this linkage of spiritual practice and scriptural study is found across tradition. The classical Hindu yogi simultaneously practices the austerities and reads his Vedas. The devout Muslim reads his Quran and observes the month of daylight fasting. These activities are seen to reinforce one another on the spiritual path.

Conclusion: In the light of this review of Scientology practice and activity, I conclude that Scientology does engage in worshipping activity, as worship is understood in the modern study of religion, in their places of worship. The activities of Scientologists in their places of worship fall into the range of patterns and practices found within the religious life of humankind.

M. Darrol Bryant

About the Author

M. Darrol Bryant is Professor of Religion and Culture at Renison College, University of Waterloo, Ontario, Canada. He has taught religious studies at the University for more than three decades; from 1987 to 1993, served as Chairman of the Department of Religious Studies.

Professor Bryant has been a Visiting Scholar at Cambridge University in the United Kingdom; the Indian Institute of Islamic Studies, New Delhi, India; the Dr. S. Radhakrishnan Institute for Advanced Studies in Philosophy, University of Madras, Madras, India; Hamdard University, New Delhi, India; and Nairobi University, Nairobi, Kenya.

Author of four volumes on the study of religion, he is a long-standing member of the Canadian Society for the Study of Religion, the American Academy of Religion, the Canadian Theological Society and the Royal Asiatic Society. He has served as a consultant to major international and interreligious conferences including the Assembly of the World's Religions.

Scientology

■

And Contemporary Definitions of Religion in the Social Sciences

Alejandro Frigerio, Ph.D.

Associate Professor of Sociology
Catholic University of Argentina
Buenos Aires, Argentina

Beginning in the middle of the current century, Western societies have observed a renewed interest in the diversity of expressions of religious phenomena. Such interest is due to:

• the rise or development of new religions, particularly in the United States of America (such as the International Society for Krishna Consciousness, the Church of Scientology, the Mission of Divine Light);

• the extension to new geographical areas of religions already established in others (such as some Eastern religions in America and Europe; Pentecostalism, the Church of Jesus Christ of Latter-day Saints and the Jehovah's Witnesses from the United States in South America and Europe; the Santeria from Cuba to the United States and countries of Central America; and the Umbanda from Brazil to Uruguay, Paraguay, Argentina, Chile and to a lesser extent the United States and Europe);

• the "revivals" of the established religions (as in the charismatic reformations in evangelism and in Catholicism, the rise of spiritualist Catholic groups, etc.) and

• the rise of a diverse, uncentralized spiritual subculture (comprised of what has been given the name New Age).

The interest in religious diversity revived old discussions within the social sciences which resulted in more accurate definitions of religious phenomena. Distinct groups of social scientists have opted for different types of definitions often responding to their immediate theoretical interests.

These different types of definitions include:

Substantive definitions of religion which attempt to characterize "from within" or in terms of the intrinsic significance;

Comparative definitions of religion which approach it by distinction from other systems of meanings;

Functional definitions of religion which characterize it in terms of its consequences over other spheres of social and personal life;

Analytical definitions of religion which characterize it by the distinct aspects which religious phenomena encompass; and

Emic definitions of religion which consider religious those phenomena which the members of its society or its institutions consider to be such.

From the viewpoint of the social sciences, the task of establishing whether a body of beliefs and practices constitutes a religion requires that one take heed of the diversity of definitions of religion in the current discussion in these disciplines.

In the following pages we propose to establish if Scientology constitutes a religion, taking into account the diverse definitions by which this term is currently characterized by the social sciences.

i. SCIENTOLOGY AND THE SUBSTANTIVE DEFINITIONS OF RELIGION

The *substantive* definitions of religion intend to characterize it in accordance with the *intrinsic traits* which the religious experiences have for those who practice it. Defined as religious from this perspective are *those experiences which individuals perceive as extraordinary, transcendent and clearly different from the quotidian reality which is perceived the majority of the time.* Those who have such experiences cannot explain them through the concepts and theories which are normally used to define and explain the events of their lives. Experience in these circumstances, however, appears to them as undeniable, more real than that which is perceived in the everyday world. Peter Berger says:

"In the context of religious experience, the reality of daily life loses in dramatic form its status as supreme reality. It appears, to the contrary, as the anteroom of another reality, one of a drastically different nature and nevertheless of immense importance for the individual. Through this change in this perception of reality all worldly activity of quotidian reality is seen as radically reduced in importance, trivialized—in the words of Ecclesiastes, reduced to *vanity*." (Berger 1974, 130-131)

From this viewpoint, religion is defined as the kingdom of the extraordinary, the sacred, "the other." In other words, religion is the sphere of activity and human thought which draws in turn on experiences which put the individual in contact with something inexplicable, marvelous, mysterious and majestic which cannot be explained through the rationality and theories through which one is aware of the events of his life. Religious institutions are those which act to regularize, define and explain religious experiences.

To ask oneself if Scientology fits the existing definitions of religions is the equivalent of investigating if it revolves around, regulates or explains some type of extraordinary experience which puts the individual in contact with a reality of another order, marvelous and surprising. The answer is, according to my understanding, affirmative.

Beyond the resolution of problems and the accomplishment of quotidian objectives, the road of Scientology promises, to one who applies himself to the understanding of its practices, gradual advancement to a lasting happiness and new states of consciousness never dreamed possible. The culmination of such states of consciousness constitutes an experience of total freedom in which

the individual would have the capacity to control the physical universe, composed of matter, energy, space and time, and reach a total omniscience. The awareness of life and death and awareness of the universe would therefore be clearly evident to one. The Church of Scientology states:

"Man consists of three parts: the body, little more than a machine; the mind divided into analytical and reactive, which computes and contains little more than a collection of pictures; and the thetan, life itself, the spirit which animates the body. ... The point being, the thetan is superior to both body and mind. ... But what are his limits? How high can he ultimately ascend?

"From the search for these answers came the subject of Scientology, and the door opened to the full realization of spiritual potential.

"That state is called Operating Thetan ... Although without mass, motion, wavelength or location in space or time, the thetan is nonetheless capable of accomplishing *anything*. Thus, the Operating Thetan or OT may be defined as one who is at 'knowing and willing cause over life, thought, matter, energy, space and time.'

"It is not for nothing, then, that Scientology has been described as realizing man's most basic hope for spiritual freedom—by stripping away the accumulated impediments of the ages and returning to our native state, with all the abilities that are inherently ours." (*The Scientology Handbook*, page 23.)

A publication of the Church describes in the following manner the results that can be obtained by reaching the ultimate level of Operating Thetan:

"These truths are essential for your survival as an Operating Thetan and your ability to reach total spiritual freedom. Your concepts of time, future and past, will change repeatedly and you will experience an incomparable and new level of stability and awareness that will stay with you this life and in future lives." (*Source* Magazine 99:21)

The difference between this experience of freedom and omniscience on the one hand and the common experience of man is clear. Furthermore, the doctrine of Scientology holds that he who follows the road it has laid out can achieve the experience of "exteriorization" in which the *thetan* (spirit) leaves the body and exists in a form independent of the flesh. Upon exteriorization the person would be able to see without the eyes of the body, hear without ears, and feel without hands, achieving the certainty that he is himself (the thetan) and not his body. According to Scientology, exteriorization of the thetan makes it obvious that the spirit is immortal and is endowed with abilities which exceed those which one could predict through quotidian reasoning:

"The thetan is able to leave the body and exist independent of the flesh. Exteriorized, the person can see without the body's eyes, hear without the body's ears and feel without the body's hands. Man previously had very little understanding of this detachment from his mind and body. With the act of exteriorization attainable in Scientology a person gains the certainty he is himself and not his body." (*What Is Scientology?* 1993:147)

In summary, like the large number of religions which internationally constitute the "religious ferment" of the last several decades (the religions of Eastern origin, Pentecostalism and the Afro-American religions, among others) religious experiences which are not ordinary and not quotidian have a central place in Scientology. As in other religions, such experiences are on the one hand motivated, regulated and interpreted by doctrine and on the other hand are taken as proof of the correctness of the cosmic vision held by the group. Therefore, Scientology fits the substantive definitions of religion in use in the social sciences at the present time.

ii. SCIENTOLOGY AND THE COMPARATIVE DEFINITIONS OF RELIGION

Some authors have approached a definition of religion distinguishing it from other systems of meaning (understood to be such bodies of thought or theoretical tradition which give meaning to reality and to life experience). Thus, for example, Stark and Gluck (1965) distinguish between the "humanist perspectives" which constitute attempts to make significant the life of man from religions which, to the contrary, assert that they have discovered or established paths to discover the *true* meaning of life. The difference between some and other systems is that in the case of the humanist perspectives one looks intentionally to grant to life a meaning which is agreed upon and relatively free-willed: in the second it is presumed that the same has a *pre-existent* meaning to that which the individual man or social group wishes to give it and that it is possible to agree to the stated meaning. On this subject, Reginald Bibby says:

"Religious perspectives imply the possibility that our existence has a meaning which precedes that which we as human beings decide to give it. By contrast, the humanist perspective leaves to one side the search for the meaning of existence in favor of a new preoccupation with giving meaning to existence." (Bibby 1983, 103)

From this perspective, to ask if Scientology constitutes a religion is to investigate if it postulates a meaning for the life of man which *pre-exists and is considered true and immutable.* In relation to this point we can note that according to Scientology, man is defined as a spiritual being. It is affirmed that man does not *have* a spirit but that a spirit is what the individual truly *is.* This spirit is called a "thetan," a name taken from the Greek letter *theta.* It is asserted that the individual exists as himself as a spiritual being. The artistic capacity, the fortitude of the person and his individual character are all manifestations of the spiritual nature of the individual. The thetan constitutes the person himself.

According to Scientology, man is composed of a body, organized physical substance or composition; a mind which consists of pictures, recordings of thoughts, conclusions, decisions, observations and perceptions; and the thetan [spirit].

According to Scientology, man is composed of a body, organized physical substance or composition; a mind which consists of pictures, recordings of thoughts, conclusions, decisions, observations and perceptions; and the thetan. The thetan is conceived as the creator of things. He has animation and life even without the mind and body and uses the mind as a system of control between himself and the physical universe. Scientologists maintain that man is a thetan and the thetan is the source of all creation, is immortal and is life itself, with potentially infinite creativity and, if not part of the physical universe, having the potential capacity to control this universe composed of matter, energy, space and time.

On the other hand, Scientology explicitly asserts that training in its doctrine furnishes a comprehension of man, his potentials and the difficulties with which he is faced which goes much further than what is taught in the humanities or social sciences. With the knowledge of the principles of Scientology the person would be able to understand, for example, why some people have success while others fail, why one man is happy while another is not, and why some relationships are stable and others fall apart. Training in Scientology would permit one who would apply himself to know the mystery of life and to attain an absolute comprehension of its immortal nature. Through the teachings of L. Ron Hubbard disseminated by the Church, the individual can achieve the development of all his abilities across the "Eight dynamics" postulated in its cosmic vision. These dynamics, or areas through which human activity is expressed, are:

1. The individual; 2. Family and sex; 3. Groups; 4. Mankind; 5. All life forms; 6. The physical universe; 7. Spirituality; and 8. The infinite or Supreme Being. (*Scientology 0-8, The Book of Basics* 1990: 25-26)

The object of the teachings of the Church is to increase the level of awareness of the individual so that he can control and influence all of the dynamics of life.

In summary, like most religions, Scientology claims to have revealed the mystery of life. It does not propound an arbitrary meaning for the life of man, but claims to have discovered the *true* meaning. In doing so, it differentiates from humanist perspectives: It does not propound or suggest ethical norms and values to make human life meaningful. On the contrary, *it claims to truly know what is man and what is the meaning of his life.* At the same time, and in spite of using a vocabulary similar to the sciences, it can be clearly differentiated from these, given that it does not intend to describe how things happen, it does not formulate questions, nor present a hypothesis for its opposition and eventual modification. Rather, it claims to have discovered the *true causes* and invites one to share in said knowledge.

iii. SCIENTOLOGY AND THE FUNCTIONAL DEFINITIONS OF RELIGION

Another class of definitions characterizes religion by the consequences that it holds in other areas of life. The first *functional* definitions of religion came out of the work of Emile Durkheim and put the stress on the feelings of solidarity which religious ceremonies evoked and its effects on social cohesion and community unity. These definitions have been criticized on the basis that, on the one hand, there frequently exist multiple religions in the same society putting in doubt the cohesive function of religion for the community as a whole and, on the other hand, other non-religious symbols and rituals, such as those which belong to the nation, the state or ethnic group, can serve the same function of creating ties of solidarity and community sentiment.

Actually a certain number of social scientists now define religion by its consequences not in social life but in the personal life of individuals. These authors define religion as "*a combination of forms and symbolic acts which relate the individual to the ultimate conditions of his existence*" (Bellah 1964:358) or as "*a system of beliefs and practices through which a group of people faces the fundamental problems of life.*" (Yinger 1970:7) Such fundamental problems would include: the perception of injustice, the experience of suffering and the awareness of what life lacks in meaning and purpose. Religions propound two types of answers to such problems of humanity. On one side, they would offer explanations for them giving them meaning. On the other, they would propound methods and programs of action directed to overcome these problems.

From the current functionalist perspective a religion is therefore a combination of beliefs giving meaning to fundamental problems such as injustice, suffering and the search for the meaning of life and a combination of practices through which such problems are faced with the intent to overcome them. To ask if Scientology fits this definition is therefore to investigate if it presents a combination of practices designed to overcome these fundamental problems of life and a system of beliefs that serve to explain them.

In this respect it is possible to observe, in the first place, that the *central practice of Scientology, auditing, is presented in effect as a way to overcome suffering.* It affirms that through active and voluntary participation in auditing one's ability to face the problems of existence, resolve them and achieve each time higher levels of consciousness and spiritual well-being, will be improved.

Scientology services strive to raise the individual to a point in which he is capable of putting the factors of his own life in order and resolving his problems. According to Scientology the tensions of life cause the individual to fix his attention on the material world reducing his awareness of himself as a spiritual being and of his environment. This reduction of awareness would have as a consequence that problems would arise, such as difficulty in relations with others, suffering, illness and unhappiness. The objective of Scientology is to revert the reduction of awareness, awakening the individual. It therefore propounds solutions to the fundamental problems of life through procedures which cause the individual to increase his awareness and freedom and to rehabilitate his decency, power and

basic abilities. Individuals who are more aware and alert would be capable of better comprehension and greater capacity to handle their lives. Through auditing and training in Scientology, people would come to know that life is something valuable and that they could live satisfactory lives in harmony with others.

Scientology postulates that through its practice and training persons will free themselves from suffering such as irrational fears and psychosomatic illnesses, become more calm, more in a state of equilibrium, more energetic and communicative, will repair and revitalize their relations with others, achieve their personal goals, discard their doubts and inhibitions and acquire certainty and confidence in themselves, feel joy and clearly understand how to achieve happiness. In summary, Scientology presents itself as a means of overcoming suffering and the inequalities of individual ability.

Another of the elements which is included in the current functional definitions of religion is the giving of a meaning or explanation for the fundamental problems of life. Through the explanation of the reasons for human suffering, most religions alleviate in an indirect manner the tensions which such suffering produces. For those who are followers of such religions the problems of life become less perceived as senseless, unjust and inexplicable through acquiring a meaning. The doctrinal explanations for suffering give a foundation at the same time for the justification of religious practices designed to overcome such suffering: the postulating of the causes of the problems of life may be regarded as the basis for the development of programs of actions to overcome them.

In this respect it can be observed that Scientology also *propounds answers to human suffering by giving an explanation*. The doctrine of Scientology expounds particularly in describing the reasons for suffering. According to this doctrine the individual is basically good and happy and the reasons for suffering are found in the "reactive mind" which is clearly differentiated from the analytical mind and is made up of "engrams." In *The Dynamics of Life*, the founder L. Ron Hubbard states:

"Man is not a reactive animal. He is capable of self-determinism. He has willpower. He ordinarily has high analytical ability. He is rational and he is happy and integrated only when he is his own basic personality. The most desirable state in an individual is complete self-determinism. ...

"The reactive mind consists of a collection of experiences received during an unanalytical moment which contain pain and actual or conceived antagonism to the survival of the individual. ... When injury or illness supplants the analytical mind producing what is commonly known as 'unconsciousness,' and when physical pain and antagonisms to the survival of the organism are present, an engram is received by the individual. ... By stripping the reactive mind of its past painful content the analytical mind may be placed in complete command of the organism. The moment a man or a group becomes possessed of this ability, it becomes possessed of self-determinism. So long as these possess reactive minds, irrationalities will persist." (Hubbard 1990:31-32)

In Scientology, therefore, the human being is basically good, happy and integrated and the root of his unhappiness is found in engrams. Thus, the practice of auditing is propounded as the only suitable means of removing the individual's engrams and enabling him to become a "Clear," which is to say, returning him to his state as "basic individual." Both terms mean: "the unaberrated self in complete integration and in a state of highest possible rationality; a *Clear* is one who has become the basic individual through auditing. ... The *basic individual* is invariably responsive in all the dynamics and is essentially 'good.' ...The virtues of the basic individual are innumerable. His intentional vices and destructive dramatizations are non-existent. He is cooperative, constructive and possessed of purpose. In short he is in close alignment with that ideal which mankind recognizes as an ideal. This is a necessary part of an auditor's working knowledge, since deviations from it denote the existence of aberration, and such departures are unnatural and enforced and are no part of the self-determinism of the individual." (Hubbard 1990:31-32)

In summary, Scientology furnishes an answer to human suffering giving it, like the majority of religious traditions, an explanation and postulating, from this explanation, a means of solution. The explanation of human suffering lies in "engrams." Engrams are described as unknown, powerful and influential mental image pictures which have mass and energy. The main solution proposed to overcome suffering consists of the practice of auditing which permits the location and conquest of engrams. Auditing is presented as a way to overcome suffering since it postulates that through the active and voluntary participation of the individual he will succeed in bettering his ability to face the problems of his existence, resolve them and achieve continually higher levels of awareness and spiritual well-being.

Scientology also *gives an answer to the experience of injustice* when perceived as an unequal distribution of abilities among men, postulating that the loss of abilities is due, at least in part to transgressions and irresponsibilities of the past. At the same time it gives a solution to this loss presenting itself as a way to regain these abilities. Additionally, *Scientology provides an answer to the experience of life lacking meaning and the experience of death* postulating that man is an immortal spiritual being whose experiences extend beyond one life and affirming that death is a transition through which the individual makes his passage while continuing to be aware. As stated by the Church of Scientology:

"Needless to say, ethics is a subject that Scientology takes very seriously. As he moves up the Bridge (The Bridge to Total Freedom, the path of Scientology) and becomes more and more himself, he likewise grows more ethical, but he also views it as a matter of personal responsibility that extends well beyond this life. For unlike the materialist who believes death to be an end to life, conscience and accountability, the Scientologist sees it as a transition through which one carries his past—a past for which one continues to be accountable. He also knows that the abilities he is regaining were, in part, lost because of transgressions and irresponsibilities. Thus, honesty, integrity, trust and concern for his fellows are more than just words. They are principles to live by." (*The Scientology Handbook*, 1994: xxvi)

Consequently, Scientology fits the concept of religion as it is currently defined from a functionalist perspective constituting a body of beliefs by means of which a group of people gives meaning to fundamental problems such as injustice, suffering and the search for the meaning of life and a body of practices through which they confront such problems and intend to overcome them.

iv. SCIENTOLOGY AND THE ANALYTICAL DEFINITIONS OF RELIGION

Another of the forms in which religion is currently defined in the social sciences is in the *analytic* manner, that is, characterizing it by the different ways in which the religion manifests itself. From this perspective there is considered to exist considerable consensus among all religions regarding the forms through which the religious person expresses his religiosity, by which it becomes possible to establish those aspects which constitute such religiosity. These aspects include:

a) Sharing the beliefs which constitute the body of doctrine of the group;

b) Participating in rituals and acts of devotion;

c) Experiencing direct contact with ultimate reality;

d) Acquiring religious information; and

e) Experiencing changes or results in quotidian life derived from the other aspects of religiosity. (Stark and Gluck 1985)

From this point of view to ask if Scientology constitutes a religion is the equivalent of investigating if the Church of Scientology as an institution expects that its adherents will be religious, which is to say that they manifest religiosity in the different ways which are considered universal.

iv.i. Sharing a Body of Doctrine

It has been maintained that religious institutions expect their adherents to share their doctrinal principles. (Stark and Gluck 1985:256) In this respect it can be observed that the Church of Scientology propounds an interrelated whole clearly structured so that its adherents acquire its body of doctrine. In effect, the practice of Scientology is composed in equal parts of auditing and training in its principles. The Church affirms that while auditing permits one to see how something happens, training teaches why.

The material used in the courses of training consists of books, publications, films and recorded lectures of the founder of the Church which are studied in a pre-arranged order. This material has the equivalent status of scriptures of traditional religions: It is not interpreted or explained. On the contrary, considerable attention is placed on the disciple receiving the word of the founder in its "pure form." Scientologists believe that Mr. Hubbard found an exact and workable path to spiritual salvation: If following one of the procedures of the founder of Scientology does not achieve the expected results it is because it was not understood or applied correctly. Thus, the possibility that there could exist an error in the original version of the word of Mr.

Hubbard is not considered.

Those who direct training in Scientology are called "supervisors" and are recognized as experts in the technology of study and skilled at finding and resolving the obstacles that the students may encounter. The role of the supervisor is also defined as ensuring that the doctrine is properly imparted and does not produce different versions or divergent interpretations. The supervisor does not give lectures and does not propound to the students his own version of the subject. It is scrupulously forbidden that the supervisor propound any type of verbal interpretation of the materials to prevent any alterations of the original.

iv.ii. Participation in Rituals and Acts of Devotion

Another of the forms through which religions seem to expect that their adherents demonstrate their religiosity is through participation in rituals and acts of devotion. In this respect, it is possible to observe in the first place that the Church of Scientology celebrates the same rituals as other religious institutions such as Sunday services, weddings, funerals and naming ceremonies for newborn children.

However, these are not the only activities which are ritually structured in Scientology. Auditing, the central practice of Scientology, is a ritual activity in the sense that an anthropologist gives to this term: a highly structured procedure which fits rigorous rules and is repeated meticulously. In effect, auditing is accomplished through a series of carefully established steps developed by the founder of the Church which are to be followed without variation. For the Church of Scientology, auditing demands a precise path, an exact route to reach higher states of awareness. Auditing is defined as a precise activity, precisely codified and which follows exact procedures:

"Auditing uses *processes—exact* sets of questions asked or directions given by an auditor to help a person find out things about himself and improve his condition. There are many, many different auditing processes, and each one improves the individual's ability to confront and handle part of his existence. When the specific objective of any one process is attained, the process is ended and another can then be run to address a different part of the person's life.

"An unlimited number of questions *could*, of course, be asked—which might or might not help a person. The accomplishment in Dianetics and Scientology is that L. Ron Hubbard isolated the *exact* questions and directions to invariably bring about improvement." (*What Is Scientology?* 1993:156)

It can thus be observed that auditing is an exact ritual and the repeated participation in this rite is a condition for an individual to be considered a Scientologist.

iv.iii. Direct Experience of Ultimate Reality

It has been suggested that most traditional religions expect that their adherents will reach at some moment a more or less direct experience of ultimate reality. This dimension of religios-ity relates to the substantive definitions of religion and we have expounded on this in reviewing the substantive definitions of religion. We therefore mentioned that religious experiences which are not ordinary or quotidian have a central place in Scientology. As with other religions such experiences are encouraged in accordance with and interpreted under the doctrines of the religion and are also taken as evidence of the correctness of the group's cosmic vision.

Scientology presents itself as a gradual, clearly defined and certain route to improve awareness guiding individuals from a condition of spiritual blindness to the happiness of spiritual existence. It promises to its adherents that such increased awareness will enable them ultimately to become aware of their own immortality, achieve total freedom, omniscience and understand directly the meaning of life, death and the universe.

The stated aim of Scientology is to achieve the complete and total rehabilitation of the innate capabilities of the individual as an immortal spiritual being. Such capabilities would put him at cause, with full knowledge, over matter, energy, space, time, thought and life. By reaching this state, the individual would be capable of a direct understanding of the infinite:

"At the level of Operating Thetan one deals with the individual's own *immortality* as a spiritual being. One deals with the thetan himself in relationship to eternity; not to the eternity that lies *behind* him, but to the eternity which lies *ahead*." (*What Is Scientology?* 1993:222)

We can note therefore that the Church of Scientology expects that its adherents, through their participation in its practices and training in its doctrine, attain a gradual improvement of awareness resulting ultimately in a direct experience of ultimate reality.

iv.iv. Religious Knowledge

The analytical definitions of religion hold that religious institutions expect that their adherents have a modicum of information about the basic postulates of their faith, its rites, its scriptures and traditions. In relation to this expectation we note that the practice of Scientology consists of equal parts of auditing and training. The commitment expected of its adherents includes that they acquire knowledge of its principal doctrines. In this respect the Church states:

"Through auditing one becomes free. This freedom *must* be augmented by knowledge of how to *stay* free. Scientology contains the anatomy of the reactive mind in its axioms and the discipline and know-how necessary to handle and control the laws of life. The practice of Scientology, then, is composed in equal parts of auditing and training in Scientology principles which includes the technology of their application. Knowing the mechanisms by which spiritual freedom can be lost is itself a freedom and places one out-

Scientology presents itself as a gradual, clearly defined and certain route to improve awareness guiding individuals from a condition of spiritual blindness to the happiness of spiritual existence.

side their influence. Auditing lets one see *how* something happened, training teaches one *why*." (*What Is Scientology?* 1993:164)

It can be noted therefore that, like most religious traditions, imparting the teachings of the movement is viewed favorably by the Church of Scientology. The acquisition of religious information is assured by the same doctrine through the symbolic reward for those who grasp for it: Whoever acquires knowledge of its principles can control the laws of life and be free of the dangers which threaten his spiritual freedom.

iv.v. Consequences in Quotidian Life

It has been noted that most religious institutions expect that their religious beliefs, the participation in rituals, religious experience and knowledge of the principal doctrines will have consequences in the daily lives of their adherents. As discussed in referring to the functional definitions of religion, Scientology postulates that through its practice and training people free themselves from irrational fears, psychosomatic illnesses, become more calm, achieve a better state of equilibrium, energy, communicate better, repair and revitalize their relationships with others, achieve personal goals, discard their doubts and inhibitions acquiring confidence in themselves, feel joy and clearly understand how to achieve happiness.

Another change which the Church of Scientology expects of its adherents is that they will help others to change conditions that they wish to improve, urging them to become auditors:

"The need for auditors is great since it is plain that individuals can be salvaged only one at a time. Unlike congregational religions, this salvation ultimately occurs in Scientology in the one-on-one relationship between auditor and preclear. Many Scientologists train to become auditors, and anyone who wishes to help his fellow man can do the same. But of no less importance, one can gain greater skill in handling life than he ever thought possible. There is no more worthwhile purpose than helping one's fellows and no better way to accomplish this purpose than by becoming an auditor. Auditors apply what they have learned to help others with auditing and to change conditions wherever they find that conditions need improving.

"This is the mission of the trained Scientologist, and it is in his understanding, his compassion and his skill that the dreams of a better world reside." (Church of Scientology 1993:169)

It can be observed therefore that like most religious institutions, the Church of Scientology expects that sharing its beliefs, participating in its rituals, directly experiencing ultimate reality and knowledge of its principal doctrines will have consequences in the daily lives of its adherents. These consequences include improvement of the ability to handle their own lives, improvement of their own abilities and an improved disposition and ability to help others.

In summary, it can be observed that the Church of Scientology expects that its adherents will be religious persons, in the sense that the analytic definitions of religion give to this term. In effect: It provides a framework so that its adherents may share in its principal doctrines and expects that those who participate achieve a direct experience of ultimate reality, acquiring information on the principles of their faith and experiencing consequences in their daily lives. Therefore, per the analytical definitions of religion, the Church of Scientology constitutes a religious institution, since its expectations in relation to its adherents correspond to what such institutions expect of religious individuals.

V. SCIENTOLOGY AND THE EMIC DEFINITIONS OF RELIGION

The "emic" point of view in anthropology is that which gives attention to the classification of ideas of those who participate in a given culture. This is opposed to the "etic" point of view which is that derived from the conceptual classifications of one of the theories of the social sciences. Until this point we have employed definitions of religion taken from the theoretical viewpoint, which is to say from the viewpoint of social scientists who participate in current discussion regarding what constitutes a religion and what are its characteristics. In this section we will consider the *emic* point of view of the participants in society.

To ask if Scientology is a religion from the *emic* point of view is to ask if it is considered as such in the specific cultural contexts in which it conducts its activities. As the Church of Scientology is an international institution, these contexts are found in many countries. Because these are complex societies this includes numerous subgroups: The Scientologists themselves, governmental institutions and students of religious subjects are included among those who have made public pronouncements on this subject.

In the first place it is possible to observe that *Scientologists themselves* present Scientology as a religion in their writing and public documents. (See for example, *What Is Scientology?* 1993: 1, 7, 141, 147; LRH Book Compilations of *What Is Scientology?* 1994:iii).

With regard to *governmental institutions,* Scientology has been found to be, for legal purposes and tax exemption, a religion in the countries in which it has carried out its activities. The governmental organizations which have explicitly declared that Scientology is a religion include:

Organizations of the Executive Branch:

Ministry of Education and Culture of Bavaria, 1973; Department of State of the United States, 1974; Social Security Agency of Angers, France, 1985; National Office of the Immigration and Naturalization Service, United States, 1986; District of Shoneberg, Berlin, Germany, 1989.

Tax Organizations:

Department of Administration and Finance of Zurich, Switzerland, 1974; Tax Department of Florida, United States, 1974; Australian Tax Office, 1978; California Franchise Tax Board,

1981; Department of Taxes and Customs of Canada, 1982; Tax Service of Pau, France, 1987; Corporate Tax Inspector of Amsterdam, Holland, 1988; Utah Tax Commission, United States, 1988; New York City Tax Commission, United States, 1988; Federal Office of Finances, Germany, 1990; Tax Commission of Monza, Italy, 1990; Tax Commission of Lecco, Italy, 1991; Internal Revenue Service of the United States, 1993; California Employment Development Department, United States, 1994.

Judicial Bodies:

Appeals Court of Washington, D.C., United States, 1969; Court of the District of Columbia, United States, 1971; Court of St. Louis, Missouri, United States, 1972; Australian Court of Perth, Australia, 1970; Court of District of Stuttgart, 1976; Court of Munich, Germany, 1979; Appeals Court of Paris, 1980; Appeals Court of the State of Oregon, 1982; District Court of the United States in Washington, 1983; Superior Court of Massachusetts, 1983; Attorney General's Office of Australia, 1973; High Court of Australia, 1983; District Court of Central California, United States, 1984; Appeals Court of Vancouver, 1984; Court of the District of Stuttgart, Germany, 1985; Appeals Court of Munich, Germany, 1985; Court of Padua, Italy, 1985; Court of Bolonia, Italy, 1986; Regional Court of Hamburg, Germany, 1988; Court of Berlin, Germany, 1988; Court of Frankfurt, Germany, 1989; Court of Munich, Germany, 1989; Court of Hanover, Germany, 1990; Court of Milan, Italy, 1991; Administrative Court of Hamburg, Germany, 1992; Superior Court of Germany, 1992; Court of New York, 1994; Tax Court of

Italy, 1994; District Court of Zurich, Switzerland, 1994; Supreme Court of Italy, 1995.

Finally, *studies carried out by social scientists* usually refer to Scientology as a religion, considering it part of the growing group of *new religious movements*.

One of the first studies on Scientology, an article by Harriet Whitehead in the book *Religious Movements in Contemporary America*, places it within the "growing collection of religious movements totally outside of the Judeo-Christian tradition." (1974:547)

In a similar manner, the monograph by Roy Wallis, "The Road to Total Freedom: a Sociological Analysis of Scientology" (1977) which analyzes the historical development and doctrinal and organizational transformations which occurred during the transition from Dianetics into Scientology, clearly places the object of the study within the new religious groups. Wallis considers Scientology to be a religion particularly adapted for the religious market of contemporary Western society — as Wilson would state years later. The emphasis on the benefits which the members will receive from their religious practice in this world, the utilization of distinctive rhetoric and a bureaucratic and rationally constructed organization reflect contemporary Western values, since "the rationalization of life in the world has brought the institutions through which salvation is obtained to rationalism." (1976:246)

[W]e can conclude that Scientology is a religion from all perspectives which exist in the current discussion of the definition of this term.

Frank Flinn, in his paper "Scientology as Technological Buddhism" included in the volume *Alternatives to American Mainline Churches*, affirms that Scientology is "the most interesting of the *new religious movements*" (1983:89) and because it "bears many close resemblances to Buddhism." (93)

In a chapter of his 1990 book *The Social Dimensions of Sectarianism*, Bryan Wilson affirms that Scientology would be a "secularized religion" and then shows that it fits a list of 20 items usually characteristic of religions, suggesting that "Scientology must indeed be regarded as a religion, and this in respect of the metaphysical teachings it canvasses (and not because it describes its organization as a church), but it is a religion which mirrors many of the preoccupations of contemporary society." (1990:288) He completes his analysis asking: "If one had to propose what would be a modern religion, perhaps Scientology would not appear as fitting in the secularized world in which it operates, and from which it takes the greater part of its organized structure and therapeutic preoccupations." (1990:288)

Scientology is included as one of the groups reviewed in some of the most important books studying new religious movements: *New Religious Movements: a Practical Introduction* by Professor Eileen Barker (1992) as well as in both the *Encyclopedia of American Religions* and *Encyclopedic Handbook of Cults in America* by J. Gordon Melton. (1992) It is also discussed, together with other new religious groups, in *Cult*

Controversies: Societal Responses to the New Religious Movements by James Beckford (1985); in *Cults, Converts and Charisma: the Sociology of New Religious Movements* by Thomas Robbins (1991) and in *L'Europe delle Nuove Religioni* by Massimo Introvigne and Jean Francois Mayer, (1993).

In summary, adopting an experiential point of view, we can observe that Scientology has been considered a religion in the cultural contexts in which it has carried out its activities, including the pronouncements of government agencies, by members of the Church and by social scientists conducting studies of new religious movements.

vi. CONCLUSIONS

As a result of the analysis undertaken here, we can conclude that Scientology is a religion from all perspectives which exist in the current discussion of the definition of this term in the social sciences and which we have reviewed in the present work.

Like most religions which internationally constitute the "religious ferment" of the last several decades (the religions of Eastern origin, Pentecostalism, and the Afro-American religions among others) religious experiences which are not ordinary and not quotidian have a central place in Scientology. Just as with the other religions such experiences occur in part motivated, regulated and interpreted by doctrine and in part taken as proof of the correctness of the cosmic vision held by the group. Consequently, Scientology fits the *substantive* definitions of religion currently in use in the social sciences.

Scientology also fits the concept of religions as it is currently defined from the *functionalist* perspective, constituting a body of beliefs through which a group of people give meaning to fundamental problems such as injustice, suffering and the search for the meaning of life and together with practices through which they face these problems and intend to surmount them.

Like most religions, Scientology claims to have revealed the mystery of life. It does not propound an avowedly arbitrary meaning for the life of man; it claims to have discovered the true meaning. In doing so, it differentiates itself from the humanist perspectives: It does not propose or suggest values and ethical norms to give meaning to human life; on the contrary it claims to know what man *truly* is and what is *the* meaning of his life. At the same time, and because of using a similar vocabulary to the sciences, it is clearly different from them, given that it does not intend exclusively to describe how things happen, does not formulate questions nor present hypotheses for their opposition and eventual modification but asserts to have discovered the true causes and offers to share its knowledge. Therefore, Scientology fits the *comparative* definitions which characterize religion, distinguishing it from the humanist perspectives.

The Church of Scientology expects that its adherents become religious persons, in the sense which the *analytical* definitions of religion give to this term. In effect: It provides an inter-related system of beliefs so that its adherents may share its principal doctrines and expects that they will participate in ritual activities, achieving a direct experience of ultimate reality, acquire information about the principles of their faith and experience results in their everyday lives. Therefore per the analytical definitions of religion, the Church of Scientology constitutes a religious institution, since its expectations with respect to its adherents correspond to what such institutions expect of religious people.

Finally, adopting an *emic* point of view, it is observed that Scientology is considered a religion in most of the cultural contexts where it has carried out its activities, including the pronouncements of governmental institutions, of the members of the Church and of social scientists who have studied new religious movements.

In this paper we have considered the correspondence between Scientology and the modern definitions of religion employed in the field of the social sciences. However, Scientology also seems to fit the definitions of religion considered "classical" in both anthropology and sociology. In the field of sociology, Max Weber, considered the "father" of the sociology of religion, preferred not to define the term. (Weber 1964:1) Rather, he minutely classified the known religions into a large number of different types divided according to a large number of criteria. Scientology seems to correspond to a certain type of the "salvation religions" which are presented as a path to the freedom of the spirit from reincarnation or the cycle of birth and death. (Weber 1964: 146) Among salvation religions Scientology would be classified according to Weberian criteria among those which:

• have been founded by a prophet who instituted a doctrine directed to making possible the salvation of mankind (Weber 1964:46);

• possess systemized rituals in a body of comprehensive laws the knowledge of which requires special training (Weber 1964:154);

• affirm that salvation can be reached through a religious endeavor directed at self-perfection (Weber 1964: 156);

• have developed a procedure intended to reach the religious consecration of the personality (Weber 1964: 156) and

• assert that the consecration of the personality implies the acquisition of superhuman powers and the possibility of accomplishing superhuman actions. (Weber 1964:157)

The correspondence between Scientology and this type of salvation religion specified in accordance with the categories of Weber is clearly expressed in the following paragraph of *What Is Scientology?*:

"Contrary to those who teach that man cannot improve and that some seventy years in a body are all one can expect, there are states higher than that of mortal man. The state of OT does exist and people do attain it. Like any other gain in Scientology it is attained gradiently. ... Some of the miracles of life have been exposed to full view for the first time ever on the OT levels. Not the least of these miracles is knowing immortality and freedom from the cycle of birth and death. The way is true and plainly marked. All one needs to do is place his feet upon the first rung of the ladder and ascend to Clear and then walk upward to the level of Operating

Thetan. Auditing enables the individual to span the distance from Homo Sapiens with his drugs, his pains, his problems, upsets and fears to higher states and freedom as a spiritual being. Such states are obtainable only through auditing. But they do exist and they are attainable and they fully restore a being to his native potential. (*What Is Scientology?* 1993:222-223)

In the field of anthropology the definition of religion considered most classical is that of Sir Edward Tylor who characterizes it as "the belief in spiritual beings." (Evans-Pritchard 1976:14-15) In relation to this definition and as already stated,

the central belief of Scientology is that man is a thetan, that is to say, a spiritual being. In this respect the Manual of Scientology says to its readers:

"You are a thetan, a spiritual being. Not your eyes, your brain, but you. You do not *have* a thetan, something you keep apart from yourself, you *are* a thetan. You would not speak of *my* thetan; you would speak of *me*. Although much of what Scientology holds true may be echoed in many great philosophic teachings, what it offers is entirely new: An exact route through which anyone can regain the truth and simplicity of his spiritual self. ..." (*The Scientology Handbook*, 1994:iii)

Alejandro Frigerio

About the Author

Alejandro Frigerio, Associate Professor of Graduate Studies in the Sociology Department of the Catholic University of Argentina and Associate Researcher at the National Council for Scientific Research, received a Licenciatura en Sociologia from the University of Argentina in 1980 and a Ph.D. in Anthropology from the University of California in Los Angeles in 1989.

Currently Associate Editor of the journal Sociedad y Religión, since 1982 Professor Frigerio has published extensively on the topic of religion in scientific journals of Argentina, Brazil and the United States. He has edited four volumes on the scientific study of new religious movements and has co-authored *Gimenez, el Pastor: El fenómeno religioso de la década*, a book which provides an analysis of the work of Argentina's most famous Pentecostal pastor.

Professor Frigerio regularly helps to organize the "Conferences on Religious Alternatives in Latinamerica," which is attended annually by religious scholars from countries throughout Latin America.

Scientology

■

A *True Religion*

Urbano Alonso Galan

Doctor in Philosophy
and Licenciate in Theology
Gregorian University and
Saint Bonaventure Pontifical Faculty, Rome

i. INTRODUCTION

In recent years some controversy has arisen regarding Scientology in some sectors in Europe, particularly in Germany, which seem to misinterpret the real social intentions of this religious group.

From the viewpoint of someone who knows philosophy and religion there is no question of any polemic, but it is easy to understand that the lack of knowledge of the religious phenomenon as a whole and the variety of the possible manifestations of this phenomenon can unjustly lead to antagonistic and intransigent attitudes.

It is for this reason that I decided to publish my conclusions about the religion of Scientology in this report, a religion which I have studied for several years, both in its formal aspects (writings, books and philosophy) and in its more day to day aspects (ceremonies, internal and external organization, practices of religious observance and community activities), both in our country as well as in other countries (France and Denmark).

ii. THE CONCEPT OF RELIGION

The theological tradition does not give us many resources when we wish to analyze the objective characteristics which define a religion and differentiate it from other types of beliefs, ideologies or social groups.

For that purpose we need to use concepts and modern bases which allow us to provide a scientific viewpoint about the religious phenomenon, but without forgetting that this is an individual and intimate experience of spirituality and as such evades some of the commonly used arguments of other social sciences.

This approach of tolerance and inter-religious dialogue constitutes a challenge and an absolute necessity in our current society, as is stressed by renowned theologians such as Leonard Boff and Hans Kung.

Just as the word religion is defined (from the Latin *re-ligare:* unite or re-unite) as a community of persons united by a faith, a practice or form of worship, so may religion itself be considered. Of course, this community must be united by a search for "the divine," and defined by its manner of confronting the problems of human life. That is why in the history of religions much is said of the experience and personal contact with "the sacred."

An elevated concept of the dignity of the individual, the knowledge and recognition of something called "sacred" are not exclusively Christian but are the essence of all religions. This was recognized by Vatican Counsel II itself in its document *Dignitatis Humanae* concerning religious faith and purity.

There are other religious phenomena, such as Buddhism and Jainism, which, although lacking an idea of God in terms of reference, do practice a form of respect and reverence of the "sacred divinity," as a generic element with characteristics much more general than the Christian, Muslim or Judaic "particular gods."

Maintaining a unitary concept of religion based solely on one's own experience and excluding other particularities, cannot be other than a form of fundamentalism which violates the most elemental test of religious freedom.

As Max Muller affirmed, "he who knows only one religion knows none," which would express the idea with complete precision. Durkheim himself explains the key to this phenomenon: "... religion is a universal phenomenon which appears in all known human societies. ..."

It is routine to use known models to attempt to define the unknown. This is a procedure used to excess by social investigators in many cases. Abusing comparative analysis will lead without a doubt to blindness when faced with standards of behavior, beliefs or experiences, which cannot be explained except by omitting any other factor and their similitudes.

Religion is evidently the search, inherent in man, which the spirit makes in order to apprehend the "infinite"; the longing and endeavor of the being with regard to his sense of unfulfilled desire for infinity. Religion is, then, an absolute necessity, nothing less than a constituent of human existence, which the individual feels in order to "communicate with the infinite"; it is the source of what sustains the human being and on which man depends in many of its aspects. The definite proof of this is anthropological analysis in which distinct religious creeds or the lack of them are a determining factor for scholars in understanding social and individual standards of the behavior of societies.

To understand a religion like Scientology it is necessary to evaluate very diverse aspects, such as those indicated by modern experts on this subject (see Bryan Wilson: *The Social Dimension of Sectarianism*, 1990, and Eileen Barker: *New Religious Movements: A Perspective to Understand Society*, 1990). Among the many possible approaches, I have selected what could be an objective and scientific view of the matter based on the aspects which I will enumerate here:

1) **The philosophical and doctrinal aspect.** In this I include the complete body of beliefs, scriptures and doctrines which hold the three fundamental parts of religious knowledge: the Supreme Being, Man and Life.

2) **The ritual aspect.** This includes the totality of ceremonies, rites and religious practices applied to the religious phenomenon experienced by the Scientologists.

3) **The ecumenical organizational aspect.** This is an aspect of great importance, because it serves to define the dividing line between religions and beliefs in formation, with those which are already completely formed and evolved.

4) **The aspect of the purpose or final objective.** Here is the definition of a purpose of life and the final attainment of the spiritual objective which leads to the goal Scientology offers to its parishioners.

iii. PHILOSOPHICAL AND DOCTRINAL ASPECT

Scientology is based on the works of L. Ron Hubbard. Scientologists recognize the works and investigations of its creator; philosopher and humanitarian L. Ron Hubbard as the sole source of the Scriptures of the religion.

Starting with Dianetics (see *Dianetics: The Modern Science of Mental Health*, 1950) the evolution of Scientology offers enormous similarities to the majority of religions, including Christianity, Judaism, Islam and Buddhism. Its history is one of discovery or systematic "revelation" of the basic "philosophic truths" which progress step by step and lead to the construction of a complete doctrinal body.

With Dianetics its founder seeks to relieve man of the sufferings the mind produces in the body and the life of men.

For some years, Dianetics has been the tool used by its followers to attain the state of *Clear*. This state, which the book itself defines, signifies an important advance in the eradication of the conditions of unwanted suffering and elevates the human being to a category in which he can better experience his own spiritual self (called the *Thetan*). If we analyze this in depth, the mystical experiences, Nirvana and other spiritual states described in most religions; they could have been looking for the same spiritual state which is sought by Scientologists in the state of Clear.

Later on, Hubbard discovered, when studying the manifestations of many people who had already attained Clear, that there existed a clear proof of the existence of a spiritual being, and additionally, that the person himself was a spiritual being, immortal and with enormous potentials which had been cancelled by the sufferings and experiences of the "constant spiral" of life, death of the body, new body.

He developed a spiritual technology which leads to "freeing" the being (the thetan) from this spiral and returns to him his complete awareness and his spiritual freedom. In this way he developed the principles and practices of spiritual counseling (called *auditing*) which lead to the highest states of awareness and being, called OT levels (OT: *Operating Thetan*, because he does not have the compulsive need to be in a body and can operate without one).

All of this is expounded in clear steps which are outlined in the route (*The Bridge*) toward "Total Freedom." The emphasis in all of the Scriptures given to knowledge of the being himself as well as life, God and the relations of man with the different universes in which he acts (the material or physical universe and the spiritual or theta universe) must be noted as important.

From this belief arise two fundamental activities of Scientologists in their path to spiritual salvation: the study of truths of life according to the Scriptures of Scientology (*training*) and the liberation (*auditing*) from the sufferings or aberrations which prevent the thetan from acting like himself and make him act in an irrational or harmful manner both towards himself and to others. (See *What Is Scientology?*)

Apart from an enormous volume of technical materials for the ministers of the Church of Scientology, an extensive index of materials and reference books for students of this religion exists. Particularly important and describing the basic truths of Scientology are the following books:

> *Scientology: The Fundamentals
> of Thought*
> *Scientology 0-8*
> *Scientology 8-8008*
> *Scientology: A History of Man*
> *Dianetics 55*
> *Scientology: A New Slant on Life*
> *Science of Survival*
> *Dynamics of Life*
> *The Scientology Handbook*

As a fundamental aspect, Scientologists define their religion as "an applied religious philosophy, which allows the person to know more about himself and life." (*Technical Dictionary of Dianetics and Scientology*)

L. Ron Hubbard divided life into its eight fundamental manifestations, each one of which is an impulse towards survival of the person, his vital force directed towards a goal of betterment. He called these the "eight dynamics," due to the fact that these are the dynamic impulses of life:

The **first dynamic** is the impulse towards survival of the person as himself.

The **second dynamic** is the impulse towards survival in the sexual sense: the couple, family and the rearing and education of children.

The **third dynamic** is the impulse towards survival of groups or as a group, including those in which the individual is part (friends, business, club, nation, race).

The **fourth dynamic** is the impulse towards survival of humanity or as humanity.

The **fifth dynamic** is the impulse towards survival of living species (animals, plants) or as a living being.

The **sixth dynamic** is the impulse towards survival of the physical universe or as the physical universe.

The **seventh dynamic** is the impulse towards survival of spiritual beings or as a spiritual being.

The **eighth dynamic** is the impulse towards survival of the infinite or as part of the infinite. This is the dynamic of the Supreme Being or God for Scientologists.

In these eight manifestations of life are contained the areas in which the person has to progress spiritually and act, maintaining ethical behaviour (which does not harm the dynamics) in order to achieve spiritual betterment. Good and bad are defined by Scientologists as a function of the benefit or harm they cause to the dynamics. Absolute good would be that which assists all the dynamics and absolute evil that which harms all of them. Of course, there would be intermediate points of good and bad which would lie on a gradient scale to the degree they benefit or harm, more or less, some of the dynamics, taking into account that all the dynamics have the same level of importance. (See *Introduction to Scientology Ethics*)

The concern with ethics and moral aspects are of the utmost importance in the doctrine of Scientology. The references to these concepts in different reference books are uncountable, and there are also complete publications dedicated to the subject, such as the one already mentioned or such as *The Way to Happiness*, the Code of Honor, The Auditor's Code and the Code of a Scientologist. (See *Handbook for Preclears*)

Taking into account that for the Scientologists the person is a spiritual and immortal being, his behaviour in each one of his different lives has great importance, not only for the benefit of his dynamics but in order to be able to reach a complete spiritual betterment. "We are in this world in order to work out our own salvation" is a statement by L. Ron Hubbard from the video *Introduction to Scientology*.

Scientologists themselves declare that they have experienced a real betterment and spiritual freedom both through study (training) as well as through spiritual counseling (auditing). They describe their "wins" as real liberations of mass, conflicts, ignorance and unwanted attitudes and sentiments.

They feel that their abilities have increased, their perceptions bettered and that they have a renewed knowledge of themselves, life and God.

The *Creed of the Church of Scientology* defines its system of beliefs which unites its believers with the ultimate meaning of life. This creed underscores the dignity of man, his inalienable and undeniable rights; it defines the natural brotherhood of man and recognizes the spiritual nature of the individual in his striving towards infinity authorizing only God the "right" to act with regard to the freedom and wisdom of men.

This creed provides a clear purpose to the practices of auditing and training as means to achieve spiritual salvation which the Scientologists promulgate in their creed.

iv. THE RITUAL OR MYSTICAL ASPECT

Part of the practices which are described in this section have already been described in the former chapter (training and auditing), therefore I will concentrate more on what can be understood as ceremonies and rites.

These are collected in the *Book of Ceremonies of the Church of Scientology*. Despite the fact that the founder himself places Scientology in the tradition of the oriental religions, inheritors of Buddhism and the Vedas, it nevertheless has ceremonies which to a large degree remind one of the western religions. This is the case with the Sunday Services and the Matrimonial Ceremonies.

But due to its tradition, it possesses various and very personal rites which, although reminiscent of the Judeo-Christian tradition, turn out to be completely coherent with the body of beliefs of Scientology. I'm referring to the Naming Ceremony, the Naming and Recognition Ceremony and the Funeral Service. In accordance with the belief in the immortality of the thetan, Scientologists conduct these ceremonies to give a name to the new body of the being which has arrived, to welcome the being to his new body and his new family or to say goodbye to a being who has abandoned his body in order to find a new one and to try to help to orient him in the new situation in which he finds himself.

All of these ceremonies are performed under the auspices of an ordained minister, or by the chaplain of the church, and the members of the community of Scientologists participate actively in them on a regular basis.

v. THE ORGANIZATIONAL ASPECT

On a worldwide basis, the Church of Scientology is structured in different churches, with various names according to their status and size.

At the lowest level are found groups and missions of Scientology and Dianetics. These are small communities of Scientologists, led by one or several ordained ministers who minister basic services of spiritual counseling, religious ceremonies and who come together to study the Scriptures of Scientology, but at the lowest level. They can not ordain nor prepare ministers nor minister the religious auditing services of the OT (Operating Thetan) levels.

At the next level there are the churches of Scientology. These can prepare and ordain ministers and they minister auditing up to the level of Clear.

Above the latter are the advanced churches. These train the ministers of the highest level and minister pastoral counseling of some of the Operating Thetan levels.

The Church of Scientology Flag Service Organization, in Clearwater, Florida, is the highest of all the advanced organizations. It trains people in the highest ministerial levels and Scientologists go there to ascend to high levels of OT.

A special case is the Church of Scientology based on the *Freewinds*, a ship operating in the Caribbean islands, which ministers a specific OT level which can not be received in any other church.

This type of structure of religious services is common to practically all known religions, insofar as the different levels of preparation of the clergy are not accessible in all the centers, but only in the central institutions (Rome, Tibet, Tel Aviv, Mecca). It is where the missionaries, the monks or priests can receive the ordination of the highest level.

With regards to the religious community of Scientology, they form a real community of ministers and religionists, who live in community, with a total dedication to the purposes of the Church and with abandon of worldly interruptions and vanities.

The Sea Organization, so named after the original crew which manned the ships commanded by its founder in the early days, has 5 principal locations in the world which carry out various functions — although there exist groups of missionaries and members in many of the countries where Scientology is present. Those 5 headquarters are situated in East Grinstead (United Kingdom), Copenhagen, Los Angeles, Clearwater, Florida and Sydney. In those 5 headquarters, more than anywhere else, one can feel the real spirit of a community dedicated to its evangelizing and pastoral work. Although there is no obligation of celibacy for the ministers of Scientology, these communities resemble in their functioning and dedication those of many other religions, including the Catholic Church. Members of the Sea Organization do follow a very strict code of ethics which includes very ethical and monogamous sexual relationships, complete abstinence from any use of drugs and complete devotion of one's life to achieving the goals of the religion.

Of course, the training of ministers of the highest levels, auditing to the highest level of Operating Thetan, ministry of the highest levels of organization and the responsibility for the level of ethics of Scientology at an international level rest only in the hands of members of the religious order called the Sea Organization, who are dedicated exclusively to this work.

vi. THE FINAL OBJECTIVE OF SCIENTOLOGY

In the words of L. Ron Hubbard himself, the goals of Scientology are: "a civilization without insanity, without criminals and without war, where the able can prosper, and honest people can have rights and where man can be free to rise to greater heights." (See *What Is Scientology?*)

As the objective for the individual, Scientology pursues the salvation of man, his spiritual liberation and the freedom of the barriers which existence has been imposing on him. But no man can be free without the society also being free. The search for responsibility is the main road through which Scientologists seek their freedom; responsibility which requires bettering our life and that of our fellow man before reaching superior goals.

Goals of such breadth could not be reached solely through pastoral work carried out by the followers. For that reason, the Church of Scientology International created different groups or associations which carry out social campaigns dedicated to those purposes. One of them is ABLE (Association for Better Living and Education) which sponsors several programs of help in the community: Narconon, which delivers services of prevention and rehabilitation

in the field of drugs; Criminon, which has programs in various countries to educate and rehabilitate criminals; Applied Scholastics, which conducts education and literacy campaigns in disadvantaged areas and neighborhoods; and the Way to Happiness Foundation, which is based on the book of the same title by L. Ron Hubbard and develops campaigns with children and adolescents to reestablish codes of conduct which help the community, such as programs for the protection of the environment, study programs, civil assistance programs, etc.

Another important group created by the Church of Scientology is the Citizens Commission on Human Rights, which has received international awards for its investigations and exposés carried out in the field of mental health.

Of special importance is the Volunteer Ministers Corps, formed by Scientologists around the world, who work together with experts and authorities in cases of accidents, natural disasters or tragic events in which help is needed. These volunteers are perfectly trained to give solace and first aide to people while the medical corps and civil defense workers take action.

vii. IS SCIENTOLOGY A RELIGION?

From my viewpoint as a theologian and philosopher, and having studied the religion of Scientology in its writings and practices, I can strongly affirm that Scientology is a religion, in the very fullest sense.

The community of persons united with a complex body of beliefs, in its search for the infinite, the sacred, searching to place man into his proper relationship with the divine, is what one encounters in examining the beliefs and practices of the religion of Scientology.

One can not see any religion without this factor which involves specific behavior toward this spiritual reality. Scientology seems to turn specially around the fact of survival and salvation, concepts clearly expressed by Xavier Zubiri as inherent tenets in any religious experience. The association or not with a God does not vary in any way the reality of this experience. This is not the case with Scientology, because Scientologists confirm their search for God and infinity in their eighth dynamic, although they do not glorify him. In fact, one of the accusations which separates Islam most from Catholicism is that the latter, so say the Moslems, let itself be carried away by idolatry after its continuous reforms.

The roots of Scientology (Buddhism and the Vedas) already point out that one can only through a complete knowledge of oneself commence to know and love God.

Islam, Judaism and Buddhism passed through similar stages and through a much larger duration than the few years the Church of Scientology has had to organize itself in a completely organized form and aspect.

As religion is a universal impulse, as the ecumenists maintain, one should not forget that Catholicism itself had to go through a long stage of formation and a continuous history of crisis and reforms until it adopted its "final form" which we know today. Islam, Judaism and Buddhism passed through similar stages and through a much larger duration than the few years the Church of Scientology has had to organize itself in a completely organized form and aspect.

The clear confrontation of Scientology with the "scientific" doctrines of psychology and psychiatry which deny the goodness of man, as affirmed by Scientology, frees this religion even more from any confusion. Scientology only values the spiritual essence of man, his innate goodness, his immortality and his search for infinity as a final goal. The novelty here is that its founder developed the religion of Scientology as a body of knowledge and practices which direct man towards these goals. To confuse this with an attempt at "therapy" or "healing" is easily imputed to the superficiality of poorly documented opinions.

Only a complete and bona fide religion could confirm and maintain these assumptions, while creating a body of beliefs, doctrine, practices, rites, structure and objectives directed towards the salvation of the spirit. This is part of no other field than religion and Scientology is a religion.

Without entering in administrative, juridical or tax-related considerations, I reaffirm that Scientology fulfills completely the requirements that can be asked of any religion.

Scientology responds to its true religious nature and pursues no other goals than those to do with the spiritual nature of man.

Urbano Alonso Galan

About the Author

Professor Alonso, a Doctor in Philosophy and a Licenciate in Theology (cum Laude), obtained his degree at the Gregorian University and the Saint Bonaventure Pontifical Faculty, both in Rome. He has been a moderator in Ecumenical Congresses directed by the Vatican and in this capacity has worked with Pope John XXIII and Pope Paul VI on religious matters.

Scientology

■

The Relationship Between Scientology and Other Religions

Fumio Sawada

Eighth Holder of the Secrets
of Yu-itsu Shinto

i. INTRODUCTION

This writer is Japanese, and this paper is about the similarities and differences of the Scientology religion with other religions of the world. This paper will also take a special interest in the similarities and differences from a Japanese perspective and thus will be comparing Scientology to Japanese religions.

The term religion in Japan means *to teach the origin, teach the source of the origin*. That is the Japanese definition, but may not correspond to the Western definition. For this study we shall use the Japanese definition. For the purpose of Japanese law one can add that to be a religion the religious organization must also disseminate the teachings, perform religious ceremonies and train parishioners. Scientology does all these as outlined in the following pages.

It is said in a 31-syllable Japanese poem called a "Waka" that there are many paths at the foot of the mountain, but the view of the moon is the same at the peak. This is an old poem and pre-dates Christianity's arrival in Japan. Mostly it refers to the two main religions of Japan, Shinto and Buddhism, where it was said that you end up the same no matter which sect you belonged to. The point being made was, why quarrel? But more importantly, when there are so many similarities among religions, why concentrate on differences?

The Scientology religion is relatively unknown in Japan, although many libraries contain Scientology books written not only by the founder, L. Ron Hubbard, but also by the Church of Scientology itself. Having read 30 books on the subject, this writer feels that any person wishing to know more on the subject is well-advised to read these books.

ii. WHAT IS SCIENTOLOGY?

The origins of Scientology date back to the 1930s when L. Ron Hubbard, the American who was to become the founder of Scientology, travelled the East and asked himself why man was living such a miserable life. No one had been able to answer his questions, when, as a young man, he had asked where man came from and where man was going.

In 1950, Mr. Hubbard wrote a book on a subject he called Dianetics ("through mind"), which was his early research into the mind. The book, *Dianetics: The Modern Science of Mental Health* was very popular and soon became a bestseller, and has sold more than 17 million copies. As the Dianetics movement grew and the research expanded from the mind into the spirit, another subject was born — Scientology — and the first Church was founded in 1954 in the United States. Dianetics first entered Japan shortly after that, but the first formal Scientology missionary expansion into Japan occurred in 1962, making this the actual starting point of Scientology's history in Japan. On 10 September 1962 the first official lecture on Scientology was given to a packed auditorium.

The word "Scientology" comes from the Latin *scio*, meaning "Knowing — in the fullest sense of the word," and the Greek *logos*, which means "to study."

In the book *Scientology — The Fundamentals of Thought*, Mr. Hubbard explains that the subject is actually descended from the roots of psychology, but that we must understand that it is not descended from current psychology, but rather the older psychology as was taught in the religions of the world before the spiritual essence of the study was removed in the last century.

Psychology means literally "the study of the spirit." Psychology of today has lost this meaning and no longer studies or recognizes the spirit as a bona fide field of study. In this sense Scientology is very different, as it does study the spirit, as most great religions of the world do.

Religions generally accept that the human spirit is related to the great "life-force" of this universe. However, the word "spirit" is difficult to define. Some

would argue that the spirit is in fact the human mind. But in Scientology the term "spirit" would mean "oneself" and it means much more than just the mind. In one Japanese Shinto religion, Seichi-no-Ie, it is expressed as what would be translated into "the child of God." It would correspond to the Japanese words "hime" or "hiko." In Scientology, Mr. Hubbard coined the word thetan, from the Greek for spirit, as no other existing word could fully describe it.

The concept of coining new words to explain new concepts that have no existing words is not new to religion. In Japan, Master Kobodaishi, the founder of Shingon (a very old and traditional, large esoteric Buddhist sect) coined many words that needed to be developed so that the religion could be practiced.

Yet at the same time there is no new word for God coined in Scientology. Though the framework of God may not be part of the Scientology study, and members may have their own ideas of what this term is or is not, the words used for it are "the Supreme Being," the "infinite," "the allness of all," "the author of the universe," and of course "God."

Unlike some other religions, Scientology has no particular dogma about the concept of God, but rather allows the person to develop his own understanding of how he fits into the universe and the nature of things. From there faith may follow. Thus Scientology students not only appear to come from all walks of life and nationalities, but from very diverse religious

backgrounds. Being a member of more than one religion is very common in Japan and the East. In this tradition, some Japanese students of Scientology also do not give up their other religions, but from what this writer can understand, have used their study of Scientology to strengthen their previous religious commitment and faith in God. This is slightly similar in concept to what is practiced in the relatively new Shinto religion, Seico-no-Ie, which also has followers coming from Buddhist, Christian and other faiths.

iii. SCIENTOLOGY AND ITS INTERRELATION WITH OTHER RELIGIONS

Scientology has an obvious similarity with Buddhism. So much so that Mr. Hubbard once asked the question of Buddhist leaders in Asia if it were possible that he was the Metteya who had been prophesied by Buddha. Buddha, Guatama Siddhartha, had told his followers when he was about to die that in the future a Buddha would come to complete the job he had begun, and that he was to be known as Metteya. If Mr. Hubbard is to complete the humane intentions of the great Siddhartha, only time will tell. It is not the purpose of this paper to answer the question that Mr. Hubbard raised. However, the fulfilling of prophesies is another similarity to other religions, great and small.

The first book that this writer read was *Scientology — The Fundamentals of Thought*. In reading this book, this writer immediately thought of how similar the contents were to Shinto religions. Specifically there is the understanding that life is but an apparency, and that the physical world is actually the apparent world, there to be seen by the senses. This is very similar to the teachings of the founder of Seicho-no-Ie, Master Masaharu Taniguchi. (Master Taniguchi was one of the four people to write down the Story Of The Universe for Holy Master Onisaburo Deguchi of Oomoto, another Shinto religion of Japan.) Both Oomoto and Seicho-no-Ie are relatively recent in Japanese history with Oomoto beginning at the end of the last century and Seicho-no-Ie beginning in the 1920s.

In Buddhism, this same idea of the "apparency of life" is expressed as "Shiki soku, Ku soku ze shiki" which means simply that anything that can be perceived with the five senses is simply nothingness or empty. The Buddhists also maintain that the universes of man are only manifestations of the mind. Of course Buddhism also has a much deeper meaning, as does Scientology.

Other explanations about life and the mind are also comparable to some Shinto beliefs, such as that the memories of experience are recorded in a film-like memory, each frame duplicating the events for the person. This again has similarities to Seicho-no-Ie. But one term in Scientology that was of great interest is the term *theta*. In Yui

Religions generally accept that the human spirit is related to the great "life-force" of this universe. Some would argue that the spirit is in fact the human mind. But in Scientology the term "spirit" would mean "oneself" and it means much more than just the mind.

Itsu Shinto, what could be a corresponding term means "The Great Life Force of the Universe." It is also in common with Hakke Shinto, which had been in charge of religious services for the Imperial Household until the time of the Meiji Restoration. This same concept then became the basis of newer Shinto religions such as Mahikari, which boomed after the war.

The concept of a person having lived before is old and fully accepted by Eastern religions. Scientology theory and practice is based around this concept, that one is a spiritual being which Mr. Hubbard has called a thetan, and that one can recall his past lives, and that as a spiritual being his actions of his past determine his situation in the present. There are more than 180,000 religious bodies in Japan, and I would expect that this concept is shared by most of them in one way or another. Of course this concept dates back not only to the time of Buddha, but also to the Veda, the source of the great Indian religions.

iv. SCIENTOLOGY PRACTICE–AUDITING

The central practice of Scientology is called auditing, from Latin *audire*, which means to listen. The person answering questions put to him by the *auditor* ("one who listens") brings about

for himself a senior state of mind and spirit, and a curing of bodily psychosomatic ills. This is very much in common with some of the newer Shinto religions that come from the Yui-Itsu Shinto line which dates back 1,400 years in Japan.

Scientology thought began with Mr. Hubbard's early research in the 1930s, which is the same time the newer Shinto religions were searching for a means of applicable religious practice to heal the spirit. Auditing began in the USA in 1950, when *Dianetics: The Modern Science of Mental Health* was published. In this book Mr. Hubbard outlines how one can attain the state known as *Clear* — free from what is referred to as the *reactive mind*. It could be compared to the state of "Satori" or even "Naikan" in Buddhism. In some Shinto religions, where a person meditates on his experiences of childhood or his past lives, under a teacher's direction he self-reflects on the way he is now. Auditing, which also can be described as a reflection on one's past, be it childhood or past lives, can also bring about the same reflection and understanding of one's current state in life.

How to conduct auditing is learned by a person who studies in Scientology study rooms called academies and course rooms. There, under the guidance of a supervisor, the student reads and practices the techniques of auditing. Auditing is the practice whereby this trained auditor has a person who is not Clear answer questions about his past. The person receiving this auditing is called the "preclear," as he is not yet Clear. As the preclear answers the ques-

tions put to him by the auditor, he experiences relief of stress, a betterment and peace of mind, and general spiritual well-being. The training time to become a proficient auditor will vary but it can take from months to years depending on the level of proficiency and exactitude the auditor is striving to achieve.

In the Oomoto religion, the practice of "Naikan" is still practiced and rehabilitates juvenile delinquents, resulting in regional governmental commendation for the practice. Again comparable, Scientology has juvenile rehabilitation programs operating in many parts of the world. Of course Naikan and auditing have similarities, but are also fundamentally different. This is an example, however, showing two religions approaching the same problem from two different cultures and arriving at answers that have obvious similarities. With auditing, one would tell the auditor in minute detail of what he had found troubling him in life from his past, where with "Naikan" one would reflect for himself under a teacher's tutelage. The end result for both is betterment in spiritual behaviour and a resurgence of ethical conduct.

In the practice of Seicho-no-Ie, called "Sin-So-Kan," a person is trained to confront himself through his past. This also has a similarity with auditing. In both practices one has to confront his own past.

Scientology has a graded path to enlightenment which is called the Bridge to Total Freedom. The result of travelling this Bridge, by being audited and learning how to audit, is not only great enlightenment but also a spiritual beingness comparable to "Chin-Kon-Ki-Shin," the great secret of Shinto, which means "to appease the spirit of man so that he can return to a God-like state." This is very similar in concept. This has been practiced by various Shinto religions, including Hakke Shinto, which was founded in 1025 A.D.

Making people better with the natural spiritual healing arts is not a lost practice in Japanese religions, as it is for some other religions. Religions such as Seicho-no-Ie, Sekai-Kyusei-kyo, Shinto-tenkokyo, Ananai-kyo and others are all interested in practices in Japan that bring out the state of Chin-kon-Kishin. The number of followers reach 20 million. Though their techniques may be different, their purposes and goals have a direct similarity to the Scientology practice of auditing and having its members move up the Bridge to Total Freedom, grade by grade.

In other major world religions too, such a state is not without description. In Islam, there is the term "Imam Zamam" which means a person so enlightened that he can fully perceive all the seven meanings of the Holy Koran.

One cannot reach any other decision than that Scientology is a religion. It has more similarities to Japanese religions than Western religions, and for this reason it may be misunderstood in the West, not being similar to the other mainstream religions. But, nevertheless, it is an international religion very similar to religions in Japan that have adherents numbering 20 million.

In the Christian confessional one also has to confront one's past. Again this is similar to Scientology, which also offers confessional procedure. A person has to look back into his past, confront another person with it — the auditor — and confess. The result is the same for both faiths — a betterment of the spirit and a resurgence in life.

This brings us full circle again to the prophecy of Buddha, who predicted that one day Metteya would liberate man from what is holding him back. In Japan, the Metteya prophecy is different from those of the Pali. Here the prophecy is not so much that a person will necessarily return, but rather that man could have a way of returning to the spiritual state as prophesied. Many religions in Japan have been waiting for such events to evolve, both Buddhist and Shinto. Scientology does have a means of raising man's spiritual ability. Japan is a country where religions place an accent on the raising of one's spiritual ability. From a Japanese point of view, Scientology is indeed a similar religion to others already here.

v. Ceremonies

Religion would not be complete without ceremonies, and Scientology has a book called *Background and Ceremonies*, used by ministers of Scientology Churches for funeral services, wedding services and for welcoming newborns into the world, to mention but a few of the Scientology services. In the West, Sunday services are also performed.

vi. CONCLUSION

In conclusion, one cannot reach any other decision than that Scientology is a religion. It has more similarities to Japanese religions than Western religions, and for this reason it may be misunderstood in the West, not being similar to the other mainstream religions. But, nevertheless, it is an international religion, very similar to religions in Japan that have adherents numbering 20 million.

I would also like to introduce the esteemed academic religious scholar and Emeritus Fellow of Oxford University of England, Bryan Ronald Wilson. He has written a very detailed study of Scientology, and for further details on Scientology from a Western scholastic point of view, I highly recommend this study for further reading.

Fumio Sawada

About the Author

Fumio Sawada is the eighth holder of the secrets of Yu-itsu Shinto, the oldest religion in Japan. Yu-itsu Shinto means The Way of One God, Creator of Heaven and Earth. The first holder of the Yu-itsu Shinto secret, or Tamanoya secrets, as they can also be called, was Shoto-ku Taishi (Crown Prince of Shotoku) of 1440 years ago. The second holder of the secrets was Emperor Tenmu of 712, who also wrote Kojiki, the first written historical record of Japan. The third holder of the secrets was the founder of the Shugendo religion.

Mr. Sawada was once director of Sophia University, one of Japan's most distinguished universities. He is Chairman of the Christian Democratic Party of Japan. He has been accorded the venerated Islamic title of Haji, having completed a pilgrimage to Mecca. He is president of the Ahlut-Bait (A.S.) Center in Japan. His eldest son is currently studying Islam in Iran, while his second son is studying in the Vatican.

Official Recognition of Scientology as a Religion

■

*Courts and various governmental agencies in the United States,
Europe and other countries have repeatedly determined
that Scientology is a bona fide religion. The following are examples
of some of the many court rulings and agency determinations
confirming Scientology's religiosity.*

On 8 October 1993, tens of thousands of Scientologists from all corners of the globe gathered
in Los Angeles to hear the news of this historic victory for religious freedom.

On October 1, 1993, the United States Internal Revenue Service in granting full religious recognition and tax exemption to all Churches of Scientology located in the United States as well as several Church organizations in other countries, determined that:

"... Church of Scientology International (CSI) and its related churches and related charitable and educational entities, [are] exempt from United States federal income tax as exclusively religious or charitable organizations under section 501 (c) (3) of the Internal Revenue Code."

On 27 October 1983, the High Court of Australia, in *Church of the New Faith v. the Commissioner for Payroll Tax*, found:

> The conclusion that it [the Church of Scientology] is a religious institution entitled to the tax exemption is irresistible.

In Italy, in the case of *State v. Scarsetti, et al.*, on 27 March 1990, the Trento Court of Appeals made the following finding:

> Scientology... has the objective of achieving an inner and outer freedom, one that transcends the human, one that belongs to the field of spiritual things, and that moves up to infinity; indeed, the progress toward realization of the eighth dynamic force—concerning Infinity and God—actually is the characteristic that describes Scientology as a religion and as a church.

Eighteen months later, on 11 December 1991, another Italian court, the First Tax Court of Novara, ruled similarly:

> It is [this Court's] opinion that the religious nature of Scientology must be considered to have been ascertained both for the theoretical and salvation oriented content of its teachings, for the rites practiced, and for the ecclesiastic-type organization in which it is formed, as is also clear from Court decisions.

The Superior Court of Hamburg in Germany, on 17 February 1988, found that:

> It is not clear what characteristics need to be specifically present for a group to be recognized as a religion in the sense of the referenced law. However, the possible criteria required for a Church are doubtlessly fulfilled in the present case. We are dealing with an association that is not only united for ideological purposes but also pursues a transcendental purpose. This is not only evident from their statutes but also from the Canon which were both submitted as part of the registration application.
>
> The association describes itself as a Church. Article 5 of their Canon explicitly talks about God and religion... In the course of the application for registration a number of expertises were presented, both by theologians as well as juridical experts, which all conclude that the association does have the characteristics of a Church.

On 27 February 1984, the United States District Court, Central District of California, in *Peterson v. Church of Scientology of California*, ruled:

> This court finds that the Church of Scientology is a religion within the meaning of the First Amendment. The beliefs and ideas of Scientology address ultimate concerns—the nature of

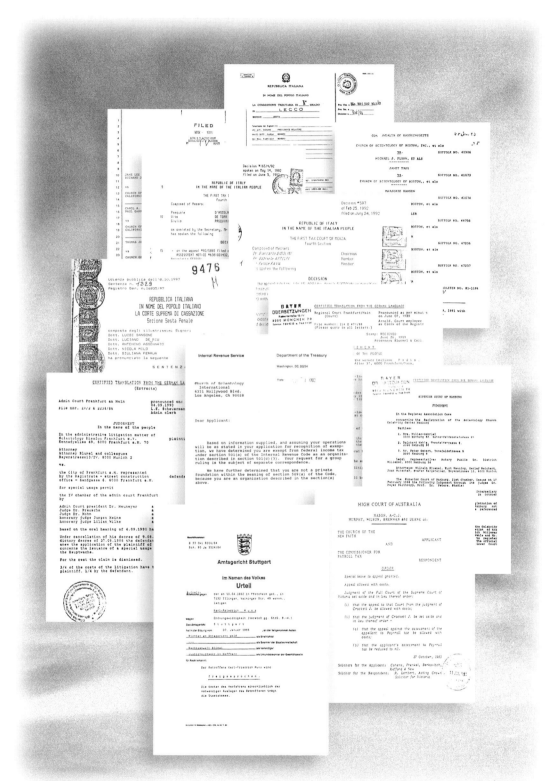

These are just some of the scores of court decisions and affirmations of the religious nature of Scientology. Such religious recognitions come from countries around the world—from Albania to Taiwan and from Costa Rica to the Russian Federation.

the person and the individual's relationship to the universe. The theories of Scientology involve a comprehensive belief system. Additional indicia of the religious status of Scientology include the following: a) Scientology has ordained ministers and ceremonial functions; b) it is incorporated as a tax-exempt religious organization; and c) it characterizes itself as a church.

On 28 June 1983, in *Church of Scientology of Boston, et al., v. Michael J. Flynn et al.*, the Boston Superior Court, Commonwealth of Massachusetts, stated:

In the present case, the court finds that the defendants have made a showing that the Church of Scientology satisfies these criteria [of what is a religion]. The teachings of Scientology, as espoused in the writings of L. Ron Hubbard, involve a theory of the spiritual nature of man, and the relationship between the spiritual nature and the universe.

...

Furthermore, these concerns are addressed as a comprehensive multi-faceted theology. The doctrines of Scientology, as embodied in the literature, set forth the theory of "auditing," a process of working towards "clear," which, in the eyes of its adherents, becomes an integral approach to life and part of the spiritual philosophy. Indeed, the practice of auditing appears to be central to

the practice of Scientology, with very stringent requirements of practicing the faith imposed upon the followers. Finally, the organization of the Church has many of the trappings of recognized hierarchical religious institutions. It has a fully developed creed and code of moral conduct, it is organized world-wide and is recognized as a religious organization for tax purposes.

In *Chiesa di Scientology della Brianza v. 2nd VAT Office of Monza*, on 25 February 1992, the First Tax Court of Monza decided:

[I]n an academic research we [the Court] found Scientology to be a prophetic-type religion as it was born from the preaching and the revelation of a charismatic founder.

...

Then we examined the doctrinal contents and ritual practice of Scientology, carried out through practices like auditing, as their initiation rite, the Naming Ceremony for the assignment of a name, etc., and came to the conclusion that what makes the religion of Scientology is not only its similarity to other religions, but above all, the fact that, while judging without any prejudice and nonetheless influenced by the western conflict between "lay" and "religious," all that is done or said in Scientology can and must find reliability within the terms of our culture only if it is considered as a religion.

On 9 December 1992, in Germany in the case of *Peter Graf v. Dianetic Stuttgart e.V.*, the Stuttgart District Court ruled:

> [Auditing] has its origin in the religious/philosophical view of defendant which is protected by German constitutional law and it is the focus of the spiritual/religious practice and pastoral counseling towards salvation within Scientology. Like most of the religious and ideological communities defendant considers man as a unity of body and soul which generally includes the promise of positive changes on a physical or spiritual level—as a so-called side effect—for the members who act according to the rules of defendant and who make use of his help.

———

The Administrative Court in Frankfurt, Germany decided on 4 September 1990:

> The classification of the plaintiff as a religious or ideological community which is confirmed by recent jurisprudence as well as in the legal expertises presented by [the Mission] cannot be objected to with the argument that the tenets of the Church of Scientology lack a dogmatically fixed "classical" creed like the Christian one nor that it lacks sufficient plausibility or seriousness. The first can be eliminated because the freedom of religion of Article 4 Constitution is not only granted to the recognized church-es and religious communities but also other religious and ideological communities which conform to the constitutional requirements of a religious or ideological community.
>
> The second objection neglects that the Constitution prohibits an evaluation of religion of ideology respective of its institutional personification based on subjective impression and viewpoints....

———

There are, in addition to these, a number of decisions and rulings confirming or upholding the religious bona fides in countries as diverse as Albania, Australia, Austria, Belgium, Canada, Costa Rica, Denmark, France, Hungary, India, Kazakhstan, New Zealand, Norway, Portugal, Russia, South Africa, Switzerland, Taiwan, the United Kingdom and the United States. These additional decisions and rulings involve matters of equal diversity, including recognition of the right to marry; income, property or VAT exemptions and, religious registration and immigration.

Copies of these court decisions and other documents are generally available.

For further information contact:

Office of the President
Church of Scientology
International
6331 Hollywood Blvd., Suite 1200
Los Angeles, CA 90028-6329
United States of America

Books by L. Ron Hubbard on Scientology

BOOKS BY L. RON HUBBARD
ON SCIENTOLOGY

Advanced Procedure and Axioms

All About Radiation

Art

Assists Processing Handbook

The Book of Case Remedies

The Book of E-Meter Drills

Child Dianetics

*Clear Body, Clear Mind:
The Effective Purification Program*

The Creation of Human Ability

Dianetics 55!

Dianetics: The Evolution of a Science

*Dianetics: The Modern Science
of Mental Health*

The Dynamics of Life

E-Meter Essentials

Group Auditor's Handbook

Handbook for Preclears

*Have You Lived Before
This Life?*

How to Live Though an Executive

Introducing the E-Meter

Introduction to Scientology Ethics

*Introductory and Demonstration
Processes Handbook*

Knowingness

Notes on the Lectures of L. Ron Hubbard

*The Organization Executive Course and
Management Series (12 volumes)*

The Problems of Work

Purification: An Illustrated Answer to Drugs

Research and Discovery Series

Science of Survival

Scientology 0-8: The Book of Basics

Scientology 8-80

Scientology 8-8008

Scientology: A History of Man

Scientology: A New Slant on Life

Scientology: The Fundamentals of Thought

Self Analysis

*The Technical Bulletins of Dianetics and
Scientology (18 volumes)*

Understanding

Understanding the E-Meter

REFERENCE WORKS
ON SCIENTOLOGY

What Is Scientology?

This encyclopedic volume provides a detailed description of the philosophy and beliefs, catechism, creeds and codes, materials and scriptures of the Scientology religion.

The Scientology Handbook

The Scientology Handbook, the companion to *What Is Scientology?*, puts the technology of Scientology into the hands of anyone who wishes to use it.

BOOKS BY L. RON HUBBARD
ARE PUBLISHED AROUND THE WORLD

Bridge Publications, Inc. publishes the works of L. Ron Hubbard in the United States and Canada, New Era Publications publishes them for the rest of the world.

While all books on *Dianetics* and *Scientology* are available in Scientology churches and missions, they can also be obtained directly from the following organizations:

BRIDGE PUBLICATIONS, INC.
4751 Fountain Avenue
Los Angeles, California 90029

NEW ERA PUBLICATIONS INTERNATIONAL APS
Store Kongensgade 55
1264 Copenhagen K, Denmark

AUSTRALIA

New Era Publications Australia Pty Ltd.
Level 3 Ballarat House
68-72 Wentworth Ave.,
Surry Hills,
New South Wales
2010 Australia

CANADA

Continental Publications Liaison Office
696 Yonge Street
Toronto, Ontario
Canada, M4Y 2A7

COMMONWEALTH OF INDEPENDENT STATES

New Era Publications Group
Str. Kasatkina, 16,
Building 1,
129301 Moscow, Russia

ENGLAND

New Era Publications United Kingdom, Ltd.
Saint Hill Manor
East Grinstead
W. Sussex RH19 4JY
England

SOUTH AFRICA

Continental Publications Pty Ltd.
6th Floor, Budget House
130 Main Street
Johannesburg 2001
South Africa

MEXICO

Era Dinamica Editores, S.A. de C.V.
Nicolás San Juan 208
Colonia Narvarte
C.P. 03020 Mexico, D.F.

FRANCE

New Era Publications France E.U.R.L.
105, Rue des Moines
75017 Paris, France

GERMANY

New Era Publications Deutschland GmbH
Hittfelder Kirschweg 5a,
21220 Seevetal-Maschen
Germany

ITALY

New Era Publications Italia S.r.l.
Via Rucellai No 39,
20126 Milano, Italy

SPAIN

Nueva Era Dinamics, S.A.
C/Montera 20, 1 Dcha,
28013 Madrid, Spain

JAPAN

New Era Publications Japan, Inc.
3-4-20-503 Sala Mita,
Minatu-ku,
Tokyo 108, Japan

Churches and Missions of Scientology

*Churches of Scientology exist throughout the world.
The address list that follows is as up-to-date as possible, but with continued
expansion, the number of organizations continues to increase rapidly.
Addresses are subject to change.*

INTERNATIONAL ASSOCIATION OF SCIENTOLOGISTS

*The International Association of Scientologists (IAS)
is the official membership association
of the Church of Scientology. It unites individuals around
the world to achieve the Aims of Scientology.
Anyone in agreement
with these aims may become a member.*

For information concerning the activities of the IAS, write to:

INTERNATIONAL ASSOCIATION
OF SCIENTOLOGISTS
c/o Saint Hill Manor
East Grinstead, Sussex
RH19 4JY England

or

UNITED STATES INTERNATIONAL
ASSOCIATION OF SCIENTOLOGISTS
MEMBERS' TRUST
1311 N. New Hampshire Avenue
Los Angeles, California 90027

CHURCH OF SCIENTOLOGY INTERNATIONAL

Church of Scientology International (CSI)
is the mother church of the Scientology religion.
It provides ecclesiastical direction,
planning and guidance to the network of churches,
missions and field auditors which make up
the hierarchy of the Scientology religion.

Information on churches, missions,
field auditors and volunteer ministers may be obtained
through the organizations listed on pages 252 through 273
of this directory or by writing to:

CHURCH OF SCIENTOLOGY INTERNATIONAL
6331 Hollywood Boulevard, Suite 1200
Los Angeles, California 90028

RELIGIOUS TECHNOLOGY CENTER

Religious Technology Center (RTC) and the Inspector General Network exist to ensure the purity of the Scientology religion. The purpose of RTC is to ensure that the religious technologies of Dianetics and Scientology remain in proper hands and are properly applied.

RELIGIOUS TECHNOLOGY CENTER
1710 Ivar Avenue, Suite 1100
Los Angeles, California 90028

THE CHURCHES OF SCIENTOLOGY
CONTINENTAL LIAISON OFFICES

The ecclesiastical management of Scientology churches within each continental zone is the responsibility of Continental Liaison Offices (CLOs). There are also Operation and Transport Liaison Offices (OTLs), which help manage churches in some larger countries, effectively functioning as a branch of the CLO in their particular country.

Continental Liaison Office Africa
6th Floor Budget House
130 Main St.
Johannesburg 2001
South Africa

Continental Liaison Office Australia, New Zealand & Oceania
3rd Floor
201 Castlereagh St.
Sydney
New South Wales 2000
Australia

Continental Liaison Office Canada
696 Yonge St.
Toronto, Ontario
M4Y 2A7 Canada

Continental Liaison Office Eastern United States
394 W. 48th Street
New York, New York
10036 USA

Continental Liaison Office Europe
Store Kongensgade 55
1264 Copenhagen K
Denmark

Continental Liaison Office Latin America
Federación Mexicana de
Dianética A.C.
Pomona # 53
Colonia Roma
CP 06700
Mexico, D.F.

Continental Liaison Office United Kingdom
Saint Hill Manor
East Grinstead
West Sussex
RH19 4JY England

Continental Liaison Office Western United States
1308 L. Ron Hubbard Way
Los Angeles, California
90027 USA

Operations & Transport Liaison Office Hungary
Magyarorszag Scientology
Izabella U. 63 1/6
1064 Budapest
Hungary

Operations & Transport Liaison Office Iberia
Iglesia de Cienciología
C/Montera 20 i'dcha
28013 Madrid
Spain

Operations & Transport Liaison Office Italy
Chiesa Nazionale di
Scientology Dell Italia
Via Cadorna 61
20090 Vimodrone
Milano, Italy

Operations & Transport Liaison Office Russia
Hubbard Humanitarian
Center
Borisa Galushkina St., 19A
129301, Moscow, Russia

THE CHURCHES OF SCIENTOLOGY ADVANCED ORGANIZATIONS

Church of Scientology Flag Ship Service Organization
118 North Fort Harrison Ave.
Clearwater, Florida
33755 USA

Church of Scientology Flag Service Organization
118 North Fort Harrison Ave.
Clearwater, Florida
33755 USA

AUSTRALIA, NEW ZEALAND AND OCEANIA

Church of Scientology Advanced Organization Saint Hill Australia, New Zealand and Oceania
19-37 Greek St.
Glebe, New South Wales 2037
Australia

EUROPE & AFRICA

Church of Scientology Advanced Organization Saint Hill for Europe and Africa
Jernbanegade 6
1608 Copenhagen V,
Denmark

UNITED KINGDOM

Advanced Organization Saint Hill United Kingdom
Saint Hill Manor
East Grinstead,
West Sussex
RH19 4JY England

UNITED STATES

Church of Scientology Advanced Organization of Los Angeles
1306 L. Ron Hubbard Way
Los Angeles, California
90027 USA

Church of Scientology American Saint Hill Organization
1413 L. Ron Hubbard Way
Los Angeles, California
90027 USA

THE CHURCHES OF SCIENTOLOGY
CELEBRITY CENTRES

INTERNATIONAL

Church of Scientology
Celebrity Centre
International
5930 Franklin Ave.
Hollywood, California
90028

AUSTRIA

Church of Scientology
Celebrity Centre Vienna
Senefeldergrasse 11/5
1100 Vienna

ENGLAND

Church of Scientology
Celebrity Centre London
27 Westbourne Grove
London, W2

FRANCE

Church of Scientology
Celebrity Centre Paris
69, rue Legendre
75017 Paris

GERMANY

Church of Scientology
Celebrity Centre
Düsseldorf
Rheinland e.v.
Luisenstrasse 23
40215 Düsseldorf

Church of Scientology
Celebrity Centre Munich
Landshutter Allee 41
80637 Munich

ITALY

Church of Scientology
Celebrity Centre Florence
Via Silvestrina 12
50129 Florence

UNITED STATES

Church of Scientology
Celebrity Centre Dallas
10500 Steppington Drive
Suite 100
Dallas, Texas 75230

Church of Scientology
Celebrity Centre Las Vegas
1100 South 10th St.
Las Vegas, Nevada 89104

Church of Scientology
Celebrity Centre Nashville
1907 Old Murfreesboro Pike
Nashville, Tennessee 37217

Church of Scientology
Celebrity Centre New York
65 East 82nd St.
New York, New York 10028

Church of Scientology
Celebrity Centre Portland
708 SW Salmon
Portland, Oregon 97205

THE CHURCHES OF SCIENTOLOGY
CLASS V CHURCHES

ARGENTINA

*Argentinian Communication
and Cultural Association*
2162 Bartolome Mitre
Capital Federal
Buenos Aires, 1039

AUSTRALIA

*Church of Scientology
of Adelaide*
28 Waymouth Street
Adelaide, South Australia
5000

*Church of Scientology
of Australian Capital
Territory*
43–45 East Row
Canberra City, ACT 2601

*Church of Scientology
of Brisbane*
106 Edward Street, 2nd Fl.
Brisbane, Queensland 4000

*Church of Scientology
of Melbourne*
42 Russell Street
Melbourne, Victoria 3000

*Church of Scientology
of Perth*
108 Murray Street
Perth
Western Australia 6000

*Church of Scientology
of Sydney*
201 Castlereagh Street
Sydney
New South Wales 2000

AUSTRIA

*Church of Scientology
of Austria*
Schottenfeldgasse 13–15
1070 Vienna

BELGIUM

*Church of Scientology
of Belgium*
61, rue Prince Royal
1050 Brussels

CANADA

*Church of Scientology
of Edmonton*
10206 106th Street NW
Edmonton, Alberta
T5J 1H7

*Church of Scientology
of Kitchener*
104 King Street West,
Kitchener, Ontario
N2G 2K6

*Church of Scientology
of Montreal*
4489 Papineau Street
Montreal, Quebec
H2H 1T7

*Church of Scientology
of Ottawa*
150 Rideau Street, 2nd Fl.
Ottawa, Ontario
K1N 5X6

*Church of Scientology
of Quebec*
350 East Charest Blvd.
Quebec City, Quebec
G1K 3H5

*Church of Scientology
of Toronto*
696 Yonge Street, 2nd Fl.
Toronto, Ontario
M4Y 2A7

*Church of Scientology
of Vancouver*
401 West Hastings Street
Vancouver,
British Columbia
V6B 1L5

*Church of Scientology
of Winnipeg*
315 Garry Street, Ste. 210
Winnipeg, Manitoba
R3B 2G7

COLOMBIA

*Centro Cultural
Dianética*
Carrera 30 # 91-96
Santa Fé
Bogotá

DENMARK

*Church of Scientology
of Jylland*
Vester Alle 26
8000 Aarhus C

**Church of Scientology
of Copenhagen**
Store Kongensgade 55
1264 Copenhagen K

**Church of Scientology
of Denmark**
Gammel Kongevej 3–5
1610 Copenhagen V

ENGLAND

**Church of Scientology
Saint Hill Foundation**
Saint Hill Manor
East Grinstead
West Sussex RH19 4JY

**Church of Scientology
of Birmingham**
Albert House, 3rd Floor
24 Albert Street
Birmingham B4 7UD

**Church of Scientology
of Brighton**
5 St. George Place
London Road
Brighton BN1 4GA

**Church of Scientology
of London**
68 Tottenham Court Road
London W1P 0BB

**Church of Scientology
of Manchester**
258 Deansgate
Manchester
M3 4BG

**Church of Scientology
of Plymouth**
41 Ebrington Street
Plymouth PL4 9AA

**Church of Scientology
of Sunderland**
51 Fawcett Street
Sunderland SR1 1RS

FRANCE

**Church of Scientology
of Angers**
6, avenue Montaigne
49100 Angers

**Church of Scientology
of Clermont-Ferrand**
6, rue Dulaure
63000 Clermont-Ferrand

**Church of Scientology
of Lyon**
3, place des Capucins
69001 Lyon

**Church of Scientology
of Paris**
7, rue Jules César
75012 Paris

**Church of Scientology
of Saint-Étienne**
24, rue Marengo
42000 Saint-Étienne

GERMANY

**Church of Scientology
of Berlin**
Sponholzstrasse 51–52
12159 Berlin 41

**Church of Scientology
of Düsseldorf**
Friedrichstrasse 28 B
40217 Düsseldorf

**Church of Scientology
of Eppendorf**
Brennerstrasse 12
20099 Hamburg

**Church of Scientology
of Frankfurt**
Kaiserstrasse 49
60329 Frankfurt

**Church of Scientology
of Hamburg**
Steindamm 63
20099 Hamburg 1

**Church of Scientology
of Hanover**
Odeonstrasse 17
30159 Hanover

**Church of Scientology
of Munich**
Beichstrasse 12
80802 Munich 40

**Church of Scientology
of Stuttgart**
Hohenheimerstrasse 9
70184 Stuttgart

ISRAEL

**Dianetics and Scientology
College of Israel**
12 Shonchino Street
PO Box 57478
61574 Tel Aviv

ITALY

**Church of Scientology
of Brescia**
Via Fratelli Bronzetti, 20
25122 Brescia

**Church of Scientology
of Catania**
Via Garibaldi, 9
95121 Catania

**Church of Scientology
of Milano**
Via Abetone, 10
20137 Milano

**Church of Scientology
of Monza**
Via Nuova Valassina, 356
20035 Lissone

**Church of Scientology
of Novara**
Via Passalacqua, 28
28100 Novara

**Church of Scientology
of Nuoro**
Via Lamarmora, 102
08100 Nuoro

**Church of Scientology
of Padova**
Via Mameli, 1/5
35131 Padova

**Church of Scientology
of Pordenone**
Via Montereale, 10/C
33170 Pordenone

**Church of Scientology
of Rome**
Via del Caravita, 5
00186 Rome

**Church of Scientology
of Torino**
Via Bersezio, 7
10152 Torino

**Church of Scientology
of Verona**
Corso Milano, 84
37138 Verona

JAPAN

Scientology Tokyo
2-11-7, Kita-Otsuka
Toshima-ku
Tokyo, 170-0004

MEXICO

**Organización Cultural
Dianética A.C.**
Avenida la Paz 2787
Arcos Sur, Sector Juarez
C.P. 44120 Guadalajara

**Asociación Cultural
Dianética A.C.**
Belisario Domínguez #17-1
Colonia Coyoacán
C.P. 04000
Mexico, D.F.

**Centro Cultural
Latinoamericano A.C.**
Rio Amazonas 11
Colonia Cuahutemoc
C.P. 06500
Mexico, D.F.

**Instituto de Filosofia
Aplicada A.C.**
Isabel La Católica #24
Colonia Centro
C.P. 06890
Mexico, D.F.

**Instituto Tecnológico
de Dianética A.C.**
Avenida Chapultepec #40
Colonia Roma
C.P. 11590
Mexico, D.F.

**Organización Cultural
Dianética A.C.**
Calle Monterrey #402
Colonia Narvarte
C.P. 03020
Mexico, D.F.

**Organización Desarrollo
Dianética A.C.**
Calle Xola y
Pitogoras
1113 Y 1115
Colonia Narvarte
C.P. 03220
Mexico, D.F.

NETHERLANDS

**Church of Scientology
of Amsterdam**
Nieuwe Zijds Voorburgwal 271
1012 RL Amsterdam

NEW ZEALAND

**Church of Scientology
of Auckland**
159 Queen Street, 3rd Fl.
Auckland

NORWAY

**Church of Scientology
of Olso**
Lille Grensen 3
0159 Oslo 1

PORTUGAL

**Church of Scientology
of Portugual**
Rua da Prata 185, 2 Andar
1100 Lisbon

SCOTLAND

**Hubbard Academy of
Personal Independence**
20 Southbridge
Edinburgh
EH1 1LL

SOUTH AFRICA

**Church of Scientology
of Cape Town**
Dorlane House
39 Roeland Street
Cape Town 8001

**Church of Scientology
of Durban**
20 Buckingham Terrace
Durban 3630

**Church of Scientology
of Johannesburg**
4th Floor, Budget House
130 Main Street
Johannesburg 2001

**Church of Scientology
of Johannesburg North**
Bordeaux Centre
Gordon Road, Corner Jan
Smuts Avenue
Blairgowrie
Randburg 2125

**Church of Scientology
of Port Elizabeth**
2 St. Christopher's
27 Westbourne Road Central
Port Elizabeth 6001

**Church of Scientology
of Pretoria**
307 Ancore Building
Corner Jeppe and Esselen
Sunnyside, Pretoria 0002

SPAIN

**Iglesia de Cienciología
de Barcelona**
Pasaje Domingo, 11
08007 Barcelona

**Iglesia de Cienciología
de Madrid**
C/ Montera 20, I' dcha.
28013 Madrid

SWEDEN

**Church of Scientology
of Göteborg**
Varmlandsgatan 16, 1 tr.
41328 Göteborg

**Church of Scientology
of Malmö**
Porslinsgatan 3
21132 Malmö

**Church of Scientology
of Stockholm**
Götgatan 105
11662 Stockholm

SWITZERLAND

**Church of Scientology
of Basel**
Herrengrabenweg 56
40054 Basel

**Church of Scientology
of Bern**
Muhlemattstrasse 31
Postfach 384
3000 Bern 14

**Church of Scientology
of Geneva**
4, rue de L'Aubepine
1205 Geneva

**Church of Scientology
of Lausanne**
10, rue de la Madeleine
1003 Lausanne

**Church of Scientology
of Zurich**
Badenerstrasse 141
8004 Zurich

UNITED STATES

Arizona

**Church of Scientology
of Arizona**
2111 W. University Drive
Mesa, Arizona 85201

California

**Church of Scientology
of Los Angeles**
4810 Sunset Blvd.
Los Angeles, California
90027

**Church of Scientology
of Los Gatos**
2155 S. Bascom Avenue,
Suite 120
Campbell, California
95008

**Church of Scientology
of Mountain View**
2483 Old Middlefield Way
Mountain View, California
94043

**Church of Scientology
of Orange County**
1451 Irvine Blvd.
Tustin, California
92680

**Church of Scientology
of Pasadena**
1277 East Colorado Blvd.
Pasadena, California
91106

**Church of Scientology
of Sacramento**
825 15th Street
Sacramento, California
95814

**Church of Scientology
of San Diego**
1330 4th Avenue
San Diego, California
92101

**Church of Scientology
of San Francisco**
83 McAllister Street
San Francisco, California
94102

**Church of Scientology
of Santa Barbara**
524 State Street
Santa Barbara, California
93101

**Church of Scientology
of Stevens Creek**
80 E. Rosemary
San Jose, California
95112

**Church of Scientology
of the Valley**
15643 Sherman Way
Van Nuys, California
91406

Colorado

**Church of Scientology
of Colorado**
3385 S. Bannock Street
Englewood, Colorado
80110

Connecticut

**Church of Scientology
of New Haven**
909 Whalley Avenue
New Haven,
Connecticut
06515

Florida

**Church of Scientology
of Florida**
120 Giralda Avenue
Coral Gables, Florida
33134

**Church of Scientology
of Orlando**
1830 East Colonial Drive
Orlando, Florida
32803

**Church of Scientology
of Tampa**
3617 Henderson Blvd.
Tampa, Florida
33609

Georgia

**Church of Scientology
of Georgia**
1132 W. Peachtree Street
Atlanta, Georgia
30309

Hawaii

**Church of Scientology
of Hawaii**
1148 Bethel Street
Honolulu, Hawaii
96817

Illinois

**Church of Scientology
of Illinois**
3011 N. Lincoln Avenue
Chicago, Illinois
60657

Massachusetts

**Church of Scientology
of Boston**
448 Beacon Street
Boston, Massachusetts
02115

Michigan

**Church of Scientology
of Ann Arbor**
2355 W. Stadium Blvd.
Ann Arbor, Michigan
48103

**Church of Scientology
of Michigan**
321 Williams Street
Royal Oak, Michigan
48067

Minnesota

**Church of Scientology
of Minnesota
Twin Cities**
1011 Nicollet Mall
Minneapolis, Minnesota
55403

Missouri

**Church of Scientology
of Kansas City**
3619 Broadway
Kansas City, Missouri
64111

**Church of Scientology
of Missouri**
6901 Delmar Blvd.
St. Louis, Missouri
63130

Nevada

**Church of Scientology
of Nevada**
846 E. Sahara Avenue
Las Vegas, Nevada
89104

New Mexico

**Church of Scientology
of New Mexico**
8106 Menaul Blvd. N.E.
Albuquerque, New Mexico
87110

New York

**Church of Scientology
of Buffalo**
47 W. Huron Street
Buffalo, New York
14202

**Church of Scientology
of Long Island**
99 Railroad Station Plaza
Hicksville, New York
11801

**Church of Scientology
of New York**
227 W. 46th Street
New York, New York
10036

Ohio

**Church of Scientology
of Cincinnati**
215 West 4th Street, 5th Fl.
Cincinnati, Ohio
45202

**Church of Scientology
of Ohio**
30 N. High Street
Columbus, Ohio
43215

Oregon

**Church of Scientology
of Portland**
323 S.W. Washington
Portland, Oregon
97204

Pennsylvania

**Church of Scientology
of Pennsylvania**
1315 Race Street
Philadelphia, Pennsylvania
19107

Puerto Rico

**Church of Scientology
of Puerto Rico**
272 JT Piñero Avenue
Hyde Park, Hato Rey
San Juan, Puerto Rico
00918

Texas

**Church of Scientology
of Texas**
2200 Guadalupe
Austin, Texas
78705

Utah

**Church of Scientology
of Utah**
1931 South 1100 East
Salt Lake City, Utah
84106

Washington

**Church of Scientology
of Washington State**
2226 Third Avenue
Seattle, Washington
98121

Washington, DC

**Founding Church
of Scientology of
Washington, DC**
1701 20th Street NW
Washington, DC 20009

VENEZUELA

**Asociación Cultural
Dianética A.C.**
Avenida Luis Ernesto
Branger EDFF
Locales PB 4 Y 5
C.P. 833 Valencia

Asociación Dianética A.C.
Avenida Principal de las
Palmas
Cruce Con Calle Carúpano
Quinta Suha
CP 1050 Caracas

ZIMBABWE

**Church of Scientology
of Bulawayo**
Suite 202
Southampton House
Corner Main and 9th Ave.
Bulawayo

**Church of Scientology
of Harare**
Braude Brothers
Building
47 Speke Avenue
Harare

THE MISSIONS OF SCIENTOLOGY

International Office

*Scientology Missions
International*
6331 Hollywood Blvd.
Los Angeles, California
90028

Continental Offices

AFRICA

*Scientology Missions
International
African Office*
6th Floor Budget House
130 Main Street
Johannesburg 2001
South Africa

AUSTRALIA, NEW ZEALAND, OCEANIA

*Scientology Missions
International
Australia, New Zealand
and Oceania Office*
201 Castlereagh Street
Sydney
New South Wales 2000
Australia

CANADA

*Scientology Missions
International
Canadian Office*
696 Yonge Street
Toronto, Ontario
M4Y 2A7

COMMONWEALTH OF INDEPENDENT STATES

*Scientology Missions
International
CIS Office*
c/o Hubbard Humanitarian
Center
Borisa Galushkina Ul. 19A
129301 Moscow, Russia

EUROPE

*Scientology Missions
International
European Office*
Sankt Nikolajvej 4–6
Frederiksberg C
1953 Copenhagen

HUNGARY

*Scientology Missions
International
Hungarian Office*
P.F. 351,
1438 Budapest

ITALY

*Scientology Missions
International
Italian Office*
Via Cadorna 61
Vimodrone
20090 Milano

LATIN AMERICA

*Scientology Missions
International
Latin American Office*
Pomona 53
Colonia Roma
C.P. 03100
Mexico, D.F.

UNITED KINGDOM

*Scientology Missions
International
United Kingdom Office*
Saint Hill Manor
East Grinstead
West Sussex RH19 4JY
England

UNITED STATES

*Scientology Missions
International
Flag Land Base Office*
118 North Fort Harrison Ave.
Clearwater, Florida 33755

*Scientology Missions
International
Western United States Office*
1308 L. Ron Hubbard Way
Los Angeles, California 90027

*Scientology Missions
International
Eastern United States
Office*
349 W. 48th Street
New York, New York 10036

ALBANIA

*Church of Scientology
Mission of Tirana*
3 Ramiz Treni Street
Tirana

AUSTRALIA

*Church of Scientology
Mission of Inner West*
4 Wangal Place
Five Dock
New South Wales 2046

*Church of Scientology
Mission of Melbourne*
55 Glenferrie Road
Malvern 3144
Victoria

AUSTRIA

*Church of Scientology
Mission of Salzburg*
Rupertgasse 21
5020 Salzburg

*Church of Scientology
Mission of Wolfsberg*
Wienerstrasse 8
9400 Wolfsberg

CANADA

*Church of Scientology
Mission of Beauce*
11925 Le Avenue
Ville de St. Georges
Beauce, Quebec G5Y 2C9

*Church of Scientology
Mission of Halifax*
2589 Windsor Street
Halifax, Nova Scotia
B3K 5C4

*Church of Scientology
Mission of Vancouver*
101 – 2182 W. 12th Ave.
Vancouver, British
Columbia V6K 2N4

*Church of Scientology
Mission of Chinatown*
1407 – 555 Jervis Street
Vancouver, British
Columbia V6E 4N1

*Church of Scientology
Mission of Victoria*
2624 Quadra Street
Victoria, British Columbia
V8T 4E4

CHILE

*Church of Scientology
Mission of Chile*
Calle Nuncio Laghi 6558
La Reyna

COLOMBIA

*Church of Scientology
Mission of North Bogota*
Avenida 13 #104-91
Bogota, D.C.

*Church of Scientology
Mission of Bogota*
Carrera 20 No. 52-27
Bogota

CONGO

*Church of Scientology
Mission de Kinshasa*
BP 1444 Fele No. 7
Kinshasa/Limete

COSTA RICA

*Church of Scientology
Mission of San Jose*
15 Mts. Este de Pali
La Florida Tibas
San Jose

CZECH REPUBLIC

*Church of Scientology
Mission of Prague*
Hornokrcska 60
14000 Praha 4

DENMARK

*Church of Scientology
Mission of Aalborg*
Boulevarden 39 St.
9000 Aalborg

*Church of Scientology
Mission of Odense*
Kongensgade 68
5000 Odense C

*Church of Scientology
Mission of Copenhagen*
Bulowsvej 20
1870 Frederiksberg C

*Church of Scientology
Mission of Lyngby*
Sorgenfrivej 3
2800 Lyngby

Hubbard Kursus Center
Virklundvej 5
8600 Silkeborg

Hubbard Kursus Center
Storgaden 78
6052 Viuf Kolding

DOMINICAN REPUBLIC

*Church of Scientology
Mission of Santa
Domingo*
Condominio Ambar Plaza II
Bloque II, Apto 302
Ave Nunez de Caceres
Esq Sarasota
Santo Domingo

ECUADOR

*Church of Scientology
Mission of Guayaquil*
Frente A La Gasolinera
Shell
A Lado De Univisa
Guayaquil

ENGLAND

*Church of Scientology
Mission of Hove*
59A Coleridge St.
Hove, East Sussex
BN3 5AB

*Church of Scientology
Mission of Bournemouth*
42 High St.
Poole, Dorset BH15 1BT

FINLAND

*Church of Scientology
Mission of Helsinki*
PL 245, Peltolantie 2 B
01300 Vantaa

FRANCE

*Church of Scientology
Mission of Bordeaux*
BP 14
33036 Bordeaux

*Church of Scientology
Mission of Marseille*
2, rue Devilliers
13005 Marseille

*Church of Scientology
Mission of Nice*
28 rue Gioffredo
06000 Nice

*Church of Scientology
Mission of Toulouse*
9 rue Edmond de Planet
31000 Toulouse

GERMANY

*Church of Scientology
Mission of Bremen*
Osterdeich 27
28203 Bremen

*Church of Scientology
Mission of Dresden*
Bischofsweg 46
01099 Dresden

*Church of Scientology
Mission of Goppingen*
Geislingerstrasse 21
73033 Goppingen

*Church of Scientology
Mission of Heilbronn*
Keilstrasse 6
74080 Heilbronn

*Church of Scientology
Mission of Karlsruhe*
Karlstrasse 46
76133 Karlsruhe

*Church of Scientology
Mission of Pasing*
Bäckerstrasse 31
81241 Munich

*Church of Scientology
Mission of Bayern*
Färberstrasse 5
90402 Nurnburg

*Church of Scientology
Mission of Reutlingen*
Heinestrasse 9
72762 Reutlingen

*Church of Scientology
Mission of Ulm*
Eythstrasse 2
89075 Ulm

*Church of Scientology
Mission of Wiesbaden*
Mauritiusstrasse 14
65183 Wiesbaden

GREECE

*Dianetics and Scientology
Centre of Greece*
Patision 200
11256 Athens

GUATEMALA

**Church of Scientology
Mission of Guatemala**
11 Avenida "A" 32-28
Zona 5
Guatemala Cuidad
01005

HONG KONG

**Church of Scientology
Mission of Hong Kong**
62-64 Peel Street
Central
Hong Kong

HUNGARY

**Church of Scientology
Mission of Baja**
Arad u. 2
6500 Baja

**Church of Scientology
Mission of Budapest**
PF.: 701/215
1399 Budapest

**Church of Scientology
Mission of Budapest**
Károly Krt. 4. III/em
1052 Budapest

**Church of Scientology
Mission of Dunaújvaros**
Tancsics M. Ut 3. I/16
2400 Dunaújvaros

**Church of Scientology
Mission of Eger**
PF.: 215
3301 Eger

**Church of Scientology
Mission of Gyor**
Dozsa Gyorgy Rakpart 1
9026 Gyor

**Church of Scientology
Mission of Kalocsa**
Tavasz Ut 44
6300 Kalocsa

**Church of Scientology
Mission of Kaposvar**
PF.: 51
7601 Kaposvar

**Church of Scientology
Mission of Miskolc**
Vörösmarty 53 I/2
3530 Miskolc

**Church of Scientology
Mission of Nyiregyhaza**
Rakoczi Ut 3 I/1
4400 Nyiregyhaza

**Church of Scientology
Mission of Paks**
PF.: 10
7032 Paks

**Church of Scientology
Mission of Pecs**
PF.: 41
7602 Pecs 2

**Church of Scientology
Mission of Sopron**
Balfi Ut 56
9400 Sopron

**Church of Scientology
Mission of
Százhalombatta**
PF.: 69
2440 Százhalombatta

**Church of Scientology
Mission of Szeged**
PF.: 1258
6701 Szeged

**Church of Scientology
Mission of Székesfehérvár**
PF.: 176
8001 Székesfehérvár

**Church of Scientology
Mission of Székszárd**
PF.: 165
7100 Székszárd

**Church of Scientology
Mission of Szolnok**
Mária Ut 19
5000 Szolnok

**Church of Scientology
Mission of Tatabanya**
PF.: 1372
2800 Tatabanya

**Church of Scientology
Mission of Tiszaújváros**
Szederkényi Ut 1
3580 Tiszaújváros

INDIA

**Church of Scientology
Mission of Ambala Cantt**
6352 Punjabi Mohalla
Ambala Cantt 133001

**Church of Scientology
Mission of Patiala**
24 Sampooran Lodge
Ajit Nagar
Patiala 147001

**Church of Scientology
Mission of Bombay**
433 Adash Magar
New Link Road Oshwara
Jogeshwari West
Mumbai 400102

IRELAND

**Church of Scientology
Mission of Dublin**
62-63 Middle Abbey St.
Dublin 1

ITALY

**Church of Scientology
Mission of Aosta**
Corso Battaglione N. 13/B
41100 Aosta

**Church of Scientology
Mission of Avellino**
Via Derna 3
83100 Avellino

**Church of Scientology
Mission of Barletta**
Via Cialdini N. 67/B
70051 Barletta (Bari)

**Church of Scientology
Mission of Bergamo**
Via Roma 85
24020 Gorle (Bergamo)

**Church of Scientology
Mission of Cagliari**
Via Sonnino 177
09127 Cagliari

**Church of Scientology
Mission of Castelfranco**
Via 8/9 Maggio N. 59
Cornuda (Treviso)

**Church of Scientology
Mission of Como**
Via Torno 12
22100 Como

**Church of Scientology
Mission of Conegliano**
Via E. Cornaro 12
31025 Santa Lucia de
Piave (Treviso)

**Church of Scientology
Mission of Cosenza**
Via Duca degli Abruzzi 6
87100 Cosenza

**Church of Scientology
Mission of Lecco**
Via Mascari 78
22053 Lecco

**Church of Scientology
Mission of Lucca**
Viale G. Puccini 425/B
S. Anna
55100 Lucca

**Church of Scientology
Mission of Macerata**
Via Roma 13
62100 Macerata

**Church of Scientology
Mission of Mantova**
Via Visi 30
46100 Mantova

**Church of Scientology
Mission of Modena**
Via Giardini 468/C
41100 Modena

**Church of Scientology
Mission of Olbia**
Centro Martini
Via Gabriele D'Annunzio
07026 Olbia (Sassari)

**Church of Scientology
Mission of Palermo**
Via Mariano Stabile N. 139
90145 Palermo

**Church of Scientology
Mission of Ragusa**
Via Cap. degli Zuavi 67
96019 Vittoria (RG)

**Church of Scientology
Mission of Seregno**
Via G. da Fossano 40
22063 Cantù (Como)

**Church of Scientology
Mission of Treviglio**
Via Massari 1
Ciserano (BG)

**Church of Scientology
Mission of Trieste**
Via Mazzini N. 44
34122 Trieste

**Church of Scientology
Mission of Vicenza**
Viale Milano 38D,
C/O Complesso Polialte
36075 Montecchio
Maggiore (Vicenza)

KAZAKHSTAN

**Church of Scientology
Mission of Almaty**
AB. Box 219
480000

**Dianetics Center of
Karaganda**
Ermekova 46
Karaganda
470061

*Dianetics Center of
Pavlodar*
AB. Box 2105
Pavlodar
637000

LATVIA

Dianetics Center of Riga
Laspesa U. 27-4
Riga 1011

LITHUANIA

*Church of Scientology
Mission of Vilnius*
Centrinis Pastas 2000
A/D 42
Vilnius

MEXICO

*Centro de Dianética
Hubbard de
Aguascalientes A.C.*
Hamburgo No. 127
Fraccionamiento Del
Valle 1A Sec.
C.P. 20080
Aguascalientes, Ags.

Mission of Satelite
Valle Verde No. 59
Club de Golf Bellavista
Atizapan, Edo 52295

Mission of Chihuahua
Ortiz Del Campo 3309
Colonia San Felipe
Chihuahua, Chihuahua

*Instituto de Filosofia
Aplica de Bajio*
Calle Manuel Doblado 111
Zona Centro,
León Gto. CP 37000

*Centro Hubbard
de Dianética*
Tecamachalco
Isabel La Catolica #32
Centro Historico
Mexico DF

*Instituto de Dianética
Monterrey A.C.*
Tulancingo 1262
Colonia Mitras
Monterrey N.L.

*Dianética y Cienciología
Valle, A.C.*
Edificio Santos
Ave. Madero 1955 Pte.
Local 712
Zona Centro
Monterrey N.L.

Mission of Tijuana
Balboa #19-S284
Lomas Hipodrom
Tijuana B.C.

MOLDOVA

*Dianetics Center of
Kishinev*
Dokuchaeva UL. 4-73
272028 Kishinev

NEW ZEALAND

*Church of Scientology
Mission of Christchurch*
PO Box 1843
Christchurch

PAKISTAN

Dianetics Centre
A-3 Royal Avenue
(Opposite URDU College
Block 13C)
Gulshan-E-Iqbal
Karachi

ROMANIA

*Church of Scientology
Mission of Bucharest*
Via Carlo Porta
34 Lissone
Bucharest

*Church of Scientology
Mission of
Szekelyudvarhely*
Odorheiu Secuiesc Str M,
Sasovenau 13
4150 Szekelyudvarhely

RUSSIA

*Dianetics Center
of Barnaul*
Vodoprovodnaja Ul., 95
Barnaul
656014

*Dianetics Center
of Briansk*
Dokuchaeva Ul., 15-72
Briansk
241037

**Dianetics Center
of Dimitrovgrad**
AB Box 189
Dimitrovgrad-12
Ulianovsk Region
433510

**Dianetics Center
of Ekaterinberg**
Mira Ul. 8-24
Ekaterinberg
610066

**Dianetics Center
of Habarovsk**
Pankova Ul. 13-332
Habarovsk
680021

**Dianetics Center
of Izhevsk**
Novostroitelnaya Ul.,
25-A, 67
Izhevsk
426006

**Dianetics Center
of Kaliningrad**
Frunze Ul. 24-13
Kaliningrad
Moscow Region
141090

**Dianetics Humanitarian
Center of Kaluga**
Engelsa Ul. 9-13
Kaluga 248016

**Dianetics Center
of Kazan**
Latyshskih Strelkov Ul.
33-171 Kazan
Tatarstan Region
420089

**Dianetics Center
of Kislovodsk**
Telmana Ul. 3-6
Kislovodsk
357746

**Dianetics Center
of Kogalym**
Mira Ul. 2-12
Kogalym
Tyumen Region
626481

**Dianetics Center
of Kostomuksha**
Geroiev Ul. 2-20
Kostomuksha
Karelia Region
186989

**Dianetics Center
of Krasnoyarsk**
Naberezhnaya Ul. 41-27
Divnogorsk
Krasnoyarsk Region
663080

**Dianetics Center
of Kursk**
Magistralny Proezd 12-2
Kursk

**Dianetics Center
of Magnitogorsk**
AB Box 3008
Magnitogorsk
455000

**Dianetics Center
of Minsk**
AB Box 4
Minsk, Belarus
220017

**Dianetics Center
of Mitishi**
2nd Shelkovsky Proezd
5/1-62
Mitishi
Moscow Region
141007

**Church of Scientology
of Moscow**
Bolshaja Semenovskaja
Ul. 42
Moscow
105094

**Dianetics Center
of Murmansk**
Pereulok Rusanova, 10-514
Murmansk
183766

**Dianetics Center
of Nizhny-Novgorod**
AB Box 123
Nizhny-Novgorod
603074

**Dianetics Center
of Nizhnekamsk**
Urmanche Ul. 3-3
Nizhnekamsk
Tatarstan
423550

**Dianetics Center
of Novgorod**
AB Box 13
Novgorod
173025

**Dianetics Center
of Novgorod II**
AB Box 120
Novgorod
173001

**Dianetics Center
of Novosibirsk**
Dostoevskogo 5-31
Novosibirsk
630104

**Dianetics Center
of Novy Urengoy**
Youbileynaya Ul. 1-41
Novy Urengoy
Tyumen Region
626718

**Dianetics Center
of Obninsk**
Gagarina Ul. 27
Obninsk
249020

**Hubbard Humanitarian
Center of Omsk**
AB. Box 3768
Omsk
644043

**Dianetics Center
of Omsk II**
AB. Box 999
Glavpochtamt
Omsk
644099

**Dianetics Center
of Orenburg**
Vystavochnaya Ul.
25-213
Orenburg
460024

Dianetics Center of Oriol
Polikarpova Pl. 32
Oriol
302000

**Dianetics Center
of Penza**
Mira Ul. 55-89
Penza
440046

Dianetics Center of Penza II
Riabova Ul. 6C
Penza
440056

Dianetics Center of Perm
AB. Box 7026
Perm
614000

**Dianetics Center
of Petropavlovsk-
Kamchatsky**
Kavkazskaja Ul. 30/1-31
Petropavlovsk-
Kamchatsky
683006

**Dianetics Center
of Samara**
Leninskaja 22-1-3
Samara
443001

**Dianetics Center
of Saratov**
AB. Box 1533
Saratov
410601

**Dianetics Center
of St. Petersburg**
Razezshaja Ul. 44
St. Petersburg
192007

**Dianetics Humanitarian
Center of Surgut**
Lermontova Ul. 6-1
Surgut
Tyumen Region
626400

**Dianetics Humanitarian
Center of Toliatti**
AB. Box 14
Toliatti
Samara Region
445050

**Dianetics Center
of Troitsk**
Sirenevya Ul. 10-87
Troitsk
142092

Dianetics Center of Tula
Krasnoarmeysky Prospect
7-127 Tula
300000

Dianetics Center of Ufa
AB. Box 7527
Ufa - 76
450076

**Dianetics Center
of Vladivostok**
AB. Box 1-147
Vladivostok
690001

**Dianetics Humanitarian
Center of Volgograd**
AB. Box 6
Volgograd
400075

**Dianetics Center
of Voronezh**
AB. Box 146
Voronezh
394000

SLOVENIA

Mission of Koper
24 Gradon 3
Koper

SOUTH AFRICA

**Church of Scientology
Mission of Norwood**
18 Trilby Street
Oaklands
Johannesburg 2192

**Church of Scientology
Mission of Soweto**
Box 314
Kwa-xuma, Soweto 1868

SPAIN

**Church of Scientology
Mission of Bilbao**
Calle Juan de Garay
3, 1A
48003 Bilbao

**Church of Scientology
Mission of Cercedilla**
Cambrils 19
28034 Madrid

**Church of Scientology
Mission of Las Palmas**
Calle Viera y Clavijo
33-2
35002 Las Palmas de
Gran Canaria

**Church of Scientology
Mission of Sevilla**
Urbanización Los Mirtos
No 65
41021 Sevilla

**Church of Scientology
Mission of Valencia**
C/ Hermanos Rivas 22-1-1
46018 Valencia

SWEDEN

**Church of Scientology
Mission of Hassleholm**
Vakken Verts Allen 8
26136 Landskrona
Hassleholm

**Church of Scientology
Mission of Stockholm**
Grev Guregatan
11438 Stockholm

SWITZERLAND

**Church of Scientology
Mission of Luzern**
Sentimattstrasse 7
6003 Luzern

**Church of Scientology
Mission of Ticino**
Via Campagna 30
6982 Serocca D'Agno

**Church of Scientology
Mission of Zurich**
Regensbergstrasse 89
8050 Zurich

TAIWAN

**Church of Scientology
Mission of Kaohsiung**
85 Tong-shin Road
Shin-Shing District
Kaohsiung

**Church of Scientology
Mission of Taipei**
Sung-Ghang Road #16
Lane 63
Taipei

**Church of Scientology
Mission of Taichung**
82-2 Wu-Chuan-5 Street
Taichung

UKRAINE

**Hubbard Humanitarian
Center of Harkov**
AB. Box 53
Harkov 52
310052

**Dianetics Center
of Kremenchug**
Mira Ul. 3-161
Kremenchug
Poltavsky Region
315326

**Dianetics Center
of Uzgorod**
Dobrianskogo Ul. 10-9
Uzgorod
294000

UNITED STATES

Alaska

**Church of Scientology
Mission of Anchorage**
1300 E. 68th Ave.,
Ste. 208A
Anchorage, Alaska 99518

California

**Church of Scientology
Mission of Beverly Hills**
109 N. La Cienega Blvd.
Beverly Hills, California
90211

**Church of Scientology
Mission of Burbank**
6623 Irvine Avenue
North Hollywood
California 91606

**Church of Scientology
Mission of West Valley**
9310 Topanga Canyon
Prairie St. Entrance
Chatsworth, California
91311

**Church of Scientology
Mission of Escondido**
326 S. Kalmia St.
Escondido, California
92025

**Church of Scientology
Mission of Capitol**
9915 Fair Oaks Blvd.
Suite A
Fair Oaks, California
95628

**Church of Scientology
Mission of Brand Blvd.**
116 S. Louise Street
Glendale, California
91205

**Church of Scientology
Mission of Bay Cities**
2975 Treat Blvd. Suite D
Concord, California
94518

**Church of Scientology
Mission of The Foothills**
2254 Honolulu Avenue
Montrose, California
91020

**Church of Scientology
Mission of Antelope
Valley**
423 E. Palmdale Blvd. #3
Palmdale, California
93550

**Church of Scientology
Mission of Palo Alto**
410 Cambridge Ave.
Suite C
Palo Alto, California
94306

**Church of Scientology
Mission of San
Bernardino**
5 E. Citrus Ave. Ste. 105
Redlands, California
92373

**Church of Scientology
Mission of Redwood City**
617 Veterans Blvd. #205
Redwood City, California
94063

**Church of Scientology
Mission of River Park**
1300 Ethan Way, Ste. 100
Sacramento, California
95825

**Church of Scientology
Mission of San Francisco**
701 Sutter Street
San Francisco, California
94109

**Church of Scientology
Mission of San Jose**
826 N. Winchester
San Jose, California
95128

**Church of Scientology
Mission of Marin**
1930 4th Street
San Rafael, California
94901

**Church of Scientology
Mission of Santa Clara
Valley**
2718 Homestead Road
Santa Clara, California
95051

**Church of Scientology
Mission of Westwood**
3200 Santa Monica Blvd.
Suite 200
Santa Monica, California
90404

**Church of Scientology
Mission of Santa Rosa**
628 Third Street
PO Box 970
Santa Rosa, California
95404

*Church of Scientology
Mission of Sherman Oaks*
13517 Ventura Blvd. Ste. 7
Sherman Oaks, California
91423

*Church of Scientology
Mission of the San
Fernando Valley*
7457 Densmore
Van Nuys, California
91406

*Church of Scientology
Mission of Buenaventura*
180 N. Ashwood Ave.
Ventura, California
93003

*Church of Scientology
Mission of the Diablo
Valley*
1327 N. Main St. Ste. 103
Walnut Creek, California
94596

Colorado

*Church of Scientology
Mission of Alamosa*
511 Main Street
Alamosa, Colorado
81101

*Church of Scientology
Mission of Boulder*
1021 Pearl Street
Boulder, Colorado
80302

*Church of Scientology
Mission of Roaring Forks*
827 Bennett Avenue
Glenwood Springs,
Colorado 81601

Florida

*Church of Scientology
Mission of Clearwater*
100 N. Belcher Road
Clearwater, Florida
33765

*Church of Scientology
Mission of Palm Harbor*
565 Hammock Drive
Palm Harbor, Florida
34683

*Church of Scientology
Mission of Fort
Lauderdale*
660 S. Federal Hwy #200
Pompano Beach, Florida
33062

*Church of Scientology
Mission of Palm Beach*
4727 Holly Lake Drive
Lake Worth, Florida
33463

Hawaii

*Church of Scientology
Mission of Honolulu*
1920 Hoolehua St.
Pearl City, Hawaii
96782

Illinois

*Church of Scientology
Mission of Champaign-
Urbana*
312 W. John St.
Champaign, Illinois
61820

*Church of Scientology
Mission of Peoria*
2020 N. Wisconsin
Peoria, Illinois
61603

Kansas

*Church of Scientology
Mission of Wichita*
3705 E. Douglas
Wichita, Kansas
67218

Louisiana

*Church of Scientology
Mission of Baton Rouge*
9432 Common St.
Baton Rouge, Louisiana
70809

*Church of Scientology
Mission of Lafayette*
104 Westmark Blvd.
Suite 1B
Lafayette, Louisiana
70506

Maine

*Church of Scientology
Mission of Brunswick*
2 Lincoln Street
Brunswick, Maine
04011

Massachusetts

*Church of Scientology
Mission of Merrimack
Valley*
142 Primrose Street
Haverhill, Massachusetts
01830

**Church of Scientology
Mission of Watertown**
313 Common Street #2
Watertown, Massachusetts
02172

Michigan

**Church of Scientology
Mission of Genesee
County**
423 N. Saginaw
Holly, Michigan
48442

Nebraska

**Church of Scientology
Mission of Omaha**
843 Hidden Hills Drive
Bellevue, Nebraska
68005

Nevada

**Church of Scientology
Mission of Las Vegas**
3355 Spring Mtn. Rd. #48
Las Vegas, Nevada
89102

New Hampshire

**Church of Scientology
Mission of Greater
Concord**
P.O. Box 112
Epsom, New Hampshire
03234

New Jersey

**Church of Scientology
Mission of Collingswood**
118 W. Merchant St.
Audubon, New Jersey
08106

**Church of Scientology
Mission of Elizabeth**
339 Morris Avenue
Elizabeth, New Jersey
07208

**Church of Scientology
Mission of New Jersey**
1029 Teaneck Road
Teaneck, New Jersey
07666

New York

**Church of Scientology
Mission of Queens**
5603 214th Street
Bayside, New York
11364

**Church of Scientology
Mission of Middletown**
45 Dolson Avenue
Middletown, New York
10940

**Church of Scientology
Mission of Rockland**
7 Panoramic Drive
Valley Cottage, New York
10989

Pennsylvania

**Church of Scientology
Mission of Pittsburgh**
37 Terrace Drive
Charleroi, Pennsylvania
15022

South Carolina

**Church of Scientology
Mission of Charleston**
4050 Ashley Phosphate Rd.
Charleston,
South Carolina 29418

Tennessee

**Church of Scientology
Mission of Memphis**
1440 Central Avenue
Memphis, Tennessee
38104

Texas

**Church of Scientology
Mission of El Paso**
6330 North Mesa
El Paso, Texas
79912

**Church of Scientology
Mission of Houston**
2727 Fondren, Suite 1-A
Houston, Texas
77063

**Church of Scientology
Mission of San Antonio**
8410 Beech Drive #207
San Antonio, Texas
78758

Washington

**Church of Scientology
Mission of Bellevue**
15424 Bellevue-Redmond
Redmond, Washington
98052

**Church of Scientology
Mission of Burien**
15216 2nd Ave. SW
Seattle, Washington
98166

**Church of Scientology
Mission of Seattle**
1234 NE 145th Street
Seattle, Washington
98155

**Church of Scientology
Mission of Spokane**
1432 W. Francis
Spokane, Washington
99205

Wisconsin

**Church of Scientology
Mission of Milwaukee**
710 E. Silver Spring Dr.
Suite E
White Fish Bay,
Wisconsin 53217

INTERNET

For more information on Dianetics, Scientology and related subjects,
visit any of the following sites on the World Wide Web.

http://www.scientology.org
http://faq.scientology.org
http://foundingchurch.scientology.org
http://on-line.scientology.org
http://www.drugfreemarshals.org
http://www.scientologyhandbook.org
http://www.smi.org
http://www.studytechnology.org
http://www.dianetics.org
http://www.lronhubbard.org
http://lronhubbardtribute.org
http://www.able.org
http://www.appliedscholastics.org
http://www.criminon.org
http://www.narconon.org
http://www.thewaytohappiness.org

Bibliography

■

BARKER, EILEEN, London School of Economics. *New Religious Movements: A Perspective for Understanding Society*, 1982.

BARKER. *New Religious Movements, A Practical Introduction*. London: HMSO, 1989.

BECKFORD, JAMES A., University of Warwick, England. *Scientology, Social Science and the Definition of Religion*, 1980.

BELLAH, ROBERT. "Transcendence in Contemporary Society" in *The Religious Situation*. Beacon Press, 1969.

BENE, WENDALL C. and WILLIAM G. DOTY, eds. *Myths, Rites, Symbols: A Mircea Eliade Reader*, 1975.

BERGLIE, PER-ARNE, University of Stockholm, Sweden. *Scientology, A Comparison with Religions of the East and West*, 1996.

BLACK, ALAN, University of New England, Armidale, New South Wales, Australia. *Is Scientology a Religion?*, 1996.

BLACK, ALAN, Edith Cowan University, Australia. "Is Scientology a Religion?" in *Australian Religious Studies Review*, published by the Australian Association for the Study of Religions, Spring 1997.

BOUMA, GARY D., Monash University, Clayton, Victoria, Australia. "Is Scientology a Religion?" 1979, in *Brief Analysis of the Religious Nature of Scientology*, 1996.

BOYLE, KEVIN and JULIET SHEEN. *Freedom of Religion and Belief*, 1997.

BROWN, LESLIE, editor. *The New Shorter Oxford English Dictionary of Historical Principles*, 1993.

BRYANT, M. DARROL, Renison College, University of Waterloo, Ontario, Canada. *Scientology, A New Religion*, 1994.

BURGER, PETER L. *The Sacred Canopy*. Doubleday, 1976.

CHIDESTER, DAVID, University of Cape Town, South Africa. *Scientology: A Religion in South Africa*, 1970.

CHRISTENSEN, DORTE REFSLUND. *Scientology: From Therapy to Religion*. The Danish Research Council for the Humanities, 1995.

CHRISTENSEN. *Scientology, A New Religion*. Munksgaard, 1997.

CRIM, KEITH, editor. *Abingdon Dictionary of Living Religions*. The Parthenon Press, 1981.

DERICQUEBOURG, RÉGIS, University of Lille III, Lille, France. *Scientology*, 1995.

ELIADE, MIRCEA. *Patterns in Comparative Religion*, 1958.

ELIADE, MIRCEA, editor. *The Encyclopedia of Religion*. MacMillan, 1987.

ELLWOOD, ROBERT S., University of Southern California. *Religious and Spiritual Groups in Modern America*. Prentice-Hall, 1973.

FLINN, FRANK, Washington University, St. Louis, Missouri. *Scientology: The Marks of Religion*, 1994.

FLINN. "Scientology as Technological Buddhism" in *Alternatives to American Mainline Churches*. Joseph Fichter, editor. New York: Rose of Sharon, 1983.

FRIGERIO, ALEJANDRO, Catholic University of Argentina, Buenos Aires. *Scientology and Contemporary Definitions of Religion in the Social Sciences*, 1996.

Bibliography

GODFREY-SMITH, ANNE, editor. and JANET HADLEY WILLIAMS. *The Australian Reference Dictionary*, 1991.

HAWKINS, JOYCE and ROBERT ALLEN, eds. *The Oxford Encyclopedic English Dictionary*, 1991.

HEINO, HARRI, University of Tampere, Finland. *Scientology: Its True Nature*, 1995.

HEXHAM, IRVING, Regent College, Vancouver, B.C., Canada. "The Religious Status of Scientology," 1978, in *Brief Analysis of the Religious Nature of Scientology*, 1996.

HINNELS, JOHN R., editor. *Who's Who of World Religions*.

HILL, SAMUEL S., University of Florida. "Scientology, A New Religion," 1979, in *Brief Analysis of the Religious Nature of Scientology*, 1996.

HOEKSTRA, E.G. and M.H. IPENBURG. "Know Your Way in Religious and Philosophical Holland," in *Handbook of Religions, Churches, Movements and Organizations*. Kampen, Holland: 1995.

INTROVIGNE, MASSIMO and JEAN-FRANCOIS MAYER. *L'Europa delle Nuove Religioni*. Torino: Elle Di Ci, 1993.

JOHNSTON, GRAHAME. *The Australian Oxford Pocket Dictionary*, 1976.

KLIEVER, LONNIE D., Southern Methodist University, Dallas, Texas. *Scientology, A Worshipping Community*, 1994.

LESSA, WILLIAM A. and EVON Z. VOGT, eds. *Reader in Comparative Religion: An Anthropological Approach*, 1979.

MELTON, J. GORDON, Institute for the Study of American Religion, Santa Barbara, California. "A Short Study of the Scientology Religion," 1981, in *Brief Analysis of the Religious Nature of Scientology*, 1996.

MELTON, *Encyclopedia of American Religions*, 4th Edition, 1993.

OOSTHUIZEN, G.C., University of Durban-Westville, Natal, South Africa. *Religious Philosophy, Religion and Church*, 1977.

OTTO, RUDOLF. *The Idea of the Holy*. Oxford University Press, 1950.

PARRINDER, GEOFFREY, University of London. *The Religious Nature of Scientology*, 1977.

PENTIKAINEN, JUHA, University of Helsinki, Finland, and **MARJA PENTIKAINEN**. *The Church of Scientology*, 1996.

PROCTER, PAUL, editor. *Longman Dictionary of Contemporary English*. Longman Group, 1978.

RENARD, MARIA-REINE, J.D. "What is a Religion?" in *La Semaine Juridique*, Edition Generale, No. 8-9, 18 Nov. 1997.

ROBERT, JACQUES, University of Paris. *Is Scientology a Religion?*, 1995.

ROBERT, PAUL and **ALAIN RAY**, eds. *Dictionaire alphabetique et analogugue de la langue francaise.*

SABBATUCCI, DARIO, University of Rome, Italy. *Scientology, Its Historical-Morphological Frame*, 1983.

SAWADA, FUMIO, Ahlut-Bait Center, Japan. *Scientology and Islam, An Analogous Study*, 1996.

SAWADA. *The Relationship Between Scientology and Other Religions*, 1996.

SCHONBECK, OLAF. "Scientology and Indian Religion," *Chaos*, No. 25, 1994.

SIVERTSEV, MICHAEL A. Board of Cooperation with Religious Organizations, Office of the Russian President, Moscow. *Scientology: A Way of Spiritual Self-Identification*, 1995.

SORENSEN, MERETHE SUNDBY. Danish Research Council for the Humanities, *Myths About New Religions*, 1988.

STUENG, FREDERICK J. *Understanding Religious Life*, 2nd. editor. Dickensen Publishing Co., 1976.

WACH, JOACHIM. *Sociology of Religion*. University of Chicago Press, 1944.

WEBB, PETER. *Australian Broadcasting Authority Annual Report 1995-96.*

WILSON, BRYAN R., Oxford University, England. *Religious Toleration and Religious Diversity*, 1995.

WILSON. *Social Change and New Religious Movements*, 1995.

WILSON. *Scientology: An Analysis and Comparison of its Religious Systems and Doctrines*, 1995.

WILSON. *The Social Dimensions of Sectarianism*. Oxford: Clarendon Press, 1990.

WILLIAMSON, WILLIAM B., editor. *An Encyclopedia of Religions in the United States — One Hundred Religious Groups Speak for Themselves*. New York: Crossroad Publishing Co., 1992.

ZETTLER, HOWARD G., editor. *Ologies & Isms, A Thematic Dictionary*. Gale Research Co., 1978.

Index

■

A

B

C

D

Z